"*Living into the Life of Jesus* is a breath of fresh ~~air whose uniqueness lies in two directions~~ its central focus is on Jesus and the Gospels, and it includes a seminal chapter on finances and the spiritual life. Issler provides the reader with new insight after new insight. But he is no mere theorist, and the reader will walk away with numerous specific suggestions as to how to live more like Jesus. I highly recommend this wonderful book."

J. P. Moreland, Talbot School of Theology, Biola University, author of *The Kingdom Triangle*

"The formation of good character is the standing human problem, generation to generation, and it is the arena of perpetual human failure throughout history, up to today. The formation of *Christian* character in companionship with Christ is the verifiable solution to the standing problem and the constant failure. For many decades, Christian sources have not done well with character formation, if they have addressed it at all. Klaus Issler has carefully worked his way through the details of how Christian character formation reliably proceeds. He knows from personal experience and scholarly research how it works. He guides you in the path and enables you to extend what you have gained to others in desperate need around you. *Living into the Life of Jesus* is a vital resource for any individual or group looking for ways to realize the powerful outcomes of spiritual transformation manifestly presented in the pages of the New Testament."

Dallas Willard, author of *The Divine Conspiracy* and *The Spirit of the Disciplines*

"*Living into the Life of Jesus* gently points us toward recognizing the gaps in our spiritual formation plan and gives us fresh tools to dive deep into the love letters of God in the Bible. Issler takes on the oft-forgotten practices of peacemaking and forgiveness, showing us practical ways to flourish in deep, real relationships designed for a lifetime instead of just a season. He also tackles the tough topics of money, the marketplace and generosity. Your walk with Jesus will be refreshed and the practices of your faith will be renewed and strengthened as you live into the life of Jesus."

Greg Leith, director, Strategic Alliances, Biola University, Board of Directors, Convene CEO Forum and The Barnabas Group

"Klaus Issler has identified the key to authentic Christian living: It is a matter of both the heart and discipline. Get ready to drink from a fire hose emanating from the well of truth, the Bible. This book will put you to work and on the road to a deeper relationship with the Lord. The work is worth the investment. Issler combines theology, Scripture, real-life experience and assignments, all designed to sharpen your understanding and Christian walk."

Ken Eldred, businessman/philanthropist, author of *The Integrated Life*

"The more Christian books I read, the more disappointed I become. As well-intended as many of these authors are, too often their final product ends up selling out to the cultural norm of shallow anecdotal responses, overly simplistic solutions, little to no rigorously applied thought processes and mediocre integration of Scripture to their subject matter. Klaus Issler's book is about as opposite of the abovementioned deficiencies as I have read in a very long time. *Living into the Life of Jesus* was such a pleasure to read; I felt the author and I were having an ongoing discussion versus being preached to in 'black and white.' Throughout the book, Issler shares his struggles, his victories, but most importantly, his personal mistakes. In doing so, Klaus has written a book that I plan on sharing with many of my clients so they may understand, appreciate and be better equipped to meet the challenge of Ephesians 4:13 '[to attain] the whole measure of the fullness of Christ.'"

Raymond P. Gleason, business executives coach, Building Champions

"The desire to become more Christlike sometimes gets translated into a list of dos and don'ts which, quite frankly, can be more burdensome than joyful. In contrast, Klaus Issler draws from the teachings of Jesus to provide a fresh perspective on achieving genuine character change. Of particular interest to me is his emphasis on the redemptive potential of marketplace activity and personal wealth. With its generous use of 'prayer projects' and review questions, I believe this book has strong potential for use in classrooms and Bible studies."

Steve Rundle, professor of international business, Biola University, and coauthor of *Great Commission Companies*

"As a pastor I am constantly seeking relevant and insightful books which stimulate not only my own personal growth but also provide an effective tool to help my church members develop the image of Christ in their lives. My criterion for such books is that they be biblically grounded with relevant application. *Living into the Life of Jesus* is one book that accomplishes that goal for me. Issler offers fresh and deep insights to familiar passages of Scripture. But this is not just an academic exercise. It will challenge your mind and also lead your heart into the practice of spiritual formation that is Christ-centered and empowered by the Spirit of God. This is an essential text for any pastor that seeks to form the character of Christ in his own life and the life of his church."

David J. Mitchell, senior pastor, Calvary Church of Santa Ana

"If you want to be changed by following the way of Jesus, immerse yourself in these penetrating, well-thought-out observations of Jesus' life alongside practical guidance for living into that life yourself."

Jan Johnson, author of *Abundant Simplicity* and *Invitation to the Jesus Life*

"This book is about learning to live like Jesus: to become more like him, to understand what it means to incorporate his way into our way, to know the heart and mind of Christ. Klaus Issler provides us a fresh and thoughtful perspective of what we can learn and apply from the life of Jesus."

Bill Pollard, chairman and CEO emeritus, The ServiceMaster Company

"Our life and relationships in Christ simply work right when we live them out from the heart. Issler's scholarship and warmth show us how clearly and deeply Jesus' teachings lead us along that path."

John Townsend, author of the bestselling *Boundaries*

The Formation
of Christian Character

LIVING INTO
THE LIFE OF
JESUS

KLAUS ISSLER

Foreword by CALVIN MILLER

IVP Books
An imprint of InterVarsity Press
Downers Grove, Illinois

InterVarsity Press
P.O. Box 1400, Downers Grove, IL 60515-1426
World Wide Web: www.ivpress.com
E-mail: email@ivpress.com

InterVarsity Press® is the book-publishing division of InterVarsity Christian Fellowship/USA®, a movement of
students and faculty active on campus at hundreds of universities, colleges and schools of nursing in the United States
of America, and a member movement of the International Fellowship of Evangelical Students. For information
about local and regional activities, write Public Relations Dept., InterVarsity Christian Fellowship/USA, 6400
Schroeder Rd., P.O. Box 7895, Madison, WI 53707-7895, or visit the IVCF website at <www.intervarsity.org>.

All Scripture quotations, unless otherwise indicated, are taken from the Holy Bible, Today's New International
Version™ Copyright © 2001 by International Bible Society. All rights reserved.

While all stories in this book are true, some names and identifying information in this book have been changed to
protect the privacy of the individuals involved.

Design: Cindy Kiple
Images: man standing on country road: © Gawrav Sinha/iStockphoto
       green vine leaf: © Martha Catherine Ivey/Getty Images

ISBN 978-0-8308-3811-0

Printed in the United States of America ∞

Library of Congress Cataloging-in-Publication Data

Issler, Klaus Dieter.
 Living into the life of Jesus: the formation of Christian character
/Klaus Issler; foreword by Calvin Miller.
     p. cm.
 Includes bibliographical references and index.
 ISBN 978-0-8308-3811-0 (pbk.: alk. paper)
 1. Spiritual formation. 2. Character—Religious
aspects—Christianity. 3. Jesus Christ—Example. I. Title.
 BV4511.I87 2012
 248.4—dc23

                                                                    2011051590

P 20 19 18 17 16 15 14 13 12 11 10 9 8 7 6 5 4 3 2

Y 29 28 27 26 25 24 23 22 21 20 19

For Beth

Contents

Foreword by Calvin Miller 9

Preface 11

PART ONE: A Process for Christian
Character Formation

  1 Form Your Heart, Not Just Your Behavior 15

  2 Wake Up to Five Formation Gaps 37

  3 Adapt Formation Practices for Your Journey 58

PART TWO: Essential Divine Resources
of Formation Grace

  4 Love
    Divine Relational Support in Jesus' Life and Ours 87

  5 Holy Spirit
    Divine Mentoring in Jesus' Life and Ours 107

  6 Scripture
    Divine Revelation of Reality and a "Jesus" Lifestyle. 135

PART THREE: Following Jesus Daily in Our Gaps

  7 Three Exemplary Jesus Practices About Relationships 159

  8 Three Exemplary Jesus Practices
    About Money and Work 184

Acknowledgments 224

Name and Subject Index 227

Scripture Index. 235

Foreword

Klaus Issler is a man for all seasons. I have known him for years, and my every visit with him has been one of joining his long, unending conversation with God. He is Emmaus—walking, heart-burning-within-him Emmaus. He has been with Jesus, but it isn't till the breaking of bread that you fully understand that. His walk is himself, and it is an unsettled walk, where questions about Christ, his life-long lover, are always popping up. I like him for this: these same questions pop up in my life too, but too often I settle into the evening news and a heavy supper, and the questions get absorbed in my own temporary lethargy.

Not so with Klaus. He mulls them over in his unsettled heart and talks to God about them, and I always think I hear God saying to him, "Klaus, I am so glad you asked."

He loves believing! He is at the height of his glory in talking about his faith discoveries. He is, with each new spiritual insight, dying to talk about it. So when I got this manuscript in the mail, I read, and read, and read some more. And when I finally got to the fifth chapter, the book organized itself around the issue he long ago settled: "Unless today's believers engage the empowering resource of the Holy Spirit—who is the divine agent of sanctification—it is impossible to be formed into the image of Christ." That is what this book is about. That is what his life is about.

Klaus doesn't want much—just to be formed into the image of Christ. And why should you read this book? Because he wants that same thing for you.

So Klaus, I know you want the best for me. I know you want nothing more from me than Jesus does. So, my dear Emmaus, thank you for this book. I walked with you today as I read, and my heart burned within me. I would like to tell you I am doing the best I can, but I know I can do more. Because of what you've written, maybe I'll turn off the news early and eat a lot lighter and ask myself, what can I do to live into the life of Christ and look forward to my being better formed in Christ?

Calvin Miller
Beeson Divinity School

Preface

If you'd like to live more like Jesus, this book is for you. But I need to warn you, I don't follow conventional wisdom about how we head in that direction. I think we've wrongly diagnosed the problem and therefore have developed strategies that don't work—which is why many of us are frustrated at the lack of deep life change. We've even given up hope that change is possible. Why do I think this book provides an alternative way?

Consider this analogy from medical history. If you lived two hundred years ago and had a terrible headache or fever, what do you think your doctor would prescribe? A good old-fashioned bloodletting. The word means just what it says: letting blood drain out of the body. For thousands of years, ever since the ancient Greeks, bloodletting was the standard medical diagnosis for almost all diseases. Why did doctors do this? Because of deeply held worldview beliefs about what a healthy body needed. Bloodletting was the most direct way to normalize the imbalance of bodily fluids, since they were all interconnected. Of course, it injured patients more than helped them. Finally in the late 1800s, germ theory—the discovery that microorganisms were the major cause of diseases—became the accepted medical perspective, doctors began using sterilizing agents, and the rest is history. What's the point? Our diagnoses and ways of solving problems are directly based on our perspectives of reality. If those perspectives are inaccurate—as they were about curing illness—then the derived methods based on those particular views are, in effect, a waste of time; worse, they can be harmful.

Similarly, I've become convinced we've got an inaccurate view about how character formation takes place. If we're going to see any long-term formation results, I suggest we must make four major shifts of perspective: We think Christian formation is mainly about using our willpower to change our external behaviors, whereas Jesus says it's really about changing the flow of our inner heart. We think Christian formation is mainly about following rules, whereas Jesus says it's really about deepening our relationship with him and relying on divine resources that make change possible. We've been persuaded—by frustrating experience—that deep Christian formation is not realistic or possible this side of heaven, whereas Jesus is convinced it is. Finally, we think of Jesus only as our Lord and Savior—which he is—but we ignore and devalue Jesus' impressive human life example. Yet Jesus says it's possible to put "words of mine . . . into practice" (Mt 7:24) and to "learn from me" (Mt 11:29).

In this book I invite you to take a fresh look at Jesus in the Gospels to benefit from what he offers. I've been doing that for the last decade and have seen Jesus bring about important, deep changes in my life—although I've still got a long way to go. In an earlier book about the Christian life *Wasting Time with God: A Christian Spirituality of Friendship with God*, I wrote about growing more deeply in our personal relationship with God. In the present book, the focus is on growing more deeply in our character and lifestyle to become more like Jesus. I'd like to share a bit of my journey, some liberating insights from Jesus' life and teachings, and some practical steps that may help you as they've helped me. So, if you would like to live more like Jesus, read on.

PART ONE

A PROCESS FOR CHRISTIAN CHARACTER FORMATION

1

Form Your Heart,
Not Just Your Behavior

Change your life. God's Kingdom is here.

MATTHEW 4:17 *THE MESSAGE*

. ℘ .

Do we think of Jesus as a hero? Of course he's our Lord God and Savior, but is he our hero as well? How is he a hero? Because Jesus was the first person to live a fully human life while dependent on the Holy Spirit, the only one to practice all that he preached. For example, Jesus didn't just talk about forgiveness (e.g., Lk 11:4; 17:4)—he lived it. On the cross he made an amazing grace-filled request to the Father for those who crucified him. Despite the false accusations during his trial, the scourging, beatings and being spit on, the agonizing journey to Golgotha, all the physical torture and emotional abuse, Jesus never responded in kind. He asked God to forgive those who tortured him. "Father, forgive them, for they do not know what they are doing" (Lk 23:34). These are the sincere words of "the champion who secures [our] salvation" (Heb 2:10).[1] *Jesus' heart had a settled grounding in God's love and peace,* formed while he lived on this earth, sustained by God's grace and power.

---

[1]"Champion" in Heb 2:10 and 12:2 ("author" or "pioneer" in other versions) is William Lane's preferred translation for *archēgos*. Lane, *Hebrews 1-8*, Word Biblical Commentary 47A (Dallas: Word, 1991), pp. 55-57.

Over the last few years I've given attention to Jesus' life and teachings. It continues to be a richly rewarding study and this book is one result of that treasure hunt. The more I examine his life and teachings, the more I come to respect and appreciate who Jesus is, how he lived his human life, and his self-giving compassion and generosity in what he accomplished for us. Jesus is my hero, someone worthy to imitate. I hope the study of Jesus' life in this book affects you in a similar way.

Change As Realistic?

This book is also about change. Is deep life change really possible? Not if we rely on our typical strategies. For example, making, then quickly breaking, New Year's resolutions is an American tradition. Even with the best of intentions our follow-through often lacks the staying power needed. Perhaps we should lower our expectations as suggested by the following "doable" resolutions in table 1.1.[2]

Table 1.1

Doable New Year's Resolutions	
1. Gain weight. At least 30 pounds.	6. Stay off the International Space Station.
2. Procrastinate more. Starting tomorrow.	7. Associate with even worse business clients.
3. Read less.	8. Wait around for opportunity.
4. Get in a whole NEW rut!	9. Focus on the faults of others.
5. Don't believe politicians.	10. Never make New Year's resolutions again.

After enough attempts with little progress, do we opt for item number ten on the list and conclude that life change is not realistic?

There's a noticeable gap between what we want to do and what we actually do. For example, I want to be a more gracious husband but am sometimes very ungracious to my wife when my controlling tendencies take over and I want to defend my turf at all costs. Each of us might be aware of these kinds of moments. We *want* to do the right thing but we don't. We know what the Bible says to do—we're *willing* to do it— but we often miss the mark. Let's call it the *willing-doing gap*. We feel

---

[2]See <www.jokesaboutnewyears.com>.

we should be doing better but can't, so frustration and guilt increase.

It's not a physical gap, as in the distance between the two banks on either side of a river. It's a gap in our potential growth, between where our character currently is and where we can imagine our character could be. For example, we can imagine the lack of competency of an Olympic gold medalist athlete at a time *before* he or she took any interest in that sport. Or consider the case of someone who fluently speaks a foreign language when earlier they couldn't. Or ponder the gap potential between beginning to play the piano and being a concert pianist.

The willing-doing gap is a universal human problem we all face. It's not unique to Christians. Some businesses actually incorporate the willing-doing gap as part of their business plan. To make it possible for these companies, such as health fitness centers, to continue offering their services to the few who actually use them, they rely on dues paid by non-participating members. But businesses also recognize the downside of this gap and take measures to counter the tendency toward non-performance. So legal contracts are required to ensure that promises are kept.

Of course, Christians have additional resources to help us decrease the willing-doing gap. God has done radical open-heart surgery at our regeneration. Furthermore, the Holy Spirit indwells each believer forever (Jn 14:16), so that we now are able to please God as we follow the Spirit's lead (Rom 8:5-11). And we've been joined to the family of God as fellow members who can give support and encouragement to each other as we intend to grow more to be like Jesus (Eph 4:4, 15-16). Finally, God has given us his written Word, a unique resource of truth and knowledge about reality (2 Tim 3:16-17). But despite all this potential help—both divine and human—we continue to sin; we continue to experience the willing-doing gap. No denying it, the gap is alive and well within each of us. As Christians, do we sometimes feel a greater sense of guilt than others because we should be trying harder and doing much better?

In various ways we attempt to close our gaps. Which of the following strategies have you tried before?

a. *more* Bible knowledge

b. *another* decision of commitment—for rededication or to receive *another* blessing

c. *more* encounters and experiences with God

d. attending or participating in *more* Christian activities

e. using *more* willpower—just decide to stop sinning

insanity

I've tried most of these at different times of my life. We redouble our efforts to grow closer to God and to become more like Jesus, yet we still reap the same limited outcomes. Isn't that the popular definition of "insanity": using the same means and hoping for different results?

Been there, done that—but I've had a perspective shift. I've become convinced that deep life change is really possible. Several years ago God convicted me of being judgmental toward certain drivers on our freeways. Jesus' teaching from the Sermon on the Mount cut me to the quick: "But I tell you that anyone who is angry with his brother will be subject to judgment. Again, anyone who says to his brother, 'Raca,' is answerable to the Sanhedrin. But anyone who says, 'You fool!' will be in danger of the fire of hell" (Mt 5:22). "Turkey!" or "You jerk!" were my outbursts as I drove each day to Biola University, where I'm a seminary professor. I can get somewhat competitive on the road and confess to mild road rage about certain unsafe drivers. I was finally willing to recognize the gap between my outbursts and Jesus' teachings, to confess it as wrong (and not just rationalize it away as I may do at other times), and to begin a plan to address it. After focusing on this for about a year, I began to experience more of God's peace during these encounters with drivers. As a result of this transformation, I became convinced that deep life change is possible and realistic today. That's why I've written this book. Perhaps you're like me and are ready to consider insights from Jesus to help diminish the willing-doing gap?

deep life change is real today

Jesus stands out among the great moral teachers of history, a truth that Lee Strobel finally became convinced of. Strobel graduated from Yale Law School and worked fourteen years in journalism; at one time he was the legal affairs editor of the *Chicago Tribune*. In 1979 his wife, Leslie, came home and shared that she had become a Christian. As an atheist, Strobel was shocked and dismayed. Yet he became intrigued by the change in her character. He had to admit he never seriously studied the unusual claims about Jesus Christ—that he had risen from the dead and that he claimed to be the Son of God. Strobel believed it was all nonsense, a legend others had concocted about Jesus for various reasons. So, employing his investigative competencies and experience, he decided it was time to check out the evidence for the claims of Christianity and what the Bible taught about Jesus Christ. After a two-year extensive study, "by November 8, 1981, my legend thesis, to which I had doggedly clung for so many years, had been thoroughly dismantled. . . . The atheism I had embraced for so long buckled under the weight of historical truth."[3] Jesus is unique—he is both divine and human.[4]

Burdensome?

Do Jesus' teachings seem burdensome? The other day I was talking with a friend about this subject, and she confessed that studying Jesus' life in the Gospels was overwhelming at times. She enjoyed reading about Jesus himself, but some of his statements seemed so extreme, making impossible standards that no one could ever fulfill, such as, "Be perfect, as your heavenly Father is perfect" (Mt 5:48). So she preferred to leave aside the Gospels and mostly study the Epistles—those teachings seemed more realistic. I can appreciate her point. I think what contributes to our problem with Jesus' teachings is our tendency to want to follow rules, which is not a bad idea in itself. But I've become convinced that when we tend toward *merely* rule making and rule following as the ultimate way to approach following Jesus, this actually moves us away from what Jesus intends.

Let me explain with an example. Have you pondered the practical challenges for those trying to adhere to strict Old Testament Sabbath rules? Consider the command not to work on the Sabbath (Ex 20:8-11). Okay, how far can you walk on the Sabbath and do no "work," a distance that became known as a "Sabbath day's journey" (cf. Acts 1:12)?

---

[3]Lee Strobel, *The Case for Christ* (Grand Rapids: Zondervan, 1998), p. 266.
[4]Calvin Miller offers a feast of varied writings and accounts about Jesus in his massive 574-page *The Book of Jesus: A Treasure of the Greatest Stories and Writings About Christ* (New York: Simon & Schuster, 1998).

It turns out the rabbis set two thousand cubits as the limit, about three-quarters of a mile.[5] Yet we need more guidance. Is that two thousand cubits a limit for that whole day, or just for each time one walks? Further discernment clarified it was for each time one walks. So you could extend your walking distance beyond that limit by planning to have a meal just within the two-thousand-cubit range, and then do more walking up to the limit after that meal. I think you get the point: it's a never-ending task to come up with more clarifications and technicalities. We can't make enough rules for every occasion.

Much of Jesus' critique of the Pharisees expressly repudiated that type of rigid rule making that focused solely on external behaviors without the corresponding heart attitudes of compassion and grace. Jesus says, "For I tell you that unless your righteousness surpasses that of the Pharisees and the teachers of the law, you will certainly not enter the kingdom of heaven" (Mt 5:20).

If Jesus' teachings have become burdensome, perhaps we've misunderstood what he intended. But how do we handle strange statements like these?

- *On seating arrangements*: "When you are invited, go and recline at the last place, so that when the one who has invited you comes, he may say to you, 'Friend, move up higher'; then you will have honor in the sight of all who are at the table with you" (Lk 14:10 NASB).

- *On guest lists for dinner:* "When you give a luncheon or dinner, do not invite your friends, your brothers or sisters, your relatives, or your rich neighbors; if you do, they may invite you back and so you will be repaid" (Lk 14:12).

- *On non-resistance:* "Whoever slaps you on your right cheek, turn the other to him also" (Mt 5:39 NASB).

- *On resisting temptation*: "If your right eye causes you to stumble, gouge it out and throw it away. It is better for you to lose one part of your body than for your whole body to be thrown into hell" (Mt 5:29).

---

[5]This decision was based on linking two unrelated passages: Exodus 16:29, commanding that one stay in one's place or village on the Sabbath, and Joshua 3:4, identifying the distance to stay behind the ark of the covenant as two thousand cubits.

Jesus himself is the ultimate reference point.

These "absolutist statements" appear like commands to be followed—until we look at the final verse, about gouging out eyes. Then we realize they're not to be taken at face value or as rules.

Christianity cannot be reduced merely to a set of rules to obey.[6] While objectively true, moral rules are not our ultimate reference point. Jesus himself is the ultimate reference point for us. We look to Jesus' own authoritative example and illustrations that present a range of ways to love God. We believe correctly that Jesus is central to salvation, as Scripture teaches. Likewise, Jesus is central to sanctification, to discipleship,[7] to Christian ethics, as Jesus himself teaches. Why else does Jesus offer this invitation—in contrast to the teachings of the Pharisees?

"Come to me, all of you who are laboring and bearing burdens, and I will give you rest. Take my yoke upon you and learn from me, because I am meek and humble in heart, and you will find rest for yourselves. For my yoke is kind and my burden is light" (Mt 11:28-30).[8]

Jesus' great invitation and offer of personal intimacy with him and personal training by him is an invitation still available today. Furthermore, Jesus offers a promise or guarantee that life change is possible if we put his teachings into practice. We'll be like a wise person who built a house on a rock—a firm and solid foundation against any storm—instead of the fool building on the unstable sand. The house "did not fall, because it had its foundation on the rock" (Mt 7:25). Our tendency to interpret Jesus' illustrations as absolute rules will hinder us from learning to follow him.

Interpreting Jesus' "Absolute" Teachings

Let me suggest three helpful guidelines for hearing the heart of Jesus in his teachings.

1. Jesus often uses a "shock" teaching method through hyperbole and

---

[6]For a helpful treatment on moral rules and other kinds of rules, see Lewis Smedes, *Choices* (New York: HarperOne, 1991), chap. 6, "Respect the Rules," pp. 43-66.

[7]Michael Wilkins, *Following the Master* (Grand Rapids: Zondervan, 1992), p. 343.

[8]Alternate translation by Donald Hagner, *Matthew 1-13*, Word Biblical Commentary 33A (Dallas: Word, 1993), p. 322.

exaggeration (a) to arrest listeners' attention and (b) to jar an openness to hear truth that counters and critiques a prevailing assumption or value gap of the day.

2. Jesus sometimes uses particular cultural references easily understood by first-century listeners, but that require more research to make sense today.

Let's pause here and look at his teaching again in light of guidelines 1 and 2. For example, within a communitarian culture that highly prized the family and respect for parents Jesus says, "If anyone comes to me and does not hate father and mother, wife and children, brothers and sisters—yes, even life itself—cannot be my disciple" (Lk 14:26). How shocking! Loyalty to Jesus must become a higher priority than family, which was considered by his listeners to be an ultimate value in that day. In this case Jesus highlights a higher priority by negating a *legitimate* priority, but a lower one. If we took such teachings literally, it would appear, for example, we shouldn't work to earn a living: "Do not work for food that spoils, but for food that endures to eternal life, which the Son of Man will give you" (Jn 6:27; cf. Mt 6:19-20).

Sometimes we don't get the power of the hyperbole and the surprise Jesus intends due to cultural references. For example, Jesus says, "Therefore, if you are offering your gift at the altar and there remember that your brother or sister has something against you, leave your gift there in front of the altar. First go and be reconciled to that person; then come and offer your gift" (Mt 5:23-24). In the verse, "altar" refers to the temple in Jerusalem. So this hypothetical person is attending a holy week feast there, whereas Jesus' audience, at the time of his speaking, lives in Galilee. Is this person supposed to stop his sacrifice, leave the feast day in Jerusalem, make an eighty-mile trip back to Galilee (usually a couple of days by foot), be reconciled with his neighbor, and then make the eighty-mile trip back to Jerusalem to make the offering? R. T. France notes, "The improbability of the scenario emphasizes Jesus' point, that the importance of right relationships demands decisive action."[9] The

---

[9]R. T. France, *The Gospel of Matthew*, The New International Commentary on the New Testament (Grand Rapids: Eerdmans, 2007), p. 203.

point is, give much more attention and effort to reconciliation. "Goug-ing out the eye" signifies giving much more attention and effort to growing one's character and reducing gaps.

In Jesus' day, a "slap on the cheek" (Mt 5:39) primarily referred to a verbal insult (often symbolized with a physical slap; see, e.g., 2 Chron 18:2; Job 16:10). France explains, "This is more a matter of honor than of physical injury, and honor required appropriate [finan-cial] recompense."[10] In a culture of honor and shame, an insult was humiliating and offensive. For an insult, Jesus says to forgo claiming the legal fine. If it was a literal slap that Jesus meant, then he didn't follow his own guidelines. After being slapped by the high priest's officer, Jesus didn't turn the other cheek (Jn 18:19-23; see Mt 5:39; Lk 6:29).

But the most important point for appreciating Jesus' teachings is guideline 3.

3. Jesus often uses concrete examples from daily life to illustrate what a Jesus-like lifestyle can look like; they're illustrations to enlarge our moral imagination, not rules to be followed absolutely. In other words, as our inner heart is changed, these kinds of Jesus-like ac-tions will become second nature for us—in many cases without really having to think about it.

Jesus uses illustrations to show what kind of actions can flow from a heart formed like Jesus' own. As it were, Jesus answers the question "How might a Jesus-like Christian respond in a given situation from a formed heart?" For example, one might not take the most prominent seat at a meal, since image is not that important (Lk 14:10). Since hos-pitality needs to be offered to all, not just friends and family, one might invite those who can't return the favor (Lk 14:12). Bottom line: the core of childhood formation is primarily rule keeping, but the core of adult formation is growing into the way of wisdom, with a heart formed like Jesus'. For some of us, such an understanding of Jesus' teaching may be the most liberating idea in this book.

Thus, Jesus presents a number of illustrations—sometimes exagger-

---

[10]Ibid., p. 220.

ations—to counter prevailing assumptions and to present a new way of living: a way of wisdom.

Focusing on the Heart of the Matter

Rather than focusing primarily on external conformity to moral rules—which becomes burdensome—Jesus teaches that we need to give closer attention to our inner life. He uses three metaphors to highlight this point: (a) contrasting inside with outside,[11] (b) the analogy of a tree bearing good or bad fruit, and (c) the term *heart,* his most frequently employed metaphor.[12]

Inside/outside contrast. "Woe to you, teachers of the law and Pharisees, you hypocrites! You clean the outside of the cup and dish, but inside they are full of greed and self-indulgence. Blind Pharisee! *First clean the inside of the cup and dish, and then the outside also will be clean*" (Mt 23:25-26, emphasis added; see also Mt 7:15; 12:27-28; Mk 7:15, 18-20; Lk 11:39-40; 16:15; cf. 1 Sam 16:7).

Fruit-bearing tree. "Make a tree good and its fruit will be good, or make a tree bad and its fruit will be bad, for a tree is recognized by its fruit" (Mt 12:33; also Mt 7:17-20; 12:33; Lk 6:43-44; perhaps based on Ps 1:3; Jer 17:7-8).

Heart. "These people honor me with their lips, but their hearts are far from me" (Mt 15:8).

"For from within, out of your hearts, come evil thoughts, sexual immorality, theft, murder, adultery, greed, malice, deceit, lewdness, envy, slander, arrogance and folly. All these evils come from inside and defile you" (Mk 7:21-23). "You have heard that it was said, 'You shall not commit adultery.' But I tell you that anyone who looks at a woman lustfully has already committed adultery with her in his heart" (Mt 5:27-28; see also Mt 6:21; 12:34-35; Lk 6:45; 12:34; cf. Jer 31:33; Ezek 36:26).

According to Michael Wilkins, "The heart is the source of all

---

[11]Larry Crabb's classic book *Inside Out* (Colorado Springs: NavPress, 1988) seems to be stimulated by this concept in Jesus' teaching.

[12]All three of these metaphors appear in Jesus' Sermon on the Mount (Mt 5–7): inside/outside (Mt 7:15), fruit-bearing (Mt 7:17-20), and heart (Mt 5:28; 6:21).

[handwritten: true purity? Their hearts need purifying.]

thoughts, motives, and actions. The greed and self-indulgence of the Pharisees and teachers of the law, especially their lust for public religious acclaim, are inner motivations that impact external behavior. In order to bring about true purity, their hearts need purifying."[13] Our actions flow from what is on the inside. If we do not focus on the source of our behaviors, we will keep battling our external words and actions—and our willing-doing gap will not change much. Jesus desires that we forgive others "from the heart" (Mt 18:35), not just mouth nice words because that is what everyone expects. *[handwritten: "from the heart"]*

Jesus himself didn't worry much about the complaints against his externally observed actions—his breaking the Sabbath, his perceived lifestyle of gluttony and drunkenness or his association with "impure" people. Richard Foster affirms, "Jesus was continually offending the religious professionals of his day because he broke their rules and moved outside the lines of convention. He forgave the transgressors and criticized the 'obedient.' You see, the condition of our hearts is more important to Jesus than how well we play by the rules."[14]

Jesus' teaching about the centrality of inner heart formation is really not new information. It is an amplification of what was already taught in the Old Testament Hebrew Scriptures—the Bible Jesus studied and meditated on. Consider Proverbs 4:23 from the Wisdom literature: "Above all else, guard your heart, for it is the wellspring of life" (NIV). Bruce Waltke explains, "This direction or bent of the heart [wise, pure or perverse] determines its decisions and thus the persons' actions. . . . Since the heart is the center of all of a person's emotional-intellectual-religious-moral activity, it must be safeguarded above all things."[15] Furthermore Waltke clarifies, "It . . . is the heart that governs all activity."[16] If we wish to make any headway in bridging the willing-doing gap, we must give attention to changing our heart flow since it directs how we live.

[handwritten: Change your heart flow.]

---

[13]Michael Wilkins, *Matthew*, NIV Application Commentary (Grand Rapids: Zondervan, 2004), p. 754.

[14]Richard Foster, *Life with God* (San Francisco: HarperOne, 2008), p. 27.

[15]Bruce K. Waltke, *The Book of Proverbs: Chapters 1-15*, New International Commentary on the Old Testament (Grand Rapids: Zondervan, 2004), pp. 91-92.

[16]Ibid., p. 298.

According to Waltke, "'Heart' *(leb/lebab)* is the most important an-thropological term in the Old Testament . . . but the English language has no equivalent. It occurs 46 times in Proverbs and 858 times in the Old Testament."[17] Throughout the Old Testament the term "heart" represents the self, including thoughts, feelings, and the will (e.g., Ps 22:26; 1 Kings 3:12; Ex 36:2); the word can even be interchangeable with "soul" (Hebrew *nephesh*, e.g., Josh 22:5; 1 Sam 2:35).[18] The New Testament mostly follows this usage for "heart" (Greek *kardia*, e.g., Lk 21:34; Acts 14:17; 2 Cor 5:12), and the term is also occasionally used in parallel with "mind" (Greek *nous*, e.g., 2 Cor 3:14-15).[19] Thus the heart will signify particularly the changeable aspects of our inner life, the source of our character.

The main focus, then, is forming the heart, becoming the kind of person who—with increasingly developed settled dispositions—keeps the moral law more routinely, rather than just trying to keep the law by trying harder and harder to keep the law. N. T. Wright notes,

> Jesus himself, backed up by the early Christian writers, speaks repeat-edly about the development of particular *character*. Character—the transforming, shaping, and marking of a life and its habits—will gener-ate the sort of behavior that rules might have pointed toward but which a "rule-keeping" *mentality* can never achieve. . . . In the last analysis, what matters after you believe [now as a Christian] is neither rules nor spontaneous discovery, but character.[20]

To the lawyer's question of rule making/rule following, "Who is my neighbor?" (Lk 10:29), Jesus responds by changing the perspective, sharing the Good Samaritan parable, and then asking a question of

---

[17]Ibid., p. 90.

[18]T. Sorg, "Heart," in *The New International Dictionary of NT Theology*, ed. Colin Brown (Grand Rapids: Zondervan, 1976), 2:181.

[19]Ibid., p. 182.

[20]N. T. Wright, *After You Believe: Why Christian Character Matters* (New York: HarperCollins, 2010), p. 7. The ethical theory most compatible with Jesus' emphasis on inner heart formation is virtue ethics. Yet even virtue ethics is ultimately deficient since it focuses primarily on indi-vidual virtues rather than on the person in whom the variety of virtues are unified, and there is no ultimate moral standard. Perhaps this label captures best the orientation of the Gospels: "a Virtuous-Exemplary-Jesus Christian Ethic," in which Jesus himself is the central moral referent. For further reading, see Joseph Kotva, *The Christian Case for Virtue Ethics* (Washing-ton, D.C.: Georgetown University Press, 1996).

inner heart formation, "Which of these . . . was a neighbor?" (Lk 10:36).[21] Similarly, in the business world, regulations and laws cannot make people act morally. Reflecting on the financial disaster of 2008, one senior banker remarked that character is the main solution. "Keeping rules is all right as far as it goes, but the real problem in the last generation is that we've lost the sense that character matters; that integrity matters. The system is only really healthy when the people who are running it are people you can trust to do the right thing, not because there are rules but because that's the sort of people they are."[22]

As another way to ponder the gap concept, consider the following situation. If you were booking a flight reservation and were given your choice, which of the following pilot competency options would you prefer for the person who flies your airplane?

- Option 1. A pilot who had studied aviation theory and successfully passed a written test for flying a Boeing 757 airplane.

- Option 2. A pilot who had accomplished "Competency 1" and also had logged many successful hours on a flight simulator.

- Option 3. A pilot who had accomplished "Competencies 1 and 2" and also had logged many successful hours actually flying a Boeing 757.

- Option 4. A pilot who had accomplished "Competencies 1, 2 and 3" and through intentional practices had formed many character-based aviation competencies, which evidenced a routine and joyful fluency in flying a Boeing 757.

Now adjust the analogy and imagine that the Christian life could be compared along a similar spectrum of competencies. Jesus lives within a "Competency 4" lifestyle, and invites us to continue to move through increasing levels of competencies toward becoming more like him. But how can our character, our heart, be changed? A pilot can't just jump to Competency 4 by willpower alone.

---

[21]In chapter three I explore the limited role that personally- and community-developed rules and principles may play as a means of establishing certain lifestyle routines to guide our practices in becoming more like Jesus.

[22]Cited in Wright, *After You Believe*, p. 10.

Willpower versus Core Beliefs

I think we've adopted the wrong diagnosis and the wrong strategy to address the willing-doing gap. We've wrongly believed that willpower is the primary factor. Perhaps because willpower works in a simple sphere—such as deciding to open a door, or getting to a certain destination—we've assumed willpower also works on a grander scale in changing our character. That's a mistake. Willpower alone was never meant to carry the weight of right living—it is too puny to defeat the various temptations we face and to change the sinful habits and compulsions we've developed over a lifetime. Remember how New Year's resolutions aren't that successful?

To narrow our gaps and become more like Jesus we need to recognize the important role that core beliefs hold in our character, from which flow our thoughts and actions. A key matter in our character formation relates to what we actually believe to be true—our *deeply held worldview beliefs and desires* about God and life. Our beliefs and desires make up the core of our character,[23] particularly those beliefs and desires that are strongly held (say with 75- or 80-percent certainty or more) and are very central in importance within our worldview. To simplify the discussion, I will use the term "worldview beliefs" or "core beliefs" as a summary phrase throughout the book for a complex set of factors within our character that influences our lifestyle, which includes a host of affective elements (e.g., desires, dispositions, attitudes, feelings), along with the more cognitive elements (e.g., beliefs, knowledge, pre-theoretical aspects, imagination). For ease of discussion, I focus more on the cognitive aspects, but realize there is much more involved in character formation.[24]

To explore further the concept of core worldview beliefs, consider the following explanations from two philosophers that emphasize how

---

[23]I rely on Richard Swinburne's model of character as mainly consisting of beliefs and desires, although his assumption of the evolutionary genesis of the soul is problematic for me. For more on the affective, see Swinburne, *The Evolution of the Soul*, rev. ed. (Oxford: Clarendon, 1997).

[24]Character formation of our inner life is more than a cognitive matter, including our emotional life as is developed in chapter four. For more on the affective aspects, see chapter three in J. P. Moreland and Klaus Issler, *In Search of a Confident Faith* (Downers Grove, Ill.: InterVarsity Press, 2008).

central and vital a role our core beliefs have for impacting our lives. Although he emphasizes the ethical aspects of our worldview beliefs, Simon Blackburn offers a useful description.

> [The moral "environment"] is the surrounding climate of [our own] ideas about how to live. It determines what we find acceptable or unacceptable, admirable or contemptible. It determines our conception of when things are going well and when they are going badly. It determines our conception of what is due us, and what is due from us, as we relate to others. It shapes our emotional responses, determining what is a cause of pride or shame, or anger or gratitude, or what can be forgiven and what cannot. It gives us our standards—our standards of behaviour. In the eyes of some thinkers . . . it shapes our very identities.[25]

From his extensive study of the history of the concept of worldview, David Naugle explains,

> A worldview . . . creates the definitive symbolic universe which is responsible in the main for the shape of a variety of life-determining, human practices. . . . The human heart is its home, and it provides a home for the human heart. At the end of the day it is hard to conceive of a more important human or cultural reality, theoretically or practically, than . . . [what] makes up a worldview.[26]

Having looked at these definitions, let's consider a few illustrations to put some flesh on the concept.

A computer analogy, though obviously simplistic, may offer a way to understand this topic from contemporary life. Imagine that each human being is composed of both hardware (physical body) and software, including a "first" operating system *(FOS)* and also a multitude of third-party-generated software applications *(3rdPSA)* from our family heritage. We know that the operating system and other software is what runs the computer. The operating system and software represents our deeply held worldview beliefs and desires. The challenge is that at birth, our *FOS* and *3rdPSA* are riddled with viruses small and large. These do not fully shut down functionality, but functionality is very limited.

---

[25]Simon Blackburn, *Being Good* (Oxford: Oxford University Press, 2001), p. 1.
[26]David K. Naugle, *Worldview* (Grand Rapids: Eerdmans, 2002), pp. 329-30.

Similarly, we have both true and false worldview beliefs and desires that affect our lifestyle.

Then God—the original designer—intervenes in our life and miraculously regenerates us and brings us into his family and orb of influence. God radically changes our potentiality at the core of our being by replacing our *FOS* with his powerful "Born-Again" operating system *(BAOS)*, a replacement only the original designer can make in this closed architecture context. Now we have the potentiality to function at optimum levels. But we still have all those *3rdPSA* riddled with viruses that distort our functionality, even affecting the *BAOS* at times. Now, our *BAOS* will never have viruses itself, but its operation is influenced by the poorly made *3rdPSA*. To continue this simplistic analogy, what God wants to do over time is to replace all those virus-tainted *3rdPSA* we currently have with his own "God-designed" software applications. These are guaranteed forever to never have any viruses! Thus, our formation involves a meticulous, difficult and time-consuming process of locating and deleting these dysfunctional *3rdPSA* and then adding in their place God's own. As these replacements take place greater computer functionality becomes possible. This upgrading can never take place without God's continuous empowerment.

An example from common life can demonstrate how influential our worldview beliefs are. In our country you don't want to drive on the left side of the road, except when it's safe to pass a car on a two-lane highway. Otherwise in the left lane you'll eventually have a head-on crash with a car coming in the opposite direction. All American drivers have developed a deep worldview belief that it's not healthy to drive in the left lane. Imagine driving a car on a two-lane highway and suddenly your car starts veering left and crosses over the dividing line into oncoming traffic. Perhaps you hit an oil slick or there's a sheet of ice on the road. Immediately your actions indicate how badly you don't want to be going over that line—a central belief about driving safely is being violated—and you do everything in your power to avert that. But if we lived in England and drove a car there, driving safely in the *left* lane would be part of our worldview beliefs.

In the last two years, the Lord has been working with me regarding a significant release of some of my controlling tendencies, moving me toward greater openness to "letting go." Many years ago, we were having a large gathering at our house during the day and I noticed that the air conditioning came on. It wasn't that warm in the house, but my first reaction the moment I heard the air conditioning starting up was to get up and turn it off to save money. However, I stopped myself in my tracks and began to muse about why I felt such urgency—had such a conditioned response like a rat in a maze—to turn off the air conditioning when I heard the sound of the unit coming on. I then realized how stingy I was, that money concerns were too highly valued in my worldview beliefs. I decided to be more generous to our guests that day and let the unit run. Our daughter Ruth had also given me similar feedback about some of our intense discussions when my first response to a new idea was "it costs too much." Facing this kind of feedback was hard, but it began a journey of inviting God's gracious work in my heart so that it's much easier now for me to be more generous.

About a year ago, after some concerted attention regarding my controlling tendencies, I sensed that a significant tectonic shift had taken place in the depth of my heart. What did it feel like? A deep joy, an awareness of more freedom in my soul, and a greater range of choices than I'd had before. I marvel at how Jesus continues to save me from these destructive sinful tendencies. I'm grateful to Jesus, and to those who've come alongside in my formation journey. I've become convinced that if we wish to reduce the willing-doing gap, our focus must include what can be called "heart flow work," deep changes that take place in our character. As Jesus clarified, "Out of *the overflow of the heart* the mouth speaks" (Mt 12:34; Lk 6:45, emphasis added).

Deep down in our character we live out of our worldview beliefs. Dallas Willard explains, "We always live up to our beliefs—or down to them, as the case may be. Nothing else is possible. It is the nature of belief."[27] So if we want to know what our worldview beliefs are, we just need to note how we act in a variety of situations. In most cases our actions exactly match our worldview beliefs. That's the basis for the prov-

---

[27] Dallas Willard, *The Divine Conspiracy* (San Francisco: HarperSanFrancisco, 1998), p. 307.

erb "Actions speak louder than words." God designed humans so that our lives are primarily directed by our deeply held worldview beliefs. It's a grace so that we don't have to be retrained every fifteen minutes. Perhaps it's also one of the factors that will ensure we won't sin in heaven: our lives will be directed by our deeply held worldview beliefs, which will all be true at that point.

But What About . . . ?

A number of questions and hesitations may arise regarding the topic of character formation. This is no moral formation project done by our own human power, but it must be initiated and sustained by God's empowering grace. The question remains, is it *all* on God to do this formation, or do I have any part to play? What comes to mind is the following disconnected, commonly held logic. When *I* do good, who is basically responsible? The answer is "God." When *I* do bad, who is basically responsible? The answer is "me." So where was *I* (i.e., me) when *I* (i.e., God) did the good? In attempting to make sure we avoid self-pride and don't rob God of his glory, must we disappear except when we sin?

It seems more consistent to affirm that, as a regenerated child of God and as an enduring self, I participate in *all* my decisions; and that when *I* do good, God and *I* cooperate in this (I'm the finite partner, God is the infinite partner). Theologians from various orthodox Christian traditions affirm some form of a cooperation or synergism between God and each believer in sanctification.[28] For example, J. I. Packer explains, "Sanctification, however, is in one sense synergistic—it is an ongoing cooperative process in which regenerate persons, alive to God and freed from sin's dominion (Rom 6:11, 14-18), are required to exert themselves in sustained obedience."[29] As Dallas Willard phrases it,

---

[28]See Keith Kettenring, *The Sanctification Connection: An Exploration of Human Participation in Spiritual Growth* (Lanham, Md.: University Press of America, 2008), pp. 26-34. He includes a representative citation from these traditions: Evangelical, Lutheran, Reformed, Dispensational, Keswick, Baptist, Wesleyan, Holiness and Anglican. For a helpful discussion of the nuances of terms such as *spiritual formation, Christian spirituality* and *sanctification,* see Evan Howard, *The Brazos Introduction to Christian Spirituality* (Grand Rapids: Brazos, 2008), pp. 17-24.

[29]J. I. Packer, *Concise Theology* (Wheaton, Ill.: Tyndale House, 1993), pp. 170-71.

"Grace . . . is opposed to *earning*, not to *effort*."[30] On a personal note, what amazes me is that the *Holy* Spirit, who indwells me forever and is the divine agent of sanctification, is willing to remain with me despite my many *unholy* gaps—what grace. God is with me in my gaps.

What about the possibility of any character formation change taking place this side of heaven? We need to avoid two extremes: concluding either that change is impossible, or that complete formation—sinless perfection—can be accomplished in this life.[31] Between these two unbiblical positions, there's a wide range for change as we learn from Jesus (Mt 11:29). Even the religious leaders observed the change in the disciples' lives following Jesus' resurrection: "When they saw the courage of Peter and John and realized that they were unschooled, ordinary men, they were astonished and they took note that these men had been with Jesus" (Acts 4:13).

Deep character formation requires that we attend to the core of our self—the heart—and cooperate with God's good work within. Whether we are female or male, whether Asian or American, whether office or factory worker, whether rich or poor, we all face the same willing-doing gap problem. None of us has an inside track to solve the willing-doing gap, except for Jesus. Willard states,

> [Jesus] knew that we cannot keep the law by trying to keep the law. To succeed in keeping the law one must aim at something other and something more. One must aim to become the *kind of person* from whom the deeds of the law naturally flow. The apple tree naturally and easily produces apples because of its inner nature. This is the most crucial thing to remember if we would understand Jesus' picture of the kingdom heart given in the Sermon on the Mount.[32]

In the Sermon on the Mount, Jesus uses the term "righteousness" (Greek *dikaiosunē*) to convey the results of this inner heart work (Mt 5:5,

---

[30]Dallas Willard, "General Introduction," in J. P. Moreland, *Love Your God with All Your Mind* (Colorado Springs: NavPress, 1997), p. 12.

[31]What of Matthew 5:48, "Be perfect, therefore, as your heavenly Father is perfect"? We cannot become divine, but since we've been created in the image of God and then regenerated with a new heart, God has built into human nature the potential to grow into moral or sinless perfection eventually, in virtues that God exemplifies for us. A parallel verse in Luke identifies one particular virtue: "Be merciful, just as your Father is merciful" (Lk 6:36). The formation process starts on this side of heaven but can only be completed after death.

[32]Willard, *Divine Conspiracy*, pp. 142-43.

10, 20; 6:1, 33). In Matthew 6:33, this righteousness and God's kingdom are linked together: "Seek first his kingdom and his righteousness, and all these things will be given to you as well."[33] Paul also connects the two in Romans 14:17: "For the kingdom of God is . . . righteousness [*dikaiosunē*], peace and joy in the Holy Spirit." What is this kingdom?

The Grand Project: The Kingdom of God

Our formation into becoming like Jesus is part of a grand cosmic project, what Jesus called "the kingdom of God." Most scholars agree that this subject was central in Jesus' teaching. For example, it appears at the beginning of his ministry (Mk 1:15), during his ministry, such as in significant teaching on the kingdom through parables (Mt 13), and until he was taken up into heaven (Acts 1:3). From Matthew 19:16-29 we learn that the concept "enter the kingdom of God" (Mt 19:24) can be a synonym for "inherit eternal life" (Mt 19:29; this is the phrase John used more often) and "be saved" (Mt 19:25; "salvation" is the term Paul used more often; Jesus' name means "Yahweh is salvation"). Regarding the kingdom of God, Darrell Bock states,

> What Jesus announced and started in almost hidden fashion, he would complete one day in a return when God's rule would decisively enter this history in judgment and prepare the way for a new world. In the meantime, those who allied themselves with Jesus are called to a life of integrity and service as they in faith embrace the hope that Jesus offered and await the completion of the promise.[34]

George Ladd adds,

> God's Kingdom in Jesus' teaching has a twofold manifestation: at the end of the age to destroy Satan, and in Jesus' mission to bind Satan. . . . This is the will of God: to conquer evil and to bring his people finally into the blessed immortality of the eternal life of the Age to Come.[35]

---

[33]Note that when Jesus teaches "Seek first his kingdom" it includes also seeking "his righteousness" (Mt 6:33). That is, God's kingdom priorities include the believers' character formation into God's righteousness. Thus engaging in one's own inner heart formation is not just a selfish pursuit, but an important priority of kingdom work, resulting in significant impact in the world as our light shines in good deeds, so that others will praise God (Mt 5:16).

[34]Darrell Bock, *Jesus According to Scripture* (Grand Rapids: Baker, 2002), pp. 590-91.

[35]George Ladd, *A Theology of the New Testament* (Grand Rapids: Eerdmans, 1974), pp. 66, 69.

The English translation of "kingdom" today indicates a location or realm, but the biblical concept also includes the dynamic reigning aspect. (To remind us of this dynamic aspect, on occasion I will use the term "kingship" as a synonym, as suggested by R. T. France.[36]) When we pray the Lord's prayer, we request "[may] your kingdom come, [may] your will be done on earth as it is in heaven" (Mt 6:10). And when we each cooperate with God in becoming more like Jesus, then our *living* like Jesus increases the effect of God's desires or wishes on earth, thus representing one aspect of an answer to that prayer.

Final Thoughts

I've become convinced that living more like Jesus is possible, but only if we take a different approach. We need to abandon an externally focused, rule-keeping emphasis on Christian living, and instead embrace Jesus' teaching and example of inner heart formation. Deep character change can take place as we rely on the essential divine resources God has made available and as we engage in relevant formation practices over time, in companionship with our brothers and sisters in Christ.

We've made a good beginning on the subject of worldview beliefs, but more is involved, as will be developed in the next chapter. Throughout the book we'll learn much from Jesus' own example. To keep this focus on Jesus, the biblical portion of our study will mainly come from the four Gospels: Matthew, Mark, Luke and John.[37] To get the most from this book, you may wish to have your Bible handy. Read the material reflectively, keeping in mind your own particular life journey and where God may be touching your heart. At the end of each chapter I summarize some key ideas and throughout the book suggest various formation practices. As one means to solidify the ideas in your mind, perhaps share with others in your community what's important to you and the questions that come to mind.

Jesus invites us to learn more about our own hearts as we follow his heart: "Come to me, all you who are weary and burdened, and I will give

---

[36]France, *Matthew*, p. 102.

[37]For a helpful guide in studying Jesus in the Gospels, see Darrell Bock, *Studying the Historical Jesus* (Grand Rapids: Baker, 2002).

you rest . . . for I am gentle and humble in heart and you will find rest" (Mt 11:29). Donald Hagner phrases it, "Jesus now promises to those who come to him and follow him in discipleship: *he* will give them rest for their souls, i.e., a realization of deep existential peace, a *shalom*,[38] or sense of ultimate well-being with regard to one's relationship with God and his commandments."[39] It's an invitation without any pressure, without any guilt for what we're not doing. Jesus demonstrates by his own life example that this is possible. I'm still on the journey myself. Will you join me?

Key Points

1. The willing-doing gap is a universal human problem that we try to fix in ways that mostly miss the source of the problem.

2. Our life is *not* primarily directed by our decisions or willpower, but primarily by our heart flow. Our heart flow is sourced in our deeply held worldview beliefs and desires, which make up our character.

3. Jesus teaches that to address the willing-doing gap effectively, we must focus on changing our heart flow, not just our behavior through rule keeping.

Reflection Questions

1. The willing-doing gap: What is it? What examples come to mind that illustrate it? In your opinion, to what extent is it a problem that needs to be addressed?

2. What are worldview beliefs? Do you agree or disagree that they are a key component of inner formation process?

3. The author encourages readers to give attention to inner formation and not just focus on external religious conformity or rule keeping. In your own words, explain what he means. Do you agree or disagree? Does Jesus actually teach this? Explain.

---

[38] *Shalom* is the best biblical term to capture the fullness of human flourishing, comparable to the classic Greek term *eudaimonia* (poorly translated as "happiness"). See Issler, "Happiness," in *Dictionary of Christian Spirituality*, ed. Glen Scorgie (Grand Rapids: Zondervan, 2011).

[39] Hagner, *Matthew 1-13*, p. 324.

2

Wake Up to Five Formation Gaps

Why do you look at the speck of sawdust in someone
else's eye and pay no attention to the plank in your own eye?
How can you say, "Let me take the speck out of your eye," when all the time
there is a plank in your own eye? You hypocrite, first take the plank
out of your own eye, and then you will see clearly to
remove the speck from the other person's eye.

MATTHEW 7:3-5

· ℮ ·

That's not me." University of New Mexico soccer player Elizabeth Lambert was responding to a video clip of her from a Mountain West Conference match in November 2009. After the game—in which the BYU women's soccer team defeated UNM 1-0—Lambert couldn't explain why she yanked BYU opponent Cassidy Shumway's ponytail with such violence as to take her to the ground in a split second. As the 2010 World Cup Soccer matches have demonstrated, there's more aggressive physical play and cheating than any referee can call, and the referee missed this Lambert-Shumway incident, but it was caught on camera. In this particular conference match, Lambert had received her share of shoves and cheap shots. The video also reveals that, prior to the ponytail incident, Lambert was elbowed in the stomach and Shumway had been tugging at her shorts. Later Lambert received a yellow card for tripping an opponent moving toward the goal, and after the game was over she was suspended indefinitely from the UNM team for her violent ponytail episode. About the emotion of the game, she admitted, "In that moment, I let it all get into my head."[1] In a formal statement of apology, Lambert included the line, "This is in no way indicative of my character or the soccer player that I am."

We tend to be clueless about our gaps—our blind spots. Jesus taught this point using a bit of humorous exaggeration in Matthew 7:3-5, the passage quoted above. Jesus acknowledges that, although we may have deep insight into the needs of others ("the speck"), we are basically clueless about the obvious "plank" in our own eye.[2] In this chapter, five particular formation gaps are identified to help us better recognize these places that hinder us from living into the life of Jesus. First we will consider three particular gaps identified in Jesus' parable of the four soils[3] and another unfruitful gap from Jesus' teaching in John 15. Then we'll examine a difficult episode in Jesus' life that offers a fifth gap, and we'll conclude with a basic strategy for how we can deal with our gaps.

Differing Heart Responses to Truth

Jesus' rich teaching of the parable of the four soils (Mt 13:3-23; Mk 4:3-20; Lk 8:5-18) offers important insights into the hindering movements of our heart. As recorded in Matthew and Mark, it is the lead story in the series of parables about God's kingship. In this teaching Jesus clarifies the spectrum of possible responses to the good news. Yet, as many Bible teachers have done in the past, we can also apply Jesus' remarkable wisdom to our own lives as his disciples.[4]

---

[1]Jere Longman, "Those Soccer Plays, In Context," *New York Times*, November 17, 2009 <www.nytimes.com/2009/11/18/sports/soccer/18soccer.html>; Michael David Smith, "New Mexico Women's Soccer Suspends Elizabeth Lambert" (November 6, 2009) <backporch.fanhouse.com/2009/11/06/>.

[2]Elton Trueblood identifies this comment as one of thirty humorous sayings of Jesus; *The Humor of Christ* (New York: Harper & Row, 1964).

[3]I appreciate colleague Joanne Jung for directing me to this parable.

[4]R. T. France suggests such an application for believers today: "But the types of soil are described not in terms of any particular group or groups, whether during Jesus' ministry or sub-

Briefly, the story involves a farmer scattering seed that fell on four different soils: some beside the road, some on rocky places, some among the thorns and finally some on the good soil—the only one that proved to be fruitful. Jesus interprets the parable and indicates that the four persons represented by the soils all hear the truth. The difference lies in *how* they hear, in the kind of heart each soil represents. We'll focus on the three unfruitful soils—the seed beside the road, the rocky soil and then the thorny soil—drawing out implications regarding barriers to receiving truth and how we might become more receptive.

Seed on the road—the dismissive gap. The seeds that fell by the road, having no opportunity to take root at all, represent the first gap. It's best summarized by that great word picture, "hard heart." Jesus was grieved at the hardened hearts of the religious leaders (Mk 3:5) and his own disciples (Mk 6:5-52; 8:17). What is a hardened heart? It's one that is closed off, even resistant to truth. For example, it could involve an arrogant refusal to hear truth from those of lesser status (e.g., Jn 9:34 [paraphrased], "Do you think you can teach us anything?"), or not pondering the implications of truths we already know, as was the case of the disciples. "Aware of their discussion [of not bringing bread with them], Jesus asked them: 'Why are you talking about having no bread? Do you still not see or understand? *Are your hearts hardened?* Do you have eyes but fail to see, and ears but fail to hear? And don't you remember [gathering up extra baskets of bread from the miraculous feedings]?'" (Mk 8:17-18, emphasis added).[5] Sadly, due to their dullness in

---

sequently, but in general categories which may be applicable in many different terms and situations within Christian history. Even as 'interpreted' the parable therefore remains open-ended in terms of its pastoral application. The careful spelling out of the successive agricultural hazards therefore probably justifies the use to which the parable has been most frequently put in subsequent Christian exposition, as a basis for those who hear it, even within the disciple community, to examine their own openness to God's message and the fruitfulness or otherwise of their response. The slogan 'Whoever has ears, let them hear' (v. 9) invites such an application" (R. T. France, *The Gospel of Matthew*, New International Commentary on the New Testament [Grand Rapids: Eerdmans, 2007], p. 518).

[5]Regarding their hard hearts, Jesus then alludes to Isaiah 6:9-10—about the rejection of receiving truth—which Jesus also quotes as an introductory note to explain his use of parables (Mt 13:13-15; Mk 4:11-12; Lk 8:10). Jesus draws an analogy, since most of the Jews of Jesus' day rejected truth just as they did in Isaiah's day. John Oswalt clarifies that the prophet Isaiah was not like one of the false prophets, preaching a message of affirmation that didn't mention their sin problem. "Rather, Isaiah is called upon to preach a message that, given the already-

remembering God's past provision (Mk 8:16-21), Jesus' disciples evidenced a hardened heart as if they were "outsiders" (Mk 4:11) or even like his opponents (Mk 3:5).

What prevents today's disciples from receiving the truth? Surprisingly, an important barrier is our current worldview beliefs, a summary term introduced in chapter one to include a complex set of beliefs, values, attitudes and desires. Specifically, we restrict our search for new-to-us truths by the ideas or concepts we regard as *not* possible or plausible. The point is that we don't expend much effort exploring ideas we don't regard as possibly true. Consider two sets of ideas: (1) ideas that might be possible but we haven't yet embraced, and (2) ideas we think are outlandish and impossible. Examples for category 1 might include that some UFOs exist, some reported near death experiences offer true accounts, more answers to prayer are possible, or there might be worlds with people outside of our galaxy. On the other hand, examples for category 2—ideas we give no credence since they're so implausible or impossible to us—might include that the earth is flat, humans can fly by flapping their arms, or it's worthwhile to pray over a person who just died to be raised to life again. However, since we're not omniscient and don't know everything there is to know, can we recognize it's likely that some things we now regard as impossible are truths?

Our false worldview beliefs can hinder us from learning new truths by bracketing off whole areas of ideas we now consider to be beyond belief. That Jesus was resurrected bodily from the tomb is a common Christian belief. Yet to the eleven disciples on resurrection Sunday morning, it was a grave matter of skepticism. The women who had visited the empty tomb came to the disciples and reported the angel's message, "He is not here; he has risen!" (Lk 24:9). But the disciples could not accept this fact. "But they [the disciples including Peter and John] did not believe the women, *because their words seemed to them like nonsense*" (Lk 24:11, emphasis added). And Thomas also resisted accepting this truth—even though his close companions tried to persuade

---

hardened heart of his generation . . . will only push them farther away from God. But some will turn, among them faithful followers of Isaiah." *Isaiah*, NIV Application Commentary (Grand Rapids: Zondervan, 2003), p. 128.

him with eyewitness accounts (Jn 20:25). Like these unconvinced disciples, we may not readily accept—or we dismiss—ideas that don't make sense to us. Hence, I label this the *dismissive* gap.

As an adult with graduate theological training, I must admit I've initially dismissed Christian truths I thought were too crazy to believe. For example, I used to think God couldn't communicate to me personally and directly. But over a period of time I became convinced that the Bible does teach this.[6]

Our false core worldview beliefs can become barriers to receiving more truth, thus hindering their potential correction. Peter, John and Thomas couldn't imagine that Jesus was alive. The town of Nazareth couldn't grasp that Jesus, who had plied his woodworking and masonry skills among them, was anything more than "the carpenter" (Mk 6:3). This limiting belief held them back from receiving Jesus' healing ministry among them: "And he was amazed at their lack of faith" (Mk 6:6). For various reasons, we may also tenaciously hold on to false worldview beliefs as these folk did—which can hinder us from formation into the greater freedom that such truths could bring.

Regarding this particular heart response in the parable, not only is the heart totally unreceptive, but Jesus also explicitly says that Satan is active to keep it that way—to hinder any further opportunity for receptivity. On two particular occasions when Jesus informed the twelve disciples about his impending suffering and death Luke records, "But they did not understand what this meant. *It was hidden from them*, so that they did not grasp it, and they were afraid to ask him about it" (Lk 9:45, emphasis added; also Lk 18:34). Nolland explains, "The disciples do not know, because they do not want to know: note how they are afraid to ask him about what they have not understood. But there is also a supernatural aspect to their blindness. They are caught up in a Satanic benightedness (see [Lk] 8:12 [parable of soils]; 18:34; 24:16)."[7] Nolland also says, "The personal responsibility is clear enough in [Lk]

---

[6]For the results of my biblical study of God's personal communication to us, see chapter 6, "Communication: Hearing the God Who Speaks," in my book *Wasting Time with God* (Downers Grove, Ill.: InterVarsity Press, 2001), pp. 151-83.

[7]John Nolland, *Luke 9:21–18:34*, Word Biblical Commentary 35B (Dallas: Word, 1993), p. 515.

24:25. It is unlikely that in 24:25 Jesus is opening minds that are to be understood as previously shut by God. The clearest analogy for such a Satanic activity is provided by [Lk] 8:12 [parable of the soils]."[8] When our hearts are hardened to truth, when we're fearful (Mk 9:32) and not open to consider a truth, we invite Satan's activity to keep us in the dark (see Jn 8:43-47; Rom 1:21; Eph 4:18; also Jn 8:43-47). Hopefully, when we don't receive truths initially, after more growth we'll be more receptive (e.g., Jn 12:16).

Rocky soil—the discrepancy gap. In the parable, the second soil was shallow, a rocky place. The seed sprang up quickly, but withered just as quickly when the sun came out. There is some initial receptivity, but "they have no firm root in themselves" (Mk 4:17 NASB). The implication is that, although we may agree with a particular Christian belief, that belief has never become incorporated into our core worldview—no deep root has taken hold in our character. Note that our deeply held worldview beliefs are not necessarily what we "profess" or say we believe. Consider Peter's brave statement at the Last Supper before Jesus was arrested. Peter—the lead disciple in Jesus' band of close companions—strongly affirmed his loyalty to Jesus. Jesus warned Peter that the devil would soon test each of the disciples ("all of you," plural, Lk 22:31), and Jesus had specifically prayed for Peter's faith to hold firm ("you," singular, Lk 22:32). Jesus added that, although Peter would fall, "when you have turned back, strengthen your brothers" (Lk 22:32). Yet Peter couldn't hear the encouragement that Jesus had prayed for him and that Jesus noted Peter's key role in encouraging the other disciples. Was it his pride or just his defensiveness that took over when he announced with bravado, "Lord, I am ready to go with you to prison and to death" (Lk 22:33)? Jesus' response? Predicting that Peter would deny Jesus three times before a rooster crowed.

In some cases our *professed* beliefs have little relation to our *worldview* beliefs—how we actually live. Note this analogy: we have an idealized perception of ourselves—an image without faults—that is in contrast with reality (we do have blind spots that are obvious to others).

---

[8]Ibid., p. 514.

C. S. Lewis illustrates these gaps as rats in a dark cellar. "Surely what a man does when he is taken off his guard is the best evidence for what sort of a man he is? Surely what pops out before the man has time to put on a disguise is the truth? If there are rats in a cellar, you are most likely to see them if you go in very suddenly. But the suddenness does not create the rats: it only prevents them from hiding."[9] We envision that our idealized self firmly holds to the truth, but an episode of reality indicates a discrepancy—as it did for that soccer player mentioned at the beginning of the chapter. As a child I used to believe it would never rain on a Sunday, since I deduced "Sunday" meant "sunny day." Imagine my disappointment—and brief crisis of trust in God—the first time it rained on a Sunday.

For me, it's getting a bit easier to acknowledge my discrepancy gaps. One year on the first day of class I was to introduce a junior adjunct professor who would be teaching one of our doctoral elective seminars. She was having difficulty setting up the PowerPoint connections for her presentation. We were now after the time when class should have begun, and students were just milling around. Instead of offering to be helpful, I walked to the front of the room with forceful direction and privately told her to forget the PowerPoint and just start the class session without it. She brushed me aside—we've been colleagues for many years and have a comfortable relationship—and she kept trying the connection, which eventually began working about five minutes later.

While sitting in the back of the class during her opening presentation I finally became aware of what I'd done. I was shocked. Was that really me? How arrogant to take charge of someone else's class. What a control freak. It just bubbled up from the core of my character. How embarrassed I felt when, *through the Spirit's awakening ministry,* I finally noticed this gap about fifteen minutes after the episode. I could have explained it away, being the senior faculty member in the classroom, or just ignored it, inferring, "That's not me." Such a response really meant that my action didn't fit with my *idealized* image of myself. But this time I could admit: Yes, it was me; yes, it is me. My anxieties had

---

[9]C. S. Lewis, *Mere Christianity* (New York: Macmillan, 1952), p. 150.

risen to such a pitch that I was worried the technical difficulties and a late start of class would reflect on my reputation. I became aware of my gap: "I'm okay trusting God for my circumstances . . . except when that controlling urge surfaces."

Becoming more aware of our gaps. As Jesus noted, we can easily spot the gaps in others, but we're usually clueless about our own discrepancies. David Benner suggests three indicators to help us become more aware of such gaps. The first discrepancy clue relates to our *pet peeves* about others. Benner explains,

> If laziness in others is what really bothers me, there is a good chance that discipline and performance form a core part of the false self that I embrace with tenacity. If it is playfulness and spontaneity in others that I find most annoying, then seriousness may be a central part of the self I protect and seek to project. If it is moral disregard that is particularly irritating in others, my false self is probably built around moral rectitude and self-righteousness. And if emotionality in others is what I most despise, emotional control is probably central to the script I have chosen to live.[10]

The second clue is the times when we're *protective* or defensive about a comment or action. Our response comes back with some extra energy. "What do you mean?!" "Of course not!" If we reflect within, we may find that we are annoyed or irritated. It's worth pondering why we're making a mountain out of a trivial matter.

Benner's third discrepancy clue is to look for the *patterns* of our compulsions, such as workaholism, perfectionism, extreme orderliness and cleanliness, being overly gracious and nice, or being controlling (as I had been in the classroom). "They often involve a good that is elevated to the status of the supreme good by the disproportionate importance we attach to it."[11]

Another guide to identifying gaps comes from Thomas Keating. He suggests that during our childhood we developed strategies—"emotional programs for happiness"—to fulfill our basic instinctual needs. When our attempts to seek happiness don't succeed, we experience various

---

[10]David Benner, *The Gift of Being Yourself* (Downers Grove, Ill.: InterVarsity Press, 2004), pp. 83-85.
[11]Ibid., pp. 84-85.

afflictive emotions, such as fear, grief, anger, hostility, jealousy, inferiority and rejection. Listed after the basic need is what our current "happiness strategy" might look like:[12]

A. Survival and safety: e.g., seek the accumulation of certain security symbols of the culture

B. Affection and esteem: e.g., seek those who can meet certain dependency needs, such as our spouse, friends and work colleagues

C. Power and control: e.g., seek to control every situation and everyone

Keating explains, "We may not remember the events of early childhood, but the emotions do. When events occur later in life that resemble those once felt to be harmful, dangerous, or rejecting, the same feelings surface."[13]

Letting go of these destructive coping strategies of the false self is an aspect of what Jesus implied in his teaching about "denying oneself" (e.g., Mt 16:24-28; Lk 9:23-24). This becomes possible as we grow into greater confidence in and dependence on God for our needs and let go of our radical independence from God, another aspect of self-denial. Jesus' teaching about self-denial is actually very life affirming. Since becoming aware of our emotions is an important element for our formation, consider the following formation exercise.

Listening to our emotions. One way I've found helpful to become aware of discrepancy gaps is to cultivate a greater awareness of my own feelings. My challenge was that I couldn't describe or label my various emotions. Like learning a foreign language, I needed to acquire a new vocabulary to name the range of feelings. After discussing this problem with a psychologist friend, Bill Roth, I developed a simple five-label checklist that continues to help me monitor how I'm feeling. I reduced the range to five broad categories, using two sets of words for ease of memory: "glad, sad, mad," and "dreads and dreams."

I ask a series of questions (listed below) in relation to a certain time frame (e.g., today, past week, past month). Within that time period, I try to identify a recent event from my life for each of these five categories.

[12]Thomas Keating, *Invitation to Love* (1992; reprint, New York: Continuum, 2002), pp. 6-9.
[13]Ibid., p. 7.

The key is to *relive* that event a bit, so that I can sense the feeling and associate the label (e.g., "glad") with it. For work on emotions, I think we can't just have a cognitive link with the term, but must also have emotional experience as a reference for the term. I take a legal pad and reflect on my week and fill in items for each category. Later, I look back over past journals to notice any patterns. These become notes of thanksgiving and prayer for divine guidance. You may wish to try it out.

1. Was I *glad* today/this past week (i.e., joyful, pleased, grateful, happy, "up," flourishing, "flow" experience, positively energized, tears of joy, relief, deep peace, freedom)? Identify an event and relive the moment—feel the emotion, and enjoy the moment again.

2. Was I *sad* today/this past week (i.e., sorrowful, "down," disappointed, depressed, tears of sadness)? Identify an event and feel the emotion.

3. Was I *mad* today/this past week (i.e., frustrated, annoyed, irritated, blocked in, "ticked off," angry, ballistic)? Identify one event and feel the emotion.

4. What did I *dread* today/this past week (i.e., concerned, bothered, worried, anxious, fearful, distressed, turbulent, obsessed, compulsively driven, negatively energized, negative expectations, burned out, chaotic)? Identify one event and feel the emotion.

5. What are my *dreams* for the future (i.e., longings, yearnings, looking forward to, wish for, hope for, positive expectations, imaginings, "it would be great if . . .")? Identify a future goal or event and feel the emotion.

Many fruitful times of conversation have opened up for my wife Beth and me by using this guide—for each category, first one sharing, then the other. The benefit of this simple practice is moving through a *wide range of feelings*. Especially the arenas where we are "sad," "mad" and have "dreads" may help us identify particular discrepancy gaps.

Thorny soil—the distracted gap. The seed among the thorns—the third soil—began to grow, but the thorns choked the plants so they didn't bear any fruit. The basic implication for Jesus' disciples today is that our way of life can cause us to become distracted, slowly drifting off course away from our priority to follow Jesus. He identifies three specific hindrances: "worries of the world [this age]," "the deceitfulness of riches" and "desires for other things" (Mk 4:19 NASB; see also Lk 21:34).

Consider a relevant enactment of this point. While Jesus was at Lazarus's house in Bethany, his sister Martha blurted out, "Lord, don't you care that my sister [Mary] has left me to do the work by myself? Tell her to help me!" (Lk 10:40). Martha was *distracted*. "Martha, Martha . . . you are worried and upset about many things" (Lk 10:41). We get busy in life, even with good things—the "desires" Jesus identified relate to general living, not necessarily to evil things—and we become easily distracted and off center.

At one point in my life I had told Jesus I really would like to go on an extended retreat and spend time with him, but I never got around to it. Then on a bright January weekend, while I was playing roller-hockey on a cul-de-sac in the neighborhood (at age forty-six), life suddenly was put on hold. I took a direct hit to my left eye with a hockey ball. I thought I might go blind—but eventually I was able to see, after a time of healing and cataract surgery. My immediate convalescence to help my eye stop bleeding was lying in our darkened bedroom for three weeks, with my head at a forty-five-degree angle. Doing nothing. It became an important season of grace for me—a divinely imposed time of retreat—that was a turning point in my life toward walking more closely with Jesus.

What chokes fruitfulness is simply getting busy and preoccupied with living without much intentionality toward Jesus' kingdom priorities. Worse, after a period of distraction, our lives may take on a destructive spiral downward; as Jesus phrases it, "[the house] collapsed and its destruction was complete" (Lk 6:49). How can we avoid the distracted gap? It requires vigilance and intentionality. One helpful means is to set aside a regular time for self-examination where we monitor our hearts, priorities and life goals. Some life goals may be worth assessing daily, some weekly, some monthly, some quarterly and some annually. In general, what we don't tend to *inspect*, we don't tend to *expect*. This is a problematic area for me. I'm great at making lists of goals, but then don't often get around to reviewing them. I'm working on that, and am requesting that an accountability partner ask me when I last reviewed my life goals. Because of the value of this particular spiritual practice, I will say more in chapter three about developing certain lifestyle routines to help us keep on track in living into the life of Jesus.

Being disconnected prevents fruitfulness. Let me suggest another major formation gap that also relates to unfruitful living: the disconnected gap. Consider Jesus' teaching about living a dependent life. Jesus depended on the Father (Jn 5:19-20, 30). He informs us we need to depend on him as well: "I am the vine; you are the branches. If you remain in me and I in you, you will bear much fruit; apart from me you can do nothing" (Jn 15:5). This fundamental relational reality for those in God's forever family involves both (a) an enduring objective status as branches—our "union in Christ" ("I am the vine, you are the branches")—and (b) an ongoing, experiential aspect—we must continually abide in Christ ("If you remain in me and I in you, you will bear much fruit").

Abiding in Jesus is the central matter of living a dependent life. The consequences of not abiding are severe: we are cut off from divine empowerment. We can't accomplish anything of lasting value—bearing fruit—unless we're dynamically relating to him while he is abiding in us. If we're *disconnected* from divine relationship and resources, we're just as fruitless as the three soils in the parable.

What does it mean to "abide" in Jesus? Whatever response we supply would fit into the category of ways we can deepen personal relationships. Individuals and communities will need to experiment with how to grow and increase their connection and intimacy with Jesus. For example, we may want our last thought at night and the first thought in the morning to be directed toward Jesus. Love is a two-way street.

Let me suggest one simple spiritual practice that can be practiced anywhere at any time and that can make an important contribution to our relationship with God and our formation. I've become aware in my own life of how much of my day I'm alone in my thoughts. Yet if I want a closer relationship with God I need to turn my mind toward him more often. This was a common practice in Jesus' life. For example, we notice that on two occasions Jesus paused briefly and offered a short prayer to God (Mt 11:25-27; Lk 10:21-22). How might we try this out today? I've found a simple way throughout my day to slow down to make room for God. Do we sometimes press a pause button on a DVD player or iPod to attend to something, and then return back to playing the movie or song? What about pressing the *pause button of life* now and then? Just stop what we're doing and take thirty seconds—like a commercial break—to have a word with God, the Sponsor of Life.

Here are the confessions of a woman in her forties and then a pastor on this practice:

> You challenged us to pause numerous times in our day and think about God. . . . As I did it, like other habits, it became easier. I have found it to be not only calming, but also truly peaceful as I allowed God to speak to me.[14]

> Ok, I confess, I thought it was goofy when Klaus made us draw a pause button on a post-it note the first day in class. But I feel sheepish now admitting how effective that little reminder has been in my life. In fact, even through those two weeks [of the course] that we spent on campus in June I used that little reminder to grab a few moments at a time for prayer and rest that helped me to pull through effectively. And I've carried the technique with me. It's become enough a part of me that I don't even need the "button" anymore as a reminder; I've just built those pause breaks right into my day.[15]

The goal is take several brief pauses during the day to talk with God. It may be helpful to use a visual support system, like small notes, to remind us to press the pause button during our day. On a sticky-note, draw a circle and write the word *pause* in the center. Place several of them at key spots in your day—bathroom mirror, refrigerator, computer screen, car dash board.

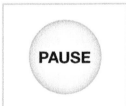

Figure 2.1

[14]Biola BOLD student, 2003.

[15]Reflection of a doctor of ministry student, October 2004.

As you pause, mention anything you want to God. You can listen to what your heart is telling you. It's a convenient way to take several brief God pauses throughout our day. That's exactly what Brother Lawrence (c. 1614-1691) has been challenging believers to do for centuries in his devotional classic, *The Practice of the Presence of God:*

> During our work and other activities, and even during our times of reading or writing, even though they may be spiritually oriented—and yes, even more during our outward devotions and prayers aloud—we ought to stop for a short moment, as frequently as we can, to adore God deep within our hearts and take pleasure in Him, even though we might have to do this momentarily and in secret.[16]

As a reminder, at the end of chapters in part two I'll suggest some additional activities to do during these thirty-second pauses.

Jesus Faces a Distressed Gap in Gethsemane

Thus far, based on a study of John 15 and the four soils parable, I have identified four formation gaps that hinder fruitful living: disconnected, dismissive, discrepancy, and distracted. Our final major gap is suggested from Jesus' experience in the Garden of Gethsemane.

Most Christians agree that in one particular event we clearly see Jesus' frail humanity. The Gospels record Jesus' emotionally wrenching experience as he entered the Garden of Gethsemane for a customary time of prayer in the evening (Lk 22:39). Except this time was different. Something suddenly hit Jesus blindside (notice the word "began," Mt 26:37; Mk 14:33). The Gospel writers describe Jesus' difficult Gethsemane experience using six different Greek terms of deep emotion. Five come from the Synoptic Gospels: "distressed" (Greek *ekthambeō*, Mk 14:33), "troubled/distressed" (*adēmoneō*, Mk 14:33; Mt 26:37), "distressed/grieved" (*lupeō*, Mt 26:37), "deeply distressed/ grieved" (*perilupos*, Mk 14:34; Mt 26:38), "distressed/anguished" (*agōnia*, Lk 22:44). The sixth comes from John's Gospel, from what many commentators agree is a prayer analogous to Jesus' Gethsemane

---

[16]Brother Lawrence, *The Practice of the Presence of God*, ed. Hal M. Helms, trans. Robert J. Edmonson (Brewster, Mass.: Paraclete, 1985), p. 125.

prayer: "troubled/agitated" (*tarassō*, Jn 12:27; also 11:33; 13:21). Looking for moral support during this trial, Jesus came back to his closest friends three times. But in this hour of struggle, even Peter, James and John could not stay awake.

From this episode, we glean helpful steps for addressing our gaps. This particular event highlights some kind of inner turbulence, a lack of peace, a troubled heart. This *distressed* gap need not be sinful, since Jesus experienced it and he never sinned. But if we allow ourselves to give way to such internal pressure and succumb to it, then it can become sinful anxiety and excessive worry.[17] To address his distress, Jesus looked to God the Father. So can we, by pressing the pause button in our moment of need. Perhaps Paul's helpful teaching is based on Jesus' Gethsemane encounter:[18] "Do not be anxious about anything, but in every situation, by prayer and petition, with thanksgiving, present your requests to God. And the peace of God, which transcends all understanding, will guard your hearts and your minds in Christ Jesus" (Phil 4:6-7).

In table 2.1 I've displayed all five formation gaps. The disconnected gap is listed first, since it seems foundational to all the other gaps. The distressed gap is included second, since it can be experienced at any time, and if not addressed in a timely fashion, it can become a hindrance to addressing the other gaps. The third column suggests a question to ask to attend to the gap, and the final column some possible practices to begin addressing the gap. Jesus' question reminds us of our gap: "Why do you call me 'Lord, Lord,' and do not do what I say?" (Lk 6:46). We can seek help to move beyond our current core beliefs, but only if Jesus is our teacher, for "everyone who is fully trained will be like his teacher" (Lk 6:40).

---

[17]A helpful resource in dealing with distress and anxiety is *The Anxiety Cure* by Archibald Hart (Nashville: Thomas Nelson, 1999).

[18]Although Paul's writings were written earlier than the four Gospels, there is New Testament evidence that Paul knew of Jesus' teachings (Paul quotes or alludes to Jesus' known teachings; see, e.g., Acts 20:35; 1 Cor 9:14 with Lk 10:7; 1 Cor 7:25; 11:23). Jesus himself played a significant role in Paul's learning, in light of Paul's personal encounters with Jesus (Acts 9:5; 18:9; 23:11; 2 Tim 4:17) and Paul's claims about receiving direct revelation/teaching from the Lord to Paul (e.g., Gal 1:11-12; 2 Cor 12:1; 1 Thess 4:15).

Table 2.1. Five Formation Gaps

"Whoever has ears to hear, let them hear" (Mt 11:15).

Gap	Biblical Basis	Key Question	Possible Practice
1. Disconnected Gap No/little intentional dependence on God	No fruitfulness without abiding in Jesus Jn 15:4-5	Am I regularly, consciously connecting with God?	Develop cues as reminders (e.g., 30-second Pause Button, hourly clock chime, object in nature like a cloud). (Rev 3:20; Jas 4:8)
2. Distressed Gap A disturbing moment of distress arises within	Jesus' temptation in Gethsemane Mt 26:37-39; Mk 14:33-36; Lk 22:42-44	Attend to distress; ask, Lord, what is this distress/ turbulence in my soul about?	Cultivate receptivity when the Spirit awakens us to distress gaps; do "glad, sad, mad, dreads, dreams" exercise. (Jn 14:27; Phil 4:6-7)
3. Dismissive Gap No/little receptivity to explore ideas further; Satan persuades us to remain in the dark	Four Soils Parable Seed on the road: No fruitfulness Mt 13:15, 19; Mk 4:11-12, 15; Lk 8:12	Am I open to consider this new-to-me idea? Why do I hesitate to consider this new-to-me idea, Lord?	Study other viewpoints within orthodox Christianity. Look to "credible witnesses" who are seeking to know God more deeply. (Lk 8:18; Phil 4:8)
4. Discrepancy Gap False self: a professed belief without yet being rooted in character	Rocky soil: No fruitfulness Mt 13:20-21; Mk 4:16-17; Lk 8:13	Following a confession to God, ask, How can I cooperate with you, Lord, in forming my heart?	Cultivate receptivity when the Spirit awakens us to character gaps; also cultivate receptivity to feedback from others. Be engaged in at least one formation project. (Mt 5:20-48; 1 Tim 4:7-8)
5. Distracted Gap Slowly drifting away from Jesus' priorities	Thorny soil: No fruitfulness Mt 13:22; Mk 4:18-19; Lk 8:14	Review a list of Jesus' priorities and life goals; ask, Where am I off course and now needing realignment, Lord?	Study Scripture; examine Jesus' priorities and life goals regularly. Ask for feedback from trusted mentors and friends. (Lk 21:34-36; Rev 2:1-7)

Unintentionally Reinforcing Formation Gaps

There's a special challenge for readers who are teachers and those offering guidance to others (spiritual directors, pastors, counselors, ministry leaders, mentors, seminary professors, parents, etc.). Jesus' warning to the educational gatekeepers of his day has often gripped me in application as a teacher: "Woe to you experts in the law, because you have taken away the key to knowledge. You yourselves have not entered, and you have hindered those who were entering" (Lk 11:52). We tend to teach out of our current, limited storehouses of worldview beliefs and, in effect, can shortchange our charges if we don't continue to be persistent seekers of truth. That is, our "dismissive gaps" hinder those we lead or teach from being exposed to all of God's truth (see Mt 5:19). Listed below are some practices we use that may actually reinforce particular gaps among those we care for.

When presenting an "altar call" of commitment to turn over a new season of dedicated living, we must be careful not to communicate that all one must do is *make a decision* to bring about a new pattern of Jesus-like living by walking the aisle (at a local church or conference). Such requests will not bring about the desired effect—a changed lifestyle—unless we indicate the need for continuing, intentional engagement in formation practices to root that decision deeply in character. Otherwise we'll be adding more guilt when no change takes place.

We may also reinforce gaps when we over-emphasize knowing the Bible cognitively *without* helping to nurture Christians' inner formation into actually *believing* the Bible deeply as core worldview beliefs. Since talk is easy, one can glibly profess many Bible facts and articulate sound theology without having the respective worldview beliefs represented by the facts and theology. God desires that we become *Bible-hearted practitioners*, not just Bible *knowers*. Living in the truth is the goal, not just professing it. From the parable of the soils we learned that bearing fruit is the only reliable indicator that we have a deeply held worldview belief related to that fruit genuinely rooted in our hearts.

A Framework for Formation Change

Returning to Jesus' challenging Gethsemane encounter, we can discern a framework for helping us address our gaps, whether they are related to distress or not. I suggest that four practical guidelines emerge specifically from Jesus' experience here. These steps can also help us deal with the other kinds of gaps. The first step is that Jesus became *aware* of this internal dissonance. We can't address a gap we're unaware of. It may take some time before it gets on our radar screen, but we can't make any movement forward without being awakened to our gap. Next, Jesus owns and *admits* this distress; in this case he shares it openly with his disciples. "My soul is overwhelmed with sorrow to the point of death" (Mk 14:34). Then something must be done to address the problem. Unhelpful responses would be to ignore the gap, explain it away or just medicate it without addressing the non-physical source of the issue.

Jesus recognizes his need, that he cannot face this inner turbulence alone within his own human resources, and *asks* for help. Initially he presses his three closest disciples, "Stay here and keep watch" (Mk 14:34), implying he wanted them to pray for him (Mt 26:40-41). Jesus moves a little farther away and then asks God the Father for help. Luke reports, "An angel from heaven appeared to him and strengthened him" (Lk 22:43). Thus far, three steps have been identified: becoming aware of a gap, admitting the gap and then asking for help. With Jesus' persistent prayer—three periods of praying to the Father and three times going back to Peter, James and John for their support—I see the final guideline of stepping out, taking action. In this case the action step was to keep asking for divine and human help. George Beasley-Murray explains that at the Last Supper, Jesus used the same Greek term, *tarasso*, as mentioned in John 12:27 above: "Stop letting your hearts be in turmoil. . . . Keep on believing in *God*."[19] When we become distressed we need not stay there. We can admit it and ask God for help, as Jesus did.

Below, I've organized the list of four steps from Jesus' example and have incorporated additional points—to be developed in succeeding chapters—to offer a practical guide for today's disciples.

---

[19]George Beasley-Murray, *John*, Word Biblical Commentary 36 (Dallas: Word, 1987), p. 249.

- *Awake*—We invite God the Holy Spirit and those we trust to help us *wake up* to our gaps, to help us be present in the gap, being sensitive to the Spirit's movement within.

- *Admit*—We do not hide or deny, but *admit* the gap with honesty and transparency. If the act is sinful, then we confess it to God and *accept* his forgiveness and peace. And we can continue to receive God's unconditional love for us—just as we are, gaps and all.

- *Ask*—We *ask* the Holy Spirit for help to be empowered with formation grace to live beyond our human ability as Jesus did, being bathed in God's love and anchored in truth, so we can address our gaps. On the human plane, with close Christian friends at our side, we can feel safe to share our journey, speak about our gaps and invite their help.

- *Act*—We plan, with intentionality and effort, to take some realistic initial steps to address our gaps on a more permanent basis, slowly chipping away at them, as we follow Jesus' example.

The two components "awake" and "admit" were the focus of this chapter and chapter one. In the next chapter more practical perspectives and guidelines are developed for the fourth component, "act." Part two of the book, chapters four through six, which focuses on essential divine resources for formation, offers further information about the third component, "ask." Since this four-step framework is foundational for the book, the steps are displayed in a box, as below, and will appear at the end of each chapter as a reminder.

AWAKE to gaps → ADMIT with honesty → ASK for formation grace → ACT, take a first step

---

Figure 2.2. Four-step framework

Final Thoughts

King David penned an eloquent confessional psalm in which he voices God's desire for us to be open about our gaps. "Surely you desire truth

in the inner parts; you teach me wisdom in *the inmost place*" (Ps 51:6
NIV, emphasis added). The last term, "the inmost place," is an unusual
one and often used in a physical context of "'plugging up' available water
sources."[20] Gerald Wilson draws the connection from this meaning to
Psalm 51:6: "God seeks open access to those parts of our lives that we
choose to keep deeply hidden within our inner world."[21] As the Old
Testament declares, "The heart is more deceitful than all else and is
desperately sick" (Jer 17:9 NASB). What does God really expect of us at
the moment when we realize we have gaps? Transparency. The Bible
calls it *confession*, agreeing with God about this particular sin. But we
first have to be aware of the gap, then own it, and then we're in a posi-
tion to confess it.

Changing our heart flow is a complex process and will not auto-
matically occur solely through becoming aware of the ideas in this
book. I don't make any claim that all my gaps have been reduced! I
continue to be on this formation journey as we all are. Yet I have seen
substantive changes in my character (confirmed by my wife and friends),
which encourages me to invite others to consider these profound concepts from Jesus' life and teaching. The bottom line is that throughout
life, we need to be open to becoming aware of our gaps. In the next
chapter we will look at the big picture of the formation process and at
some practical steps of action to reduce our gaps.

Key Points

1. Five particular gaps can hinder us from living into the life of Jesus:
   disconnected Gap (not regularly abiding in Jesus), distressed gap (an
   initial moment of troubling emotional stress), dismissive gap (resistance to truths that seem impossible), discrepancy gap (professed
   values that are not character deep) and distracted gap (a lifestyle
   slowly drifting off course).

2. Our worldview beliefs cannot be changed instantly by a heartfelt

---

[20]Gerald Wilson, *Psalms*, NIV Application Commentary 1 (Grand Rapids: Zondervan), p.
   779.
[21]Ibid.

commitment of our will at any time we want. But they can be changed indirectly over time, with God's grace.

3. Four steps can help us make progress regarding inner heart formation: Awake to gaps, Admit with honesty, Ask for formation grace, and Act, taking a first step.

4. Since Jesus faced the distressed gap, we need not feel we are sinning when we initially encounter it. We can then follow Jesus' example to address this particular gap and keep from sinning.

Reflection Questions

1. Why is it difficult to become aware of our gaps? How do you think we can become more receptive to being aware of our gaps? Do you think Benner's indicators and Keating's insights about instinctual needs can be helpful for this purpose?

2. The author presented Jesus' parable of the four soils to illustrate the spectrum of heart responses to truth. Consider ways we can move toward having a "good heart" response more of the time.

3. Responding to constructive, truthful criticism can be challenging at times. Reflect on some occasions of such feedback in the past. Journal or share your reflections about these instances at this time. What effects did or could the truthful comment have for changing the relevant matter? How can we improve our response to truthful feedback and learn to process further any truth in these comments?

3

Adapt Formation Practices
for Your Journey

*These words I speak to you are not incidental additions to your life,
homeowner improvements to your standard of living. They are foundational words, words to build a life on. If you work these words into your life,
you are like a smart carpenter who built his house on solid rock. Rain poured
down, the river flooded, a tornado hit—but nothing moved that house. It
was fixed to the rock. But if you just use my words in Bible studies and
don't work them into your life you are like a stupid carpenter who
built his house on the sandy beach. When a storm rolled in and
the waves came up, it collapsed like a house of cards.*

MATTHEW 7:24-27 *THE MESSAGE*

· ℘ ·

Refreshingly honest, Bill Heatley, an IT professional, admits "I lied
as easily as I breathed, especially when it involved bad news about
something for which I was responsible. I would say what I thought
people wanted to hear or what I wanted them to think and then go try
to make it true."[1] He began a formation project to reduce his lying by
making room for God to change his heart. Over a two-year period, the

---

[1]Bill Heatley, *The Gift of Work* (Colorado Springs: NavPress, 2008), p. 47. Heatley is a Theology
of Work project board member (www.theologyofwork.org) and son-in-law of Dallas Willard.

lying habit was uppermost in his mind as he spent time in solitude, in fasting, in prayer and in his regular time with God. After a relapse, Heatley acknowledged it before God, accepted his gracious forgiveness, and continued on. Then he had to report some bad news about a project at work. He prayed for divine help to resist the temptation to lie, and he told the truth. Truth telling in this situation became an important milestone—he noticed that God had changed his heart. "I was so happy I had done what was right and that [God] had blessed me with a changed heart, I couldn't stop smiling. The people around me couldn't figure out why I seemed so happy and relieved when I was reporting such bad news."[2]

A different kind of a formation process involved a woman in her late forties who experienced chronic stomach disorders and arthritis.[3] She asked for prayer. While praying, her pastor sensed the Holy Spirit informing him that the main problem was not physical, but a matter of unforgiveness, particularly bitterness toward her sister. Discerning that it was appropriate to share this insight, he posed a question about her relationship with this sister. She stiffened. "No, I haven't seen my sister for sixteen years." When the pastor pressed further, "Are you sure?" she confessed that years ago her sister had married a man she had loved and then had later divorced him. "I cannot forgive my sister for that." Relying on Psalm 32:3, the pastor counseled, "If you don't forgive her, then your bones will waste away." When she relented and asked for advice, he suggested she write a letter, forgiving her sister and asking to renew their relationship. As soon as she got home she wrote that letter, but didn't get around to mailing it for several weeks. Her physical condition worsened to the point that she feared she might die. Then she remembered the letter. She dragged herself to her car and drove to a mailbox. The moment she dropped off the letter she experienced some relief, and complete physical relief came when she arrived home.

By the end of this chapter, I hope to encourage you to try out a formation practice related to a gap that God is touching you about. Later

---

[2]Ibid., p. 48.

[3]John Wimber with Kevin Spring, *Power Healing* (San Francisco: Harper & Row, 1987), pp. 70-71.

in the chapter, we'll consider some applied matters regarding the process of formation and suggest a few practices worth trying out. But first let's step back and explore some foundational issues, in light of a question that may have come to mind.

Jesus' Own Formation

How do we think Jesus came to know about and live out the content of his teachings? Unless there was an infusion of moral virtue when Jesus was a baby—which Scripture does not indicate—then we can infer that Jesus, in his humanity, acquired his deeply held worldview beliefs and resulting heart flow of lifestyle just like we do. If we take seriously that Jesus was born and moved through the same stages of human development as all human persons, then the truths taught by the Father (Jn 12:49-50) passed through Jesus' own formation journey. Do we tend to ignore Jesus' own human formation, his acquiring wisdom and character virtues so he could practice what he preached? Note these key verses about Jesus' own formation:

- "And the child grew and became strong; he was filled with wisdom, and the grace of God was upon him" (Lk 2:40).

- "And Jesus grew up, he increased in wisdom and in favor with God and people" (Lk 2:52).

- "Everything that I learned [literally "heard"] from my Father I have made known to you" (Jn 15:15).

- "Although he was a son, he learned obedience from what he suffered and, once made perfect, he became the source of eternal salvation for all who obey him" (Heb 5:8-9 NIV).

As we look at Jesus' formation we also need to consider his childhood and private life prior to beginning his public ministry. Do you think Jesus ever had a headache or common cold? Did he have to learn his math tables? Leon Morris notes that Jesus experienced ignorance as any human would.

> Ignorance is an inevitable accompaniment of the only human life that we know. . . . Sometimes one meets people who overlook this aspect of Jesus' life. They picture him going on a serene way, knowing the

thoughts of everyone about him, knowing the outcome of every course of action in which he or they were engaging. If this was the manner of it, then the life Jesus lived was not a human life, even human life at its highest level.[4]

We need to ponder what it means for Jesus to live a human life from infancy on.

Regarding the transition from childhood into adulthood, most cultures in the past and various contemporary ones still mark a rite of passage from childhood to adulthood at around the age of twelve.[5] Thus we can divide Jesus' life into three main phases: childhood, young adulthood prior to his public ministry and later adulthood during his public ministry. Table 3.1 surveys the span of Jesus' thirty-three years.

Table 3.1. Jesus' Formation from Childhood to Later Adulthood

	Temple (12 yrs)		Baptism (30 yrs)	Cross (33 yrs)
Phase:	**Childhood**	**Young Adulthood**	**Later Adulthood**	
Years:	12 years	18 years	3 years	
Formation Passage:	Luke 2:40 John 15:15 (Hebrews 5:8-9)	Luke 2:52 John 15:15 (Hebrews 5:8-9)	Hebrews 5:8-9 John 15:15	

Note that a distinct formation verse about Jesus appears in each phase of his life, indicating his continuing learning *throughout* life. I assume that the major learning period regarding his mission as Messiah had all taken place prior to his baptism and entrance into public ministry. The two verses from Luke appear as "bookends" surrounding the only childhood experience recorded in Scripture (Lk 2:41-51). At age twelve, Jesus had a significant learning encounter with the religious teachers, which also offers evidence of his unusual wisdom at that young age ("they were amazed at his understanding and answers," Lk 2:47). We could infer that a regular part of a Jewish boy's early training was at-

---

[4]Leon Morris, *The Lord from Heaven* (London: Inter-Varsity Press, 1958), pp. 46-47.

[5]For a discussion of childhood and a biblical basis for an age of moral accountability, see my "Biblical Perspectives on Developmental Grace for Nurturing Children's Spirituality," in *Children's Spirituality: Christian Perspectives, Research, and Application*, ed. Donald Ratcliff (Eugene, Ore.: Cascade/Wipf & Stock, 2004), pp. 54-71.

tendance at sabbath school with a local rabbi. And Jesus also had his own continuing private tutorials about Scripture with his inner tutor, the Holy Spirit (a topic addressed in chapter 5).

Yet the opportunity to discuss key points of Scripture with the "seminary professors" at the Jerusalem temple was so exciting an occasion that twelve-year-old Jesus lost track of the time for three days (Lk 2:46-47)! Could it be that this special learning experience for Jesus was the first of many such encounters that he looked forward to during his subsequent annual temple visits? From age twelve through thirty—until he launched into his public ministry—Jesus could engage with these Ph.D. Jewish teachers for several days once a year about the finer points of Scripture to help clarify his own understanding as well as confirm interpretations of Scripture.

Hebrews 5:8-9 indicates there was learning after his baptism as well, especially related to his suffering experiences during his public ministry. The way Jesus phrases his learning from the Father comes from the customary manner in which boys learned their father's trade, watching them and growing in their professional skills. "The Son . . . can do only what he sees his Father doing, because whatever the Father does the Son also does" (Jn 5:19; cf. Jn 15:15).

Bruce Ware offers helpful insight on this important matter of formation.

> Through the things that Christ suffered, through the trials, temptations, and afflictions of life, he learned to obey increasingly difficult demands of his Father until at last, he was prepared—made mature, if you will, strengthened in faith and character—to go to the cross. . . . Could Jesus have gone to the cross successfully three, or five, or fifteen years earlier? The answer that seems to suggest itself is, no. He learned to obey harder and harder demands and proved himself "obedient to the point of death, even death on a cross" (Phil 2:18). . . . But he always did obey, and through this regular obedience he was made ready, strengthened, for the biggest challenge of all, death on the cross, in order that he would be the source of our eternal salvation.[6]

Jesus' life provides evidence that his formation teachings work, for they were effective while Jesus grew from childhood through adulthood, trusting God and becoming a wise person. Jesus, our Lord and Savior, was willing to undergo difficult experiences of living on this planet as a part of his own formation, to be a model for us (1 Pet 2:21-23).

Why All the Drama?

After reading thus far, we may wonder why God has permitted this kind of arrangement. Why do we have such overwhelming deficits and gaps that each of us needs to overcome to move into easier kingdom living like Jesus? Isn't there a better or less complicated way? Although a complete answer will have to wait till we see Jesus, I can suggest a few key points that Scripture hints at. Part of God's kingship project involves creating a world where good permeates all its citizens. "But in keeping with his promise we are looking forward to a new heaven and a new earth, the home of righteousness" (2 Pet 3:13). Apparently God could not (or chose not to) create that kind of world at first. Heaven must wait. The kind of humans God envisions to populate his forever kingdom must go through a certain kind of formation process to become mature adults who are able and willing to live in God's holy presence, to live in harmony with fellow citizens and to be competent coleaders with God in running his universe.

In that next age, we can continue to learn and grow into more of the potential God has designed for being fully human—and without the presence of the devil or any more evil. But in this age, since the Fall, it seems that experiences of suffering are important. Apparently human nature is so constituted that suffering can be an aid in maximizing deep character formation as we bear more of the fruit of the Spirit (Gal 5:22-23). Jesus' own formation included suffering: "Although he was a son, [Jesus] learned obedience from what he suffered and, once made perfect, he became the source of eternal salvation for all who obey him" (Heb 5:8-9 NIV). And so we follow our Lord in suffering (Rom 8:17; 2 Cor 1:5; Phil 1:29; 3:10; 1 Pet 4:13). "Therefore, since Christ suffered in his body, arm yourselves also with the same attitude, because those who have suffered in their bodies are done with sin. As a result, they do not live the rest of their earthly lives for evil human desires, but rather for the will of God" (1 Pet 4:1-2). "Arm yourselves" is a military term related to going into battle. Thomas Schreiner explains, "The point is not that believers who suffer have attained sinless perfection. . . . [But] the commitment to suffer reveals a passion for a new way of life, a life that is not yet perfect but remarkably different from the lives of unbelievers in the Graeco-Roman world."[7] On Romans 8:17 Douglas Moo asserts, "What Paul is doing is setting forth an unbreakable 'law of the kingdom' according to which glory can come only by way of suffering."[8]

God the Father "disciplines us for our good, that we may share in his holiness" (Heb 12:10). We can be formed through the trials of life: "the testing of your faith develops perseverance. Let perseverance finish its work so that you may be mature and complete, not lacking anything" (Jas 1:3-4). Certain character traits can be developed through suffering and experiences of evil (e.g., courage through fear, compassion through suffering, endurance through hardship, humility by hitting the bottom), and we can appreciate more deeply God's forgiveness from the posture of a sinner saved by grace.[9]

Jesus emphasizes the importance of giving our best effort to addressing our formation gaps by using hyperbolic statements: "If your right eye causes you to stumble, gouge it out and throw it away. It is better for you to lose one part of your body than for your whole body to be thrown into hell" (Mt 5:29; see also Mt 5:30; 18:9; Mk 9:43-47). In another context Jesus proclaims, "Make every effort [Greek *agōnizomai*] to enter through the narrow door" (Lk 13:24). I. Howard Marshall notes, "By using [this Greek] term . . . Luke stresses that moral effort is necessary in order to enter the kingdom (cf. [Lk] 16:16)."[10] Similar affirma-

---

[7]Thomas Schreiner, *1, 2 Peter, Jude,* New American Commentary 37 (Nashville: Broadman, 2003), p. 201.

[8]Douglas Moo, *The Epistle to the Romans,* New International Commentary on the New Testament (Grand Rapids: Eerdmans, 1996), p. 506.

[9]For further discussion of suffering see chapter seven in Klaus Issler, *Wasting Time with God* (Downers Grove, Ill.: InterVarsity Press, 2001), pp. 183-213.

[10]I. Howard Marshall, *Commentary on Luke,* New International Greek Testament Commentary (Grand Rapids: Eerdmans, 1978), p. 565.

tions of intentionality related to formation appear in the Epistles (emphasis added):

- "Let us therefore *make every effort* [Greek *diōkō*] to do what leads to peace and to mutual edification" (Rom 14:19).
- "*Make every effort* [*diōkō*] to live in peace with everyone and to be holy; without holiness no one will see the Lord" (Heb 12:14).
- "So then, dear friends, since you are looking forward to this, *make every effort* [*spoudazō*] to be found spotless, blameless and at peace with him" (2 Pet 3:14).

Regarding our formation, we'll need to exert effort, and we'll also go through experiences of suffering. That point leads to other questions.

Is It Worth the Effort to Address Our Gaps Now?

What does the future hold? What is God preparing us for? Ever thought about the fact that we'll be living four hundred years from now? Some of us give a lot of time to planning for later years. But do we consider making plans for our life after death? The ancient Egyptian Pharaohs gave a lot of thought to the afterlife. Some packed their glorious funeral chambers—including the amazing pyramids—with treasures, chariots and clothes they hoped to use in the afterlife. Although they left it all behind, I think the Egyptian kings got something right. It's a good idea to plan for life after death. If we're in Jesus' forever family, and the Holy Spirit dwells in us *forever* (Jn 16:14), then we'll be living more than four hundred years from now.

Imagine what it might be like to live after death. Since our few years this side of death is a small number compared to living forever, it could be helpful to take a long-term perspective about planning our life here and now. The Bible teaches that this present world is but a *temporary passageway* toward arriving at the Christian's true home in the next phase of God's kingdom in heaven, the kind of world everyone dreams about: a world of peace, love and goodness.

Unfortunately, some Christians think of "heaven"—our future eternal home—as a place that's *not* very desirable at all. Here on earth it's exciting, there's change and variability, great growth potential, and so much adventure. But heaven is often viewed as boring, static, ethereal and other worldly. The image of sitting on clouds in white robes strumming harps and singing forever isn't that appealing for most—a view that arose from those who reacted to an emphasis on heavenly life as continuous worship of God. Mark Twain (d. 1910) gave voice to such a common misperception in his novel *The Adventures of Huckleberry Finn*, in which Miss Watson, while tutoring Huckleberry, talks about the "good place": "She said all a body would have to do there was to go around all day long with a harp and sing, forever and ever. So I [Huck] didn't think much of it. But I never said so. I asked her if she reckoned Tom Sawyer would go there, and she said not by a considerable sight. I was glad about that, because I wanted him and me to be together."[11]

Randy Alcorn challenges these boring views in his book *Heaven*. He uses the term "Temporary Heaven" (or "Present Heaven") to refer to the place where those saints who have passed on before us are currently living, and "Eternal Heaven" to refer to our future, permanent mode of living, the place Jesus is preparing for us (Jn 14:1-3).[12] Alcorn explains, "The New Earth will be the same as the old Earth, just as a new Christian is still the same person he was before. Different? Yes. But also the same."[13] Major differences for us will include that we'll have resurrected bodies and will enter into greater flourishing lifestyles, all without sinning. Major differences for the new earth include a major makeover by God, the absence of evil and the creation of the kind of home we each long for. Alcorn challenges us, "We need to stop acting as if Heaven were a myth, an impossible dream, a relentlessly dull meeting, or an unimportant distraction from real life. We need to see Heaven for what it is: the realm we're made for. If we do, we'll embrace it with contagious joy, excitement, and anticipation."[14]

So God *is* in the process of creating that perfect world that we all dream of. It's just that God has a different or better idea for how to get

---

[11]Mark Twain, *The Adventures of Huckleberry Finn* (1885), chap. 1, par. 6. Available at <www .enotes.com/adventures-of-huckleberry-finn-text>.
[12]Randy Alcorn, *Heaven* (Carol Stream, Ill.: Tyndale House, 2004), p. 44.
[13]Ibid., p. 149.
[14]Ibid., p. 443.

there. Nothing in this world compares to the excitement and surprises God has in store for his children in that new place. When believers know that life is even better beyond the grave, it makes it a little easier to put up with a lot of grief and anguish now. Randy Alcorn muses, "In Heaven, God will unleash our creativity, not confine it. . . . On the New Earth, our resurrected eyes and ears will see and hear God's glory as never before, and our resurrected hearts will be moved to see beauty everywhere. We will live in a land of fascinating observations, captivating insights, wondrous adventures, and spellbinding stories."[15]

In one parable about the end-times, Jesus offered this comment for all believers: "Then the King will say to those on his right, 'Come, you who are blessed by my Father; take your inheritance, the kingdom prepared for you since the creation of the world'" (Mt 25:34). We'll have an inheritance in the age to come.

So why all the fuss and effort now? Why not just wait until heaven when we'll be perfected anyway? In one sense, we don't have the option of postponement. In some cases at least, the suffering that comes our way—whether we like it or not—seems to "force" change in us when it's the most *convenient* response, yet still difficult. But we can remain resistant in our old ways. In another sense, it might be possible to take a "minimalist effort option" to pursue Christian living now and basically ignore Jesus' teachings and promises about abundant living now (Jn 10:10). Yet we'll miss out on the potential positive influence on others in light of our becoming more like Jesus, and also the related bonus rewards in the next age (Mt 5:11-12; 10:42; Lk 6:35). "You are the salt of the earth. . . . You are the light of the world. . . . Let your light shine before others, that they may see your good deeds and praise your Father in heaven" (Mt 5:13-16).

Storing Up Treasure for the Next Age?

A friend of mine recently reminded me that there's never a U-Haul trailer attached to a hearse at a funeral. We come into this life as babies, empty handed, and we exit through death in the same way, empty

---

[15]Ibid., pp. 404, 406.

handed. "We brought nothing into the world, and we can take nothing out of it" (1 Tim 6:7; see also Job 1:21; Eccles 5:15). But if we can't take any material possessions, is there something we can take into eternity? Although we leave this life empty-*handed*, we don't leave empty-*hearted*.[16] There are at least three arenas in which we can invest our time and effort into immaterial realities now that will last beyond the grave: (a) our relationships, with God and those within God's family, (b) the inner heart transformation of our character, including our knowledge and competencies, and (c) our good deeds, which can have continuing good effects for which God rewards us with a bonus. Perhaps these kinds of eternal investments are also included in Jesus' concept of storing up "treasures in heaven" (Mt 6:20; Lk 12:33).

Relationship with God and others. We can take with us our relationship with God that began on this earth. In the next age we'll continue to get to know God, building on the friendship we've been developing with him here.[17] The disciples took up where they left off when they met Jesus after his death and resurrection (Jn 21). Also, we can grow our relationships with those in Jesus' forever family. God is building his *kingdom community;* it begins here and continues there.

Inner heart transformation. We can take with us our *character,* the kind of person we're becoming. We'll continue learning and building on what we've gained here, in knowledge and wisdom, in skill and talent, in attitudes and desires—all purified from any taints of evil.[18] We are becoming the kind of kingdom citizens God desires in his eternal kingdom. "Train yourself to be godly. For . . . godliness has value for all things, holding promise for both the *present life* and the *life to come*" (1 Tim 4:7-8, emphasis added). Also, we'll take with us any leadership/life skill competencies we've been developing, to be used to assist God in running his universe: "You have made them to be a kingdom

---

[16]For further discussion of *empty-handed* and *empty-hearted,* see my 64-page booklet using a game analogy for life, *What Does It Mean to Be Human? Participating in the Game of Life* (Atlanta: Ravi Zacharias Ministries International, 2002).

[17]For further discussion on developing our relationship with God, see my book *Wasting Time with God.*

[18]That we'll learn in eternity is suggested by Ephesians 2:7. For a brief discussion of this topic, see Gary Habermas and J. P. Moreland, *Immortality* (Nashville: Thomas Nelson, 1992), p. 146.

and priests to serve our God, and *they will reign on the earth*" (Rev 5:10, emphasis added; see also Lk 12:32; 2 Tim 2:12; Rev 2:26; 20:6; 22:5). There are a wide range of leadership competencies that can be developed in a variety of ways, such as being a CEO, being a mid-level manager, being a parent, being a good ministry team member and being a good manager of personal finances. The key is being faithful with what God has loaned us, including our physical bodies, our possessions, our time and our competencies. In the parable of the talents Jesus places these words on the landowner's lips, "Well done, good and faithful servant! You have been faithful with a few things; I will put you in charge of many things. Come and share your master's happiness!" (Mt 25:23). If we're faithful in growing our *leadership competencies* here, God grants us increasing responsibilities and possessions in the next life.

Continuing effects of good deeds as rewards. Finally, we can also take with us the effects of our good deeds on others in that our deeds will be rewarded in the next life. "For we must all appear before the judgment seat of Christ, that each one may be recompensed for his deeds in the body, according to what he has done, whether good or [worthless]" (2 Cor 5:10 NASB; see also Mt 6:1; Lk 6:23; 1 Cor 3:14; Rev 22:12). It's a bonus, so trying to earn such a reward can't be the sole motive for engaging in good deeds, otherwise we forfeit the reward (Mt 6:1). Yet it's a legitimate motivational factor to keep in mind. Often we're unaware of the good impact of our deeds on others (Mt 25:34-40). In his generosity God honors us with a bonus for serving others as part of his kingdom project.

Expending effort for one's formation yields future benefits as well as current benefits. If truth can make us more free (Jn 8:32) and if worldview beliefs (both true and false ones) significantly influence our lives, then even now our lives will experience greater flourishing as we embrace an increasingly greater set of true worldview beliefs than we currently hold. As Jesus promises, "I have come that they may have life, and have it to the full" (Jn 10:10; see also Mt 7:24-27; Lk 6:46-49).

Now we'll transition to some practical matters related to developing formation practices.

Formation Change Is a Process

Core worldview beliefs change over time through a process. For example, as noted earlier, Jesus' own formation involved a process (in the NASB translation, "increasing" appears in both Lk 2:40 and Lk 2:52). Although early on resurrection Sunday morning the disciples didn't believe Jesus was alive, by the end of the day they did, except for Thomas who was not present when Jesus physically appeared. It may seem as though their worldview beliefs were changed in a day, but let me suggest that they were aware at some level that three people had already been raised from the dead. Initially, Jesus' appearance did nothing for them except scare them, so strong was their worldview belief against Jesus' resurrection. "They were startled and frightened, thinking they saw a ghost. [Jesus] said to them, 'Why are you troubled, and why do doubts rise in your minds?'" (Lk 24:37-38 NASB). When Jesus ate the piece of fish, they couldn't deny the fact that he was alive in "flesh and bones." Thomas took a little longer, since he didn't have the undeniable fact of Jesus' physical sense as the others had. Eight days later Jesus appeared to Thomas and he finally believed (Jn 20:26-28).

For Peter during his evangelistic tour outside of Jerusalem, it was a two-day process of weighing the evidence to welcome Gentiles as genuine believers (Acts 10). The apostle Paul changed from fanatic Pharisee jailing Christians to bold evangelist for Jesus three days later (Acts 9). But it was many years before Barnabas invited Paul to join him as a teacher in the new Gentile church in Antioch (Acts 11:19-26, c. A.D. 39). Perhaps the intervening years permitted Paul a time for his worldview beliefs about the gospel to become more settled in mind and character for his future role as the early Church's chief theologian and missionary. Deep heart formation involves a process over time.

These cases, along with other New Testament passages, teach us that our formation is a process that occurs over time. "Consider it pure joy, my brother and sisters, whenever you face trials of many kinds, because you know that the testing of your faith develops perseverance. Let perseverance finish its work so that you may be mature and complete, not lacking anything" (Jas 1:2-4; see also Rom 5:1-5; 2 Pet 1:5-11; 1 Jn

2:12-14).[19] There is no "silver bullet" or "quick pill" available for us to become instantly mature, living like Jesus. Putting Jesus' words into practice is a process that God enables and in which we have a significant role.

Illustrating A Process of Formation Change

How might this process unfold? Since it's a complex process that involves some mystery it cannot be fully explained. Yet the formation process is something we're already familiar with, if we reflect on the way we learned our current competencies. It's a process that takes time and effort, similar in many ways to gaining fluency in a foreign language, becoming proficient with a musical instrument or acquiring mastery of some complex skill in a sport or at work. Some readers may wish for an illustration of such progressive steps of formation change. What might be involved when moving from becoming aware of a particular gap to incorporating a new habit or virtue into one's lifestyle?

To illustrate the kinds of decisions that formation involves from a human perspective, I've adapted a model that offers a bird's-eye view of the process.[20] Keep in mind three major phases with the letters A, B and C. Each phase will have subphases within it, resulting in seven distinctive steps of formation change.

Phase A, "Becoming Aware of a Gap," involves the transition from being unaware of a gap to the point of considering whether or not to expend the effort to work on a change. In Phase B, "Carrying Out a

---

[19]Jesus teaches that when believers engage in spiritual practices "in secret" rather than for show, the Father who sees in secret will reward believers (Mt 6:4, 6, 18). I wonder if that "reward" includes the mysterious heart change that only God can accomplish? The section on fasting (Mt 6:16-18) seems to suggest this possibility, since it has no benefit to anyone else, whereas alms-giving does benefit another. If this is the case, then when believers engage in practices for show, there would be no inner formation change, but only when the spiritual practice is done for inner motives.

[20]The framework I adapt is based on the Transtheoretical Model (TTM) of Change proposed by James Prochaska and Carlo DiClemente. See James Prochaska, John Norcross and Carlo DiClemente, *Changing for Good* (New York: HarperCollins, 1994); and Carlo DiClemente, *Addiction and Change* (New York: Guilford, 2003). I appreciate my colleague Jim Wilhoit for directing me to their research. It's based on years of helping those with addictive habits, such as physiological dependence (e.g., smoking, illegal drugs), problematic relationships and excessive work behaviors. If such addictions can be reduced—perhaps achieved without conscious dependence on God's empowerment—doesn't that give us more hope for us who have additional divine resources to access?

Table 3.2. Three Major Phases in Heart Flow Change

Awake and Admit	**PHASE A: Becoming aware of a gap** **A-1:** Basically unaware of gap	*That's not me!*
	A-2: Now aware of gap and considering whether to change or not	*Is it really worth changing?*
Ask and Act	**PHASE B: Carrying out a formation practice** **B-1:** Planning formation practice and committing to change; dependence on Spirit	*Okay, how can I go about a change?*
	B-2: Implementing formation practice; dependence on Spirit	*It isn't easy but I'm working my plan with God's help.*
	B-3: Practicing new habit is much easier than before (moved beyond the "tipping point"); dependence on Spirit (see figure 3.1)	*I'm changing! Thank you, Lord.*
	PHASE C: Settling into a changed character and lifestyle **C-1:** Integrating change more into one's lifestyle, with less focus and effort needed; dependence on Spirit	*I feel more freedom. Thank you, Lord.*
	C-2: Living routinely without much effort in this area; little or no temptation; dependence on Spirit	*What freedom and flow!*

Formation Practice," we make a commitment to change and we plan a formation practice, implement it and get to a place where practicing the new habit is easier than not doing it. Finally Phase C, "Settling into Changed Character and Lifestyle," relates to the later period where the new habit has been increasingly incorporated into one's lifestyle. In some cases it may involve a transition to a point where one experiences little (or no) temptation to discontinue the new habit, the seventh step.

Table 3.2 surveys each phase and subphase. One of the key points is the critical step of moving from sub-phase A-1 into A-2, becoming aware of our gaps. Without awareness of a particular gap, it's very difficult to make any formation progress in that area (see Lev 4:22-23, 27-28). Figure 3.1 provides a visual depiction of the dynamic movement between phases. This figure is only an illustration based on my understanding of the model, although the time parameters are suggested by the researchers mentioned in note 20.[21]

As depicted in figure 3.1, within Phase B, subphase B-3 indicates when the new habit becomes easier to do than not to do. I call this getting past the "tipping point." We now are carried along more and more into routine obedience by our heart flow, requiring much less effort. What comes to mind is a ski outing with my son Daniel. He was in high school at the time and I think he had skied once or twice before. I bought passes for us at Mount Bachelor in central Oregon. By the afternoon on the first day, Daniel was very discouraged. His skiing wasn't going well. He wanted to quit and go home. I was sorry for him and suggested a few tips to navigate the terrain and stay upright on his skies longer. I skied alongside him and encouraged him to keep trying. (I had bought *three-day* passes, so I had mixed motives about quitting so soon.) He was

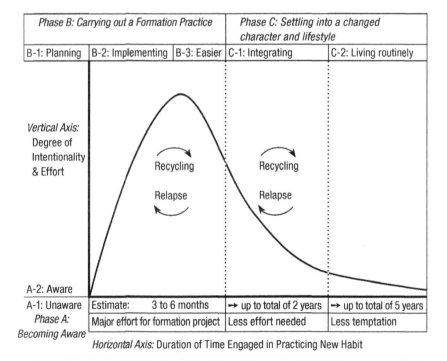

Figure 3.1. Effort and time for a formation practice

[21]DiClemente, *Addiction and Change*, pp. 140, 191, 193.

courageous and kept at it. As we were driving home he said he was willing to try it again. The second day was much better. He got the hang of it and did very well. On the third day he was zipping past me on the slopes, a veteran skier. Daniel had made it over the tipping point.

Eventually, with persistence, patience and God's empowerment, we move into Phase C in which the particular practices we're engaged in become more embedded within our character and lifestyle. Now the gap has been reduced noticeably. After arriving in subphase C-1, we're still open to temptation and to potential slips or lapses (one or two lapses) or a major relapse and collapse (return to practicing the gap) in which we move back to subphase B-3 or even B-2.[22] We can adapt some intentional practices to regain the measure of stability in heart flow we previously had and eventually return to C-1. In a few cases we may gain such formation change that gaps may become virtually eliminated and our lifestyle evidences full fruit of the Holy Spirit in that particular area. Yet we must remain aware of falling into temptation. Jesus encouraged his disciples in Gethsemane, "Keep watching and praying that you may not enter into temptation; the spirit is willing, but the flesh is weak" (Mt 26:41 NASB).

An Example of a Formation Practice

In chapter one I alluded to a personal formational experience from over a decade ago that convinced me my heart could change. My case of reducing mild "road rage" and increasing peacefulness involved moving through these various phases and subphases, although I was not aware of this particular framework at the time. My problem was my anger at drivers who wove in and out of freeway lanes as I drove each day to Biola where I'm a seminary professor. In the Sermon on the Mount the first vice Jesus targets is anger (Mt 5:21-26). It was Dallas Willard's use of the word *contempt* that arrested my attention, in his discussion of this passage in *The Divine Conspiracy*.[23] *Contempt* is an ugly word, and it

---

[22]DiClemente, *Addiction and Change*, pp. 182-83.

[23]Dallas Willard, *The Divine Conspiracy* (San Francisco: HarperSanFrancisco, 1998), p. 141. My views on formation into Christlikeness have been significantly influenced by Dallas Willard. His *Renovation of the Heart* (Colorado Springs: NavPress, 2002) provides the best presentation of his perspectives on formation. For an overview of Willard's writings, see Steve Porter, "The Willardian Corpus," *Journal of the Spiritual Formation and Soul Care* 3, no. 2 (Fall 2010): 239-

helped to uncover my ugly attitude for certain drivers. Jesus' focus is not on the external act of murder but on the internal sources for anger, hostility and unreconciled relationships. Furthermore, he wasn't laying down a new law that we can never say *"raca,"* or "fool." Jesus uses the word himself in his own teaching ("blind fools," Mt 23:17; "You fool!" on God's lips, Lk 12:20). The point is, does that spoken word "fool" come from an angry heart? At the time, I didn't think I was an angry person, but I was awakened to my gap when I realized I had an attitude of contempt. It was a gap I couldn't deny. I entered a season of working on this attitude toward some freeway drivers and developing a more peace-filled heart on the road.

For my formation practice I recited some relevant verses and invited the Spirit to make me aware of my mild road rage. As I became aware (at first, hours after the occasion), I'd confess my sin and thank God for his forgiveness and invite his supernatural peace to wash over me as promised in Philippians 4:6-7. Over several months I worked through this process numerous days each week, and the time between the spoken word of contempt and the awareness became shorter. Eventually I became aware *before* I would hurl "you turkey" (with contempt). Then "graduation day" came, about twelve months later, when a driver cut in front of me and *nothing* stirred in my heart except peace. In that moment—as I experienced such freedom and peace in my heart—I was stunned by the grace of God. I still experience internal turbulence on the road, but hardly like before. I could've invited a close friend to help me on this project—perhaps it might not have taken so long—but at the time I was too embarrassed to share it with anyone.

Engaging Spiritual Practices as a Means of Formation

Formation change requires our time and effort. Our core character beliefs that guide our life are fairly stable, but they can be changed, not directly by our willpower but indirectly over time. Many of our deep beliefs were formed during childhood, mostly without our awareness.

66, a special issue devoted to Willard's contributions to spiritual formation.

As we approach adolescence and young adulthood, it's likely we have little idea of all the deeply held worldview beliefs that have been formed into our character.[24] Through the pursuit of truth and regularly engaging in spiritual practices or disciplines, we can indirectly influence changes in our character. Willard explains, "A discipline is any activity within our power that we engage in to enable us to do what we cannot do by direct effort."[25]

We can't change worldview beliefs directly, partly because of how settled worldview beliefs are and also because we're not the only ones involved in the process. The Holy Spirit has an essential role in our formation process, along with a community (and culture). Yet with personal intentionality and persistence, worldview beliefs can be changed. As Richard Foster notes, "Indirection affirms that spiritual formation does not occur by direct human effort, but through a relational process whereby we receive from God the power or ability to do what we cannot do by our own effort. We do not produce the outcome. That is God's business."[26] Cloud and Townsend illustrate this point by advising, "The alcoholic who tries to stop drinking by using willpower and commitment is wasting his time. He's much better off using that willpower to take himself to the next support meeting."[27] Our goal is to place ourselves in accommodating circumstances—with our heart open, asking for God's empowering grace, engaging formation practices, supported by our Christian community—so that over time, our worldview beliefs can change and become more aligned with God's reality.

That's why the regular study and meditation of Scripture is an important means for encountering truth: because it offers an accurate view of reality like no other source of knowledge (Ps 1:1-6). Scripture indicates Jesus engaged in various spiritual practices as part of his lifestyle routines, such as celebration (Jerusalem feasts, Lk 2:41; Jn 5:1; wedding, Jn

---

[24]For further discussion on this topic, see my article "Inner Core Belief Formation, Spiritual Practices, and the Willing Doing Gap," *Journal of Spiritual Formation and Soul Care* 2, no. 2 (Fall 2009): 179-98.

[25]Willard, *Divine Conspiracy*, p. 353.

[26]Richard Foster, *Life with God* (San Francisco: HarperOne, 2008), p. 155.

[27]Henry Cloud and John Townsend, *12 "Christian" Beliefs That Can Drive You Crazy* (Grand Rapids: Zondervan, 1995), pp. 59-60.

2:1-2), community (Mk 3:14), fasting (Mt 4:2; Lk 4:2; Mt 6:16-18), giving to the poor (Jn 13:29; Mt 6:2-4), prayer and solitude (Mk 1:35; Lk 5:16; 6:12; 11:1; Jn 6:15; Mt 6:5-6), retreat (Mk 6:31), rule of life ("custom," Mk 10:1; Lk 4:16; 22:39), sacrifice (Mt 8:20), Scripture study and memorization ("it is written," Mt 4:4, 7, 10), service (Mk 10:45), submission (Mt 26:52-54; Jn 18:36) and witness (Jn 4:4-43).[28]

It will take time for worldview beliefs to be adjusted. As we persist in our formation practices we patiently wait for growth, and it will become evident. Dallas Willard clarifies,

> We know that we must, instead of just trying to obey, find a way to become the kind of person who does, easily and routinely, what Jesus said—does it without having to think much about it, if at all, in the ordinary case. . . . In engaging the [spiritual] disciplines we go to the root of the tree of life, the sources of behavior. We do the things that will transform our minds, our feelings, our will and our embodied and social existence, even the depths of our soul, to "make the tree good, and its fruit good" (Mt 12:33 NASB). We cultivate and fertilize the tree (Lk 13:8). We don't try to squeeze fruit out of the ends of the branches. . . . And in this way we become, by divine grace, the kind of person who does the things Jesus said to do and avoids what he said not to do.[29]

We'll need to take a long-term view. The race in formation is not a sprint, but a marathon—it requires endurance over time.

Formation Through Upgrading Our Lifestyle Patterns

Engaging in individual formation practices may be likened to specific battles and skirmishes in a larger war. We want to win these battles, but

---

[28]For a helpful list of sixty-three spiritual practices, see Adele Ahlberg Calhoun, *Spiritual Disciplines Handbook* (Downers Grove, Ill.: InterVarsity Press, 2005). For a helpful discussion of various character strengths from the social science literature, see Christopher Peterson and Martin Seligman, eds., *Character Strengths and Virtues: A Handbook and Classification* (New York: Oxford University Press, 2004). For further practical help on habit formation, see David Watson and Roland Tharp, *Self-Directed Behavior*, 9th ed. (Belmont, Calif.: Wadsworth, 2006).

[29]Dallas Willard, "Spiritual Formation as a Natural Part of Salvation," in *Life in the Spirit: Spiritual Formation in Theological Perspective*, ed. Jeffrey P. Greenman and George Kalantzis (Downers Grove, Ill.: InterVarsity Press, 2010), pp. 55-56.

we also want to win the war. One particular formation strategy that keeps that broader lifestyle perspective in view is attending to our *rule of life* or *lifestyle patterns*. As Ruth Haley Barton explains, "Living into what we want in any area of our life requires some sort of intentional approach. Building a solid financial base, retirement planning, home improvements, career advancement, further education, losing weight or becoming more fit—all . . . require a plan."[30] Do we tend to shy away from modifying our lifestyle patterns for personal formation because we think it's too constrictive? Yet we're okay with making plans in other areas of our life, as Barton notes. Are we being inconsistent? Can we reframe the picture, and appreciate how structure in this case can lead to greater freedom rather than hinder it? Doing such life planning helps us address the range of gaps identified in the last chapter, especially the distracted gap, where our lifestyle slowly drifts away from the key values we wish to embrace.

We're already familiar with lifestyle patterns in that we each have various set ways for how we go about the regular features of our lives (e.g., brushing teeth daily, washing clothes weekly, paying bills monthly and filing our income tax returns annually). The problem is that most of our habits just evolved over time from necessity. We may not give much thought to how we can include more of the key values from Jesus' teaching into these regular patterns. Our life may be mostly on autopilot in the bad sense—moving through our day pursuing the most demanding tasks in front of us, distracted from considering the eternal value of the sum of our activities. It's probably focused mainly on material and urgent needs, with little thought to developing routines and patterns to prepare us for living four hundred years from now.

The key question, according to Barton, to pose is "How do I want to live so that I can be who I want to be?"[31] To guide the updating of our lifestyle patterns, Barton suggests these points. A life plan needs to be *personal* and unique to that person, *realistic* in light of their stage of life,

---

[30]Ruth Haley Barton, *Sacred Rhythms* (Downers Grove, Ill.: InterVarsity Press, 2006), p. 146. Chapter nine of her book offers some practical steps and examples for updating lifestyle routines. For an approach on this from the context of the business world see Daniel Harkavy, *Becoming a Coaching Leader* (Nashville: Thomas Nelson, 2007).

[31]Barton, *Sacred Rhythms*, p. 147.

balanced among easy and challenging spiritual practices, and *flexible* at times when we've taken on too much to do.[32] We need to avoid the tendency to view these guidelines as absolute standards equal to Scripture itself. Personal guidelines we formulate probably need to be adjusted as we experiment with what works for us in our season of life, fitting in with our particular circumstances, personality, gifts, strengths and gaps.

The ultimate goal is living in a loving relationship with God and his people, and becoming more like Jesus in our character. Intentionally updating our lifestyle patterns is a way of planning to reduce our gaps. When beginning to work on gaps in a new area of emphasis, it can be helpful to borrow the guidelines of others.[33] Eventually we'll need to adapt, experiment and custom-fit them to our own formation journey. We'll also need to be careful that our personal guidelines don't become the source of judgmentalism toward others, in that we implicitly require others to follow our personal guidelines as The Standard for a robust Christian life. These are just *personal* guidelines, and each of us will need to set about developing our own response to God and his Word that is sensitive to our context. A life plan is only a *means* toward an end, not an *end* in and of itself.

Looking at Our Daily and Weekly Routines

"Daily" and "weekly" are important time markers. We can easily get busy and be distracted from what Jesus values. Two particular practices may prove helpful for pondering our routines. One involves imagining a traffic signal with three lights: green, yellow and red. Compare the

---

[32]Ibid., pp. 148-50.

[33]A classic corporate rule of life with various ideas to consider was developed and compiled for monastics by Benedict of Nursia (A.D. 480–547), *The Rule of St. Benedict in English*, trans. Leonard Doyle (Collegeville, Minn.: Liturgical Press, 2001). Although I attend a non-liturgical church, I appreciate the routines of the liturgical/church calendar. For further reading, see Robert Webber, *Ancient-Future Time: Forming Spirituality through the Christian Year* (Grand Rapids: Baker, 2004), and Joan Chittister, *The Liturgical Year: The Spiraling Adventure of the Spiritual Life* (Nashville: Thomas Nelson, 2010). My wife, Beth, and I occasionally use structured prayers from the *Book of Common Prayer*, as compiled by David Stancliffe and Brother Tristam SSF, in *Celebrating Common Prayer: Pocket Version* (New York: Mowbray/Continuum, 1994).

daily and weekly routines with each light: the green light represents life-energizing activities, the yellow light includes partially life-energizing and partially draining activities, and the red light represents draining activities that tend to deplete our life energies. Do the sum of the routines tend toward being life-energizing or life-draining, more "green" than "red" activities? Such awareness is an important step in assessing our life routines. Is it possible to make minor adjustments to certain activities to increase their life-giving value?

Or, perhaps we need to make some major adjustments. We don't always have a choice about all of our activities, but there are some over which we have a measure of discretion. Here, the "4 Ds" may be a helpful evaluation exercise. Among our discretionary activities and routines, is it possible to make any of these adjustments?

a. *Drop it*—Do I really need to continue doing this activity?

b. *Delegate it*—Is it possible that another person could do this activity who might enjoy it more and do a better job? Or can I do the task along with someone else, sharing the load together?

c. *Delay it*—Do I really need to do this activity/project right now? Can I postpone doing part or all of it until a later time?

d. *Diminish it*—If it's an important task I need to keep doing, is there a way I can realistically limit the time and effort I give to doing this task?

Periodically working through this exercise may stimulate some creative ideas regarding our routines. When it comes to our daily routines, are we engaged in activities that are needful and good? Ralph Winter challenges us with a statement worth pondering: "Nothing that does not occur daily will ever dominate your life."[34]

Take an Energizing Break from Our Daily Routines

Do we recognize that the week was instituted by God? "By the seventh day God had finished the work he had been doing; so on the seventh

---

[34]Ralph Winter, "Join in the World Christian Movement" (August 29, 2006) <www.perspectives.in/perspectives/fastrak/PSP09.shtml>.

day he rested from all his work. Then God blessed the seventh day and made it holy, because on it he rested from all the work of creating that he had done" (Gen 2:2-3). From this passage, we glean a "sabbath" or "rest" principle, initiated prior to the Mosaic law. When this concept was explained in the law, a key part was *not* to do what they normally did each day, to take a break from their work, from their lifestyle routines ("not do any work," Ex 20:11-12; "do no regular work," Num 28:26; 29:1, 7, 12, 35).

My application is that I need to take a break from my work and daily routines to do things that I usually don't do get a chance to do—something I look forward to doing. The focus is on engaging in life-giving and energizing activities that restore our souls. It's not a focus on doing nothing. This will include spending time with God, the main source of our rest (Heb 4:9-11; cf. Mt 11:29), on an individual basis, and also with other believers, as the New Testament teaches (Heb 10:24-25). Some try to make Sunday a whole day of rest, but that's not always practical—and it's not required by the New Testament. The main point is, are we taking sufficient time aside, on a weekly basis, to do some life-giving activities that energize and restore our soul? I'm now asking myself, *Am I resting* weekly *or am I resting* weakly—*and am I tending toward the old "being busy and in a hurry" mode?* We might take a break daily, or periodically throughout the week, or take a block of time weekly. Either we can take a break from our life routines, or eventually our life routines will break us.

For example, here are some suggested practices to attend to our rest needs and avoid being distracted from living more like Jesus. With much patience we can extend grace to ourselves and others, granting permission to grow and fail.

- Time for personal reflection (e.g., journaling, "glad, sad, mad, dreads and dreams" reflection guideline in chap. 2)

- Time for personal study and meditation as a lifelong learner (e.g., Scripture, books, conferences, seminars, DVDs, courses)

- Time for feedback from trusted others (e.g., close friends, mentors, small group, spiritual directors, counselors)

Businesspersons know how important it is to regularly monitor the key indicators of business health, such as customer satisfaction, product quality, employee competency and morale, and profit and positive cash flow. Without periodically looking at these key indicators, the business will eventually lose market share and margins, which could result in business failure. Regular monitoring is just as important for our own formation and lifestyle.

I'm suggesting that we balance daily and weekly routines with weekly times for rest and play. Life is not only about structure and routines. Gerald May challenges us to value spontaneity and creativity. Using the concept of our "inner wilderness," he encourages us to leave plenty of room for "this inner wilderness [which] is the untamed truth of who you really are."[35]

Final Thoughts

I used to give much more attention to my words and external behaviors—what I said and how I acted— in my attempts to follow God's commands in the Bible. But in light of the insights above, I am giving myself more grace and taking a long-term view of formation. What is now more important is to give attention to my reactions to discern what is going on inside. And, as I become aware, to be transparent with God and admit I need help and ask for his grace to grow my heart. In some cases, I may take on a related spiritual practice so both my soul and body are attending to this area of need. Although it's a slow process, I have been affirmed recently by trusted others who have noted some deep changes in me.

God hasn't left us alone without any help. God is ready to support our growth into Christlikeness. We will explore these essential formation

---

AWAKE to gaps → ADMIT with honesty → ASK for formation grace → ACT, take a first step

Figure 3.2. Four-step framework

---

[35]Gerald May, *The Wisdom of Wilderness* (New York: HarperCollins, 2006), p. xx.

resources in part two. These resources are not one more thing to add to your to-do list but are to be received as gracious gifts to benefit us.

Key Points

1. The formation of our heart flow to become more like Jesus involves a process that can be illustrated as three phases, from being clueless about the particular gap (A), to being transformed so that we routinely live like Jesus in that particular area (B and C; table 3.2 and figure 3.1).

2. We take with us into eternity our relationship with God and relationship with others in Jesus' forever family, the kind of persons we are becoming, and the effects of our good deeds.

3. Members of Jesus' forever family will be living four hundred years from now. Taking a long-term view in life planning is important for living now, monitoring our daily routines and taking our weekly breaks.

4. Jesus himself, in his humanity, acquired his deeply held worldview beliefs and resulting heart flow of lifestyle in a similar manner as we all do.

Reflection Questions

1. What insights and questions come to mind about Jesus' own formation as human (see table 3.1)?

2. Look over table 3.2 and figure 3.1. Try to explain in your own words what each is attempting to communicate about the process of inner heart formation. Which one is more helpful? Explain. Would you make any adaptations to either of them? Explain.

3. Reflect on the discussion about heaven. What topic was most interesting to you in that discussion? Explain.

4. What are some life-giving activities you would like to do as part of a weekly break?

PART TWO

ESSENTIAL DIVINE RESOURCES

OF FORMATION GRACE

4

Love

Divine Relational
Support in Jesus' Life and Ours

That brought him to his senses. . . . He got right up and went home
to his father. When he was still a long way off, his father
saw him. His heart pounding, [his father] ran out,
embraced him, and kissed him.

LUKE 15:17, 20 *THE MESSAGE*

· ℘ ·

The main question addressed in this book is, What can we learn from Jesus' life and words about Christian living and character formation? Jesus' invitation is still available, "Come to me, all of you who are laboring and bearing burdens, and I will give you rest" (Mt 11:28), so that we might have life "to the full" (Jn 10:10). Part one described components of a four-step formation framework: awake, admit, ask and act. Yet we can't be formed solely through the power of our own human resources. In part two we consider three essential divine resources from above to support our formation journey here below: God's unconditional love (chap. 4), empowerment by the Holy Spirit (chap. 5) and reality-checks from Scripture (chap. 6). Without regularly accessing each of these divine resources, little formation progress can take place.

Explaining why this is the case is what we'll explore in these three chapters.

I Love You

"Son, I love you. Everything is going to be all right."[1] Jack Frost couldn't fathom this statement from his father. Jack, age nineteen, was at a hospital in a semi-comatose state recovering from an LSD overdose in 1972. Father and son had been estranged due to an infamous haircut imposed on Jack by his dad. Although Dad Frost loved his children deeply, his uncompromising rules—including the way you wore your hair—weren't balanced out by any perceived love and intimacy. A strict military man, he demanded immediate obedience and expected a crew cut or a flattop of his son. A year earlier, when he noticed that Jack's hair was touching his collar, he commanded Jack to get his hair cut by the next morning. All that rebellion bubbled up in Jack. In no uncertain terms he told his dad what he could do with his rules—and he wasn't going to cut his hair. Dad reacted as well. He dropped his son on the floor at that moment and, against Jack's will, cut Jack's hair himself. Now, with shorter hair, Jack shouted profanities at his dad and soon after left the house never to return, severing all ties with his dad.

Jack let his hair grow, got a job at a popular drug paraphernalia shop in downtown Daytona, Florida, during the 1970s, and got stoned as often as he could while "working." It just happened that his dad's mail delivery route included Jack's shop. Daily, when his dad came to the shop on his route, he'd go inside looking for Jack, but Jack would hide. "I rejected my father every single day for over a year."[2] But there in the hospital room was his dad, holding Jack in his arms, caressing his shoulder-length hair, tenderly whispering how much he loved Jack. "Even though I was in a drug-induced fog, his words sank deep into my soul, 'Son, I love you.'"[3] Don't we all long to hear those special words, "I love you"?

When you think of the concept of love what image comes to mind? A

---

[1]Jack Frost, *Experiencing Father's Embrace* (Shippensburg, Penn.: Destiny Image, 2002), p. 21.
[2]Ibid., p. 76.
[3]Ibid., p. 21.

heart shape? A Valentine's Day special date with a loved one? A mother nursing a baby? A dad playing with a child? A grandmother caring for a sick child? A love poem? A favorite song? A kind act someone did for you recently? Group hugs? Counselors tell us we need a couple of hugs each day. What is loving to you? What fills up your love tank?

Gary Chapman suggests there are five basic love "languages" or ways to show someone they are loved:

- *Words* of affirmation (e.g., regular praise and compliments)
- Giving *gifts* (e.g., flowers, cards, a favorite candy)
- Acts of *service* (e.g., fixing a leaky faucet, cooking a meal)
- Physical *touch* (e.g., holding hands, back rubs)
- Quality *time* (e.g., focused attention, a walk in the park together)[4]

Think back over this week or month or year. When was it that you felt especially loved? For *each* of the categories above, when did you experience some moments of grace and expressions of love in your life?

Barriers to Deeper Love and Intimacy

Yet we need to move beyond love languages to open up a greater flow of love in our lives. Unfortunately we develop certain deeply held worldview beliefs at the core of our being that can hinder our receptivity to love and our ability to give love. I should know; I'm a recovering loner. Having been steeped in the radical individualism of our culture for over half a century, it's been difficult for me to acknowledge that I have relational needs for intimacy. Perhaps this is more common among men than women in our culture. I've been on a long and slow journey to move toward deeper relationships and deeper intimacy. This chapter touches a particular gap of mine. Working on the issues of this chapter is opening up some key insights to help me become more able to receive the Father's love. I hope God may use an insight from this chapter to help diminish gaps you may have in this area of love. An important first step toward wholeness is recognizing how each of us has a limited re-

---

[4]Gary Chapman, *The Five Love Languages* (Chicago: Northfield Publishing, 1995).

serve bank out of which we love others. The following account highlights how early life experiences can impact our present relational capacities.

The overthrow of the communist state of Romania in 1989 made
public to the world their outrageous care of orphans.[5] Inspectors were
horrified at what they found in the orphanages: children had been tied
to cribs and chairs, bodies were emaciated, children were hosed down
in their cribs for washing, few playthings were available and there was
infrequent verbal or physical interaction between caregivers and children. In one adult psychiatric hospital, some of the older children had
been restrained with head-to-toe sheets wrapped around them. When
a sheet was removed from one seventeen-year-old, part of the sheet
actually lifted off the skin making a raw open wound.

Several countries developed programs for adopting these children.
Much research has been conducted to follow up on the development of
these Romanian orphans. Michael Rutter, one of the main researchers, reports that at the time of the adoption, among one group that
came to the United Kingdom "over half had a weight below the third
percentile, and three-fifths were functioning developmentally in the
severely retarded range."[6] For adopted Romanian orphans who came
to the United Kingdom before age two, there was in general by age six
dramatic evidence of catching up both in weight and in basic cognitive
functioning with average U.K. children. Yet regarding psychological
aspects of relational and attachment functioning there were continuing problems—especially for those children who had remained longer
in the orphanage prior to adoption—such as inattention, overactivity
and autistic-like features.

In his book summarizing the major themes and research on social
attachment theory, Robert Karen notes that "a child needs to be lovingly attached to a reliable parental figure and that this need is a pri-

---

[5]Craig S. Smith, "Romania's Orphans Face Widespread Abuse, Study Finds," *NYTimesOnline*
(May 10, 2006) <www.nytimes.com/2006/05/10/world/europe/10iht-romania.html>.
[6]Michael Rutter, "Adverse Preadoption Experiences and Psychological Outcomes," in *Psychological Issues in Adoption*, ed. David M. Brodzinsky and Jesus Palacios (Westport, Conn.: Prae-
ger, 2005), p. 80.

mary motivating force in human life."[7] Included in his list of basic themes of attachment are "the need for proximity, for felt security, for love; the need to be held, to be understood, to work through our losses. . . . We have mixed feelings about these [attachment themes]. But they are there."[8]

Love is fundamentally experiential and relational. As newborns, we enter life with basic love needs that remain throughout our life, yet we're totally dependent on others to love us and to help us grow our capacities to receive and to give love. In an imperfect world, these love needs remain to some degree unmet and our love capacities will have had limited formation—with influences ranging from significantly debilitating experiences, such as those of the Romanian orphans, to very affirming and nourishing communities. Regardless, we all have room to grow into greater depths of love.

Moving Toward the Source of Deep Love

Part of Jesus' mission is to help stretch our perspectives and expectations about unconditional love. What does it look like? What does it feel like? On the topic of unconditional love, most of us are probably moving into foreign territory. The fact is, none of us—in our own power—can *give* absolute unconditional love because we're finite humans in a fallen world. The corollary is that we really haven't had significant opportunities to *receive* absolute unconditional love from others. Each of us may have moments of grace now and then, where a close approximation of this unique kind of love breaks through, but these are limited and short term. Almost all of our experience is of conditional love—love conditioned on what we do or say. For some who have had significant abuse in their life, unconditional love probably seems like a topic of make-believe. Yet Jesus' truth and love can heal us in the deep places.

What is Jesus' love message for us? Bottom line, at the core of our identity, God . . . loves . . . us unconditionally. We are God's beloved

---

[7]Robert Karen, *Becoming Attached* (New York: Oxford University Press, 1994), p. 441.
[8]Ibid.

sons and daughters. Jesus' most famous story captures the heart of God to welcome us all. It's often referred to as the return of the "prodigal" son (recklessly wasteful son). This tale is told in response to a grumbling comment by some religious leaders, "He takes in sinners and eats meals with them, treating them like old friends" (Lk 15:2 *The Message*). Jesus shares a series of three parables, all to communicate the heart of God: the lost coin, the lost sheep and the lost son.

A father had two sons. The younger son (unmarried, perhaps around twenty years old) requests his portion of the inheritance. The first twist is that the father graciously gives him his portion rather than beating him for this brash offense. The inheritance was normally only passed on at the father's death. With his wallet full, the younger son leaves the dad (and his family business duties) to travel to a distant country where he wastes all his money on parties and friends. Then, alone and without a dime to his name, he takes a job feeding hogs, a most demeaning line of work in Jewish culture. Here Jesus attempts to depict the worst kind of degradation a person could fall into. Life becomes so meager that the younger son even considers eating the hog slop. Finally he comes to his senses, realizing even his father's own servants are better off than he is. So he swallows his pride and decides to return home and beg his father to let him take on the role of a servant in his household. The journey home is slow as he rehearses his apology and request.

When he gets closer to home, his father happens to see him a long way off. Here's the next twist: The old man, overcome with great joy, doesn't wait for his son to come to him, but takes off running to welcome him home. Running wasn't what dignified, elderly men did in that day—in Middle Eastern culture such behavior is viewed as a humiliating act, worthy of scorn. But the father doesn't care about his reputation; he's overcome with great joy because his son has returned. Embracing his son, the father lavishes him with kisses. The son begins his memorized speech, but the father interrupts him. Instead of "I told you so," or "Shame on you!" he immediately orders his servants to get the best clothes and sandals and a family ring for his beloved son. These tokens represent the father's complete forgiveness and welcoming reception of his son with all the authority and rights of a son.

More surprises. The father can't contain his enthusiasm and throws a lavish welcome home party that very day so the whole village can celebrate this momentous event. Such a public affair demonstrated to the family and household, to neighbors and to the rest of the community that he fully accepted his son back without punishment, forgetting what was past—that his son was honored and under his protection.[9]

But the story doesn't end there. The elder son is not around when the lavish celebration begins. He learns from a servant what all the noise is about and he's irritated that his brother was welcomed back in such a gracious way without any punishment or shame. His father comes out to invite the elder son in, but he argues with his father and disagrees with such treatment of a person who wasted his inheritance. Jesus' listeners would have considered the greater sin of the younger son as not having any resources to help care for an aging father. The elder son is angry toward the younger son and toward his father and doesn't go to the party, thus dishonoring his father before the villagers at the feast. He complains that he always obeyed his father but never got such a party. The father reminds his elder son that all the possessions are his—the elder son is legally vested with the estate—but that he had to welcome his son back this generous way. Notice how the elder son represents a primary focus on external actions with little regard for matters of the heart—for the heart of repentance and humility of the younger son, and the heart of love and generous forgiveness of the father.

Jesus' story is a marvelous portrayal of two contrasting ways to respond to sinners. Do some of us side more with the self-righteous elder son, expecting God to harangue repentant sinners with "I told you so" and other forms of abusive shaming? I think our view of God may have been skewed by past experiences of conditional love solely focused on correcting external actions. According to Jesus, the father in the story is the more accurate depiction of God's heart—gracious, forgiving, extravagant, always welcoming and ready to enter into a closer relationship with anyone—no matter how badly that person seems to have degraded

---

[9]Some of these insights came from Robert Stein, *An Introduction to the Parables of Jesus* (Philadelphia: Westminster Press, 1981).

themselves or dishonored God. God leaves the ninety-nine sheep still in the fold and seeks after the one that has gone astray (Mt 18:12-14). All are welcome within God's family; no one is shamed or turned away. God is ready to forgive us and embrace us as true children.

Yet as a result of our experiences to date, have we developed an incomplete view of what love is, a distorted view of who God is and a confused view of who we are? These factors can become a barrier to fully receiving God's unconditional love.

What Is Our Image of God?

Imagine you were having a conversation with God on your phone. What do you think God might say to you now in that conversation? Be honest. Do any of these negative messages come to mind?

"Can't you try a little harder?"

"Do you know you've already asked me ten times to forgive you for that?"

"I'm sorry. I've got an emergency. I'll call you back later."

Unfortunately for many of us, old tapes of negative messages from life experiences interfere with hearing God's genuine messages to us.

And how do our circumstances affect the way we perceive God's love for us?

I got a raise. *He loves me!*

I didn't get the promotion I wanted; I lost my job altogether. *He loves me not!*

Something in the Bible inspired me today. *He loves me!*

My child is seriously ill. *He loves me not!*

I gave money to someone in need. *He loves me!*

I let my anger get the best of me. *He loves me not!*

Something for which I prayed actually happened. *He loves me!*

I stretched the truth to get myself out of a tight spot. *He loves me not!*

A friend called me unexpectedly to encourage me. *He loves me!*

My car needs a new transmission. *He loves me not!*[10]

Like picking off the petals of a flower and saying "He loves me," or "He loves me not" with each petal removed, do we experience such a pendulum swing of back and forth in our experience of God?

What if God clearly sent the following message directly to us? Could we receive it deep down in our soul?

"I love you. My heart is very tender toward you. You're special to me."

How often does *that* thought cross our mind? God's message of love and tenderness sadly may not connect for many of us. As mentioned before, we may feel unworthy or unlovable. But that's not God's view of us. Remember Jesus' story about how the father rushed out to embrace the wayward son, smothering him with kisses. God loves us, in spite of our self-image and our particular image of God.

On that matter, our view of God may probably be much too puny and distorted. Distortions in our God-image can prevent us from re- ceiving God's gracious love—in effect, rendering various aspects of God's character as nonexistent. For it's hard to assign the word *love* to a relationship with God when God *feels like* a judgmental parent who criticizes us without any display of affection, or like a legalistic police officer who makes us toe the line whether we like it or not, or like a distant relative who never seems to show up. Or, if our parents were overly affectionate, we may struggle with seeing God's love as smother- ing and negatively overwhelming.

Reflect on your initial responses to the exercise above about what God would personally say to you now. Are there any hints there to your current "God-image"? Our views of God are largely formed through our experiences with authority figures such as parents, relatives, teach- ers, pastors and coaches. The obvious fact is that none of these persons can fully represent a majestic, all-wise, all-loving God. I know. I'm imperfect and I've played or still play some of these human roles. Those of us in such roles will always represent both good and bad qualities to those in our care. Can you trace any similarity between experiences

---

[10]Wayne Jacobsen, *He Loves Me! Learning to Live in the Father's Affection* (Newbury Park, Calif.: Windblown Media, 2007), p. 4.

you've had in the past and your current view of God and his relationship with you?

Why is this important to discuss? Because the quality of our life experience is linked to *our view of God* and *what we expect God to do*. The devil's ploy in the Garden of Eden was to deceive Adam and Eve about God's love for them—implying that God was hindering them from becoming wise and enjoying all that creation had to offer, and that God was selfish for banning them from eating from the tree of life (Gen 3:1-5). Adam and Eve listened to these implicit lies defaming God's character and they trusted the devil more than God at that moment. To what degree do our own actions evidence how much we trust in God at a *deep level within?* If we're honest we might admit how limited our own God-confidence is—how we have difficulty placing more trust in God. That's why our God-image needs a makeover. To live a more flourishing life, it's important that we keep developing a more accurate view of God.

Try out an exercise and finish this sentence: "God is always greater than . . ."

Some possible responses: God is always greater than

- my current view of God

- my pastor's view of God

- the view of the author of this book (or any book I read)

- what's included in the Bible

God is still always "greater than."

Ponder again the story Jesus told of the Father's warm welcome of a wayward son. Henri Nouwen reflects on our own waywardness. "I am the prodigal son every time I search for unconditional love where it cannot be found. Why do I keep ignoring the place of true love and persist in looking for it elsewhere? Why do I keep leaving home where I am called a child of God, the Beloved of my Father?"[11] Can we really hear God's message in the depths of our heart: "I love you. My heart is very tender toward you. You're special to me"? We can't get that kind of

---

[11]Henri Nouwen, *The Return of the Prodigal Son* (New York: Image, 1992), p. 43.

love from anyone on this earth. It's God's unique quality: unconditional love. And you and I are the fortunate recipients of that ever-giving love. Can't buy it. Can't earn it. Can only receive it. That's amazing grace.

God Is Our "Abba"

Jesus could share this message with us because he was convinced at the core of his own heart that he is the beloved Son. Notice how Jesus included a character portraying himself in the parable of the vineyard, depicting how the religious leaders rejected his mission and his being sent from God. The absent owner had sent various messengers so he could receive some of the harvest from the land. But instead of complying, the tenants had beaten previous messengers. The owner finally sent his own beloved son: "He [the vineyard owner] had one [messenger] left to send, *a son, whom he loved.* He sent him last of all, saying, 'They will respect my son.' But the tenants said to one another, 'This is the heir. Come, let's kill him, and the inheritance will be ours'" (Mk 12:6-7, emphasis added; also Lk 20:13-14). Jesus knew at his core that he was the beloved Son (Lk 2:49; 3:22; 9:35).

On the night of Jesus' betrayal, during his agonizing prayer in the garden, Jesus used the affectionate Aramaic term *"Abba"* (Mk 14:36), like our "Dad." That's the only time that special term is recorded on Jesus' lips in the Gospels. But just because the New Testament is written in Greek, we can't assume that Greek was Jesus' primary spoken language. Rather, Jesus mainly used Aramaic, which the Gospel writers hint at by recording Jesus' spoken Aramaic phrasing in other contexts: Mark 5:41; 7:34; 15:34; and John 1:42. Mary Magdalene spoke to the resurrected Jesus in Aramaic (Jn 20:16). When Paul reports his encounter with the resurrected Jesus on the Damascus road, he mentions that Jesus spoke Aramaic to him (Acts 26:14). Thus, in the Gospels whenever we read Jesus saying "Father" (Greek *pater*), we can infer Jesus was actually speaking the Aramaic *Abba*. In the classic study on this subject, Joachim Jeremias concluded, "We have discovered that all five strata of the Gospel tradition report unanimously and without any hesitation that Jesus constantly addressed God as 'my Father' (with the exception of Mark 15:43 par. Matt. 27:46), and show that in so doing he used the Aramaic, Abba."[12]

Jesus introduced a new way of addressing God, with familial familiarity, as Jeremias explains: "Jesus talks to his Father as naturally, as intimately and with the same sense of security as a child talks to his father."[13] Furthermore, the prayer Jesus taught his disciples begins with addressing God as Father, that is, our heavenly "Abba" (Mt 6:9; Lk 11:3), thus "authoriz[ing] them to say 'Abba,' just as Jesus did. In this way, Jesus gave them a share in his relationship with God."[14] The apostle Paul reinforces this authorization that we too can approach God with the same affectionate term of endearment: "The Spirit you received does not make you slaves, so that you live in fear again; rather, the Spirit you received brought about your adoption to sonship. And by him we cry, 'Abba, Father'" (Rom 8:15). "Because you are his sons, God sent the Spirit of his Son into our hearts, the Spirit who calls out, 'Abba, Father'" (Gal 4:6).

As Jesus' disciples, we are to use this special term, Abba, exclusively for God alone (Mt 23:9). New Testament scholar Scot McKnight offers a helpful summary.

> Jesus is decidedly lopsided when it comes to names for God: *every prayer* of Jesus recorded in the Gospels begins with *"Abba*, Father" except the famous "My God, My God, why have you forsaken me?" utterance from the cross. . . . What Jesus wants to evoke with the name *Abba* is God's unconditional, unlimited, and unwavering love for his people. In this name for God we are standing face-to-face with the very premise of spiritual formation: God loves us and we are his children.[15]

Is It Difficult to Receive God's Love Deeply?

Even though this is such a gracious gift, God's unconditional love may be hard to receive. Our painful past seems too fresh to us—times when we trusted someone, letting our guard down, but they didn't fulfill

[12]Joachim Jeremias, *The Prayers of Jesus* (Philadelphia: Fortress, 1967), p. 57.
[13]Ibid., p. 78.
[14]Ibid., p. 63.
[15]Scot McKnight, *The Jesus Creed* (Brewster, Mass.: Paraclete, 2004), p. 25.

their promise. We felt hurt and rejected. Yet God is different. At the core of our being, *God loves us unconditionally*. Brennan Manning shares the story of a seventy-year-old single woman—a Roman Catholic nun—who felt rejected by God. During a series of meetings in the Midwest, each night's sessions concluded with times for healing prayer. This particular night Manning had been praying for others till past midnight, and he finally went to bed. At 3:00 a.m. he heard a rap on the door and a voice asking, "Brennan, can I talk with you?"[16] These two sat in the hallway as she shared her pain.

> I've never told anyone this in my entire life. It started when I was five years old. My father would crawl into bed with me with no clothes on. . . . When I was nine, my father took my virginity. By the time I was twelve, I knew of every kind of sexual perversion you read in dirty books. Brennan, do you have any idea how dirty I feel? I've lived with so much hatred of my father and hatred of myself that I would only go to Communion when my absence would be conspicuous.[17]

Brennan prayed for her healing, and then suggested a spiritual practice to do daily for the next thirty days. He encouraged her to sit in a quiet place, with eyes closed and palms turned up, saying this simple prayer, and to sequence it along with her breathing: "As you inhale— [say,] *Abba*. As you exhale—[say,] *I belong to You*."[18] She agreed to try this. In a follow-up letter to Manning, she related how, having done the exercise, she had completely forgiven her father and had received such inner healing and peace unknown to her before. The letter closed with, "A year ago, I would've signed this letter with my real name. . . . But from now on, I'm Daddy's little girl."[19] At the core of our being, *God loves us unconditionally* and yearns for our deep healing.

God is love (1 Jn 4:8). That simple phrase is profound, yet receiving this truth that God really loves me, deep in my soul, has been a challenge for me much of my life. It's probably the most difficult of Jesus'

---

[16]Brennan Manning, *The Furious Longing of God* (Colorado Springs: David C. Cook, 2009), p. 45.

[17]Ibid., pp. 45-46.

[18]Ibid., p. 46.

[19]Ibid.

teachings in this book for me personally. Theologically and conceptually I understand the concept and can research and teach about it. But *experientially* it's been hard to connect at a deeper emotional level. I've had many wonderful moments of God's grace, but some kind of underlying emptiness has been a continuing theme. An important breakthrough came on a recent three-week retreat. My spiritual director encouraged me to stay outside of my cabin and let God's creation speak to me—if I would listen. At first I was puzzled as I walked on the shore, shells crunching under my feet. Then the crows started cawing loudly. At first I was annoyed, but then I woke up—was awakened— that God was trying to get through to me. For three weeks, that bay in Washington state became a classroom on God's love through his creation. "Look at the birds of the air; they do not sow or reap or store away in barns, and yet your heavenly Father feeds them. Are you not much more valuable than they?" (Mt 6:26). My reflections of that time by that bay are represented in a poem I wrote, which is shared at the end of this chapter. (I've included a few other poems in the remaining part of the book to communicate about formation through a different literary avenue.)

When I come to Abba for comfort and support, I sometimes employ an emotionally laden image that represents safety, affirmation and affection for me. Scripture is full of various metaphors for Abba, such as stronghold/fortress (Ps 31:23; 62:2, 6-7; 94:22), shelter/refuge (Ps 61:3- 4; 91:1) and sheltering wings (Ps 63:7; 91:4). I imagine myself crawling into Abba's lap, seeking his comfort and being held tightly. This is a vivid and special memory for me because of my daughter. When Ruth was still at home, she would often come to me and say "Hugs, Daddy," and crawl into my lap. It was a precious time.

What emotionally laden imagery conveys those kinds of messages to you? Whenever we become aware of our fear, anxiety, hopelessness or aloneness, we can come to our Abba who eagerly welcomes us with open arms. One morning I was reciting these phrases over and over, "Abba, I belong to you. Abba, I am loved by you." Then I was surprised when I mixed the words up a bit and said, "Abba, I'm in love with you." Perhaps my deep heart was finally speaking up.

Attending to God's Love Initiatives

Some might say, "I don't always sense God's love. Sometimes God seems so distant. Why isn't God's love more evident more often?" An important point from Jesus' story of the prodigal son is that God is willing to give us plenty of room to make our choices in our relationship with him, just as the younger son had the freedom to take his inheritance and leave home. We have the opportunity to get closer to God or to be away from God. Since God is not threatened by our absence, God partially *hides* or veils his presence to make this "relational space" possible. God could have made the world another way, with a more noticeable imprint such as angelic choirs praising God morning, noon and night, or clouds taking the shape of key Bible verses. But that's not the way our world is because that kind of world would be too coercive—God's presence would be forced on everyone, whether they welcomed him or not. Even the God of the universe will not coerce our love and friendship. We enjoy our physical space (notice how we keep our distance on an elevator) as well as our relational space (we may tend to avoid someone who demands too much of our time). God sets an atmosphere in which to woo us into a genuine love relationship. That means God won't be as obvious to us most of the time as is a tree or a mountain. But even when he seems absent—that is, not physically obvious to us—*he is always present* (see Ps 139:7-12).

Yet there are grace moments when God visits us in a special way, if we're listening. For example, God visited Parker Palmer, a noted educational consultant, during a time of depression. "Amazingly, I was offered an unmediated sign of that love when in the middle of one sleepless night during my first depression, I heard a voice say, simply and clearly, 'I love you, Parker.'"[20] But initially Palmer dismissed the event. After awakening to the importance of this message from Abba much later, Palmer became open to seeking professional help with his depression, overcoming his false belief that going to counseling was a sign of weakness.

This kind of "hide and seek" arrangement from God—the apparent

---

[20]Parker Palmer, *Let Your Life Speak* (San Francisco: Jossey-Bass, 2000), pp. 64-65.

oscillation between God's absence and presence—may frustrate us. But we need not assume God doesn't care about us. More to the point, God cares about us too much as persons with dignity and free will and is willing to leave room so we can respond to his love. From Jesus' prodigal son story it's clear that the Father is always ready to welcome us home—no matter our condition, no matter what we've done. In the story, the younger son had done all the wrong things to insult his dad, but his dad was compassionate and gracious.

What I learned on that retreat by the bay was that I need to be more attentive toward becoming aware of *God's love initiatives* toward me: sunshine that warms me in a special moment, the cheerful sound of birds singing in the morning when I need that encouragement, a beautiful sunset that overwhelms me, a specific word from a friend that goes deep and a hug from a friend that puts flesh on love. I'm reminded of an excerpt from an Elizabeth Browning (d. 1861) poem,

> Earth's crammed with heaven,
> And every common bush afire with God:
> But only he who sees, takes off his shoes,
> The rest sit round it, and pluck blackberries.[21]

How is God speaking to you? Scripture informs us that God speaks all the time and through a variety of means, such as Scripture, nature, animals, music, dreams, angelic visits, dramatic healings and his soft inner voice. Paraphrasing Jesus' oft-repeated challenge, have we got our "ears on"? ("Whoever has ears, let them hear," Mt 11:15; 13:9).

God's love is also conveyed through our human community, through our friends and mentors. Part of our journey is becoming the kind of person who is safe and trusted by others rather than someone people tend to avoid. In my own formation journey John Finch, a well-known contemporary psychologist, played a significant role by creating a safe context for me on my first three-week retreat in 1997.[22] There I had a

---

[21]Elizabeth Barrett Browning, "Aurora Leigh" (1857), bk. VII, I.812-26.
[22]For further reading on John Finch, see *A Christian Existential Psychology: The Contributions of John G. Finch*, ed. H. Newton Maloney, 2nd ed. (Pasadena, Calif.: Integration, 1990), and John G. Finch, *The Holy Spirit: The Explosive Power of a New Affection* (Gig Harbor, Wash.: Integration, 1997).

life-changing encounter with God, which has set me on a path to begin to explore my inner heart. I had no idea about my emotional life. I had no idea that the Holy Spirit was available to empower me for life and ministry. I had no idea that I was a proud and arrogant person. I was clueless (hopefully a bit less clueless about those items now). Without John's gracious welcome on that retreat, humanly speaking, I would not have the capability of offering any insights about formation.

Finch also helped me move from being a hand shaker to a hugger. After one of our meetings he commented, "You know, Klaus, you're the only one who shakes my hand after a session. Everyone else hugs me." I dutifully hugged him, but that began a journey of bodily defrosting and appreciating the role that physical touch conveys in expressing love and affection to others—somewhat like the "holy kiss" of New Testament times (Rom 16:6). Other mentors—spiritual directors and counselors—have also had important effects on my formation journey.[23]

One Christmas I had the joy of spending three weeks with Kate, our sixteen-month-old granddaughter. Walking with her hand in hand, playing house, reading books, changing diapers (a few) and hugs. There's nothing she could do to dissuade me from loving her. And that's one of the experiences God is using to break through into my heart. In a very vivid way, I know experientially the love I have for Kate. I can imagine God views me in a similar way. It's been a very helpful analogy to gain a glimpse of God's bountiful love for me.

Final Thoughts

Without a safe and loving context, it's difficult to take the risk to admit our gaps. God's unconditional and forever love for us is a gift to receive; there's nothing to earn. Can we become the little vulnerable child who is very needy, letting go of our defenses and allowing God's love to overwhelm us? God doesn't condemn believers anymore for their sin (Rom 8:1). In such a loving and safe relationship, we can honestly admit our gaps and be wooed by God's love into becoming more of the true self

---

[23]For a helpful guide on developing a "spiritual direction" approach for your small group, see David Benner, *Sacred Companions* (Downers Grove, Ill.: InterVarsity Press, 2002), chap. 8, "Spiritual Accompaniment in Small Groups," pp. 165-83.

that God created us to be. We were designed to be deeply loved by God. Only Abba's love can meet that need. It's objectively and propositionally true that God loves us. But that's only part of the reality. God's love is also something we can and need to experience personally.

God's love is one foundational resource. In the next chapter we'll explore another foundational resource: the ministry of the Holy Spirit. According to Romans 5:5, the Holy Spirit is the divine agent of God's love: "God has poured out his love into our hearts by the Holy Spirit, whom he has given us" (NIV).

Pause Button

As you practice taking thirty-second pauses throughout your day, consider using these prayers to God as a way to meditate on your relationship with God: "Abba, I belong to you. Abba, I am loved by you."

AWAKE to gaps → ADMIT with honesty → ASK for formation grace → ACT, take a first step

---

Figure 4.1. Four-step framework

The Call to Come Away . . . to Come Home

Come away, be among us, come and see
Our active movements, our passivity:
    Of drifting clouds in sun-drenched bright,
    Of seagulls and eagles aloft in flight,
    Of honking geese, of cawing black crow,
    Of shimmering waters, of tides high and low,
    Of ducks afloat or feeding near shore,
    Of little "whiteheads" diving down for more,
    Of sand-dollared sea urchins clustered in clumps,
    Of oyster shells befriended by barnacled bumps.

Stay awhile, be among us, become aware,
This bay is a place of God's loving care.
Of God's feeding our birds, that Jesus knew,
Yet, how much more valuable to God are you!

Come just as you are, we really don't mind.
This is our sanctuary, leave your worries behind.
By "green pastures," by "still waters," the psalmist foretold,
The Shepherd brings healing from want: "He restores my soul."

Relax . . . Unwind . . . Rest among us . . . Come home.

©Klaus Issler, 2/2011

Key Points

1. Our expectations about love—both unconditional and conditional love—are based on past/present experiences and relationships. Yet Jesus came to show us how much God unconditionally loves us—we who are in his forever family. The story of the loving father and wayward son powerfully demonstrates God's unconditional love for us.

2. Our (small) conception of who God is—our God-image—highly influences how we live our life—it's a deeply held worldview belief. Our view of God needs to be regularly expanding since God is infinite.

3. We need to grow in our *experiential* ability to receive God's unconditional love at a deep emotional level.

4. Jesus introduced a novel way to address God as *Abba*, an Aramaic term of familiarity and intimacy. And he taught believers to use *Abba* as well, in the Lord's Prayer.

Reflection Questions

1. Ponder or discuss the five love languages, and the idea that everyone has at least one key way they receive love.

   a. Can you remember in the recent past when you sensed being loved through your primary love language? Reflect on these experiences and on what you learn about love and about yourself.

   b. What are the primary love languages of some of your loved ones, friends or small group members? Do you notice a difference when you offer love in light of their primary love language, rather than using your primary love language?

2. As you think about a recent occasion where you sensed being loved through your primary love language(s), consider to what extent God was involved in extending his own love in this experience. Reflect on such occasions of "God's love initiatives" and what you can learn about love, yourself and God.

3. Being around children (and also friendly animals) provides an amazing opportunity to give and receive love. Why is that the case? Perhaps explore how to regularly visit with children, if you are not normally around them. Volunteer in a church nursery or a hospital pediatric ward to hold children who need human touch. Perhaps take a mission trip to an orphanage overseas. Be a support for those families that invite foster children into their home or who adopt children.

5

Holy Spirit

Divine Mentoring in Jesus' Life and Ours

I will talk to the Father, and he'll provide you another Friend
so that you will always have someone with you. This Friend is the Spirit of
Truth. . . . The Friend, the Holy Spirit whom the Father will send
at my request, will make everything plain to you. He will
remind you of all the things I have told you.

JOHN 14:16-17, 26 *THE MESSAGE*

· ℘ ·

Jesus mentioned this promise about the Spirit, in the passage quoted above, at the last meal with his disciples. Then, before he ascended to his seat at the right hand of God, the resurrected Jesus spoke with his disciples about the kingdom of God and reminded them of this promise from the Father. "You will receive power when the Holy Spirit comes on you; and you will be my witnesses in Jerusalem, and in all Judea and Samaria, and to the ends of the earth" (Acts 1:8). The coming of the Holy Spirit was a key feature of the new covenant (KJV "new testament") spoken about in the Old Testament (Jer 31:31-34 [Heb 8:10-11; 10:16]; Ezek 36:25-27; Joel 2:28-29 [Acts 2:17-18]). Jesus inaugurated this new covenant with his death and resurrection (Lk 22:20; 1 Cor 11:25; 2 Cor 3:6; Heb 9:15; 12:24; cf. Rom 8:1-17). The book of Acts notes that Stephen and Barnabas had reputations as persons who were full of the Spirit and of faith (Acts 6:5; 11:24).

Unless today's believers engage the empowering resource of the Holy Spirit—who is the divine agent of sanctification (Rom 8:13; 2 Thess 2:13; Tit 3:5; 1 Pet 1:2)—it is impossible to be formed into the image of Jesus Christ. The Holy Spirit's ministry is an important link and transition between Jesus' life and ministry and the believer's life and ministry. Why? Because Jesus himself could not have accomplished his messianic mission and his life example for us without the empowering ability of the Holy Spirit. These important points will be explored in this chapter.

Teamwork

Why would Dick Hoyt burden himself by pulling 110 pounds of extra weight in the 1999 Hawaii Ironman Triathlon event—the most prestigious event of its kind? Because of a father's love for his son. Team Hoyt consists of a father and a son who compete in these sports events together.[1] Rick was born in 1962 with cerebral palsy. During birth, the umbilical cord squeezed Rick's neck and cut off his oxygen supply, damaging his physical body but not his mind. Instead of institutionalizing him, Dick and Judy Hoyt decided to keep Rick at home and give him as normal a life as possible.

Rick cannot talk, walk or feed himself, but he can move his head and knees. He communicates with head pats on a specially designed computer. In 1979, when Rick was fifteen, he asked his dad if they could enter a five-mile charity race as father and son. Although Dick was forty years old and not a runner, he was eager to respond to Rick's request. After competing—and not finishing last—Rick grinned with joy. Back at home Rick tapped out on his computer, "Dad, when I am running, it feels like I'm not even handicapped." That was all the encouragement dad needed, and they began entering races regularly, improving their equipment and speed.

---

[1]Sam Nall, *It's Only a Mountain: Dick and Rick Hoyt, Men of Iron*, 2nd ed. (St. Petersburg, Fla.: Southern Heritage, 2002).

In 1999 at the Kona event, Team Hoyt completed this grueling contest—a 2.4 mile swim, 112 mile bike ride and 26.2 mile run—ahead of some of the other competitors, despite a mechanical delay with their bike. At that event, they achieved their personal best finish time to date: fourteen hours and twenty-six minutes. Dick tows his son in a small rubber boat with a tether tied to his waist while he swims, rides a specially designed bicycle with Rick seated out front, and then pushes a three-wheeled chair in the run. (Google "Team Hoyt" and you can watch a video of their amazing performance.)

In 1982 a reporter asked Dick Hoyt, "'Why do you do this?' 'Because Rick loves to run,' [Dick] replied truthfully. 'And I love running with him.' 'Would you ever race without him?' 'Why should I? He's what drives me.'"[2] A son's request in 1979 launched the amazing Team Hoyt into action as a powerful heroic example of what a father's love will do.

What About Jesus?

Do we regard Jesus as an amazing hero who successfully overcame enormous obstacles like Dick and Rick Hoyt have? Deep down do we believe that Jesus genuinely struggled against the challenges of life *just like they did,* or *like we do?* Or do we picture Jesus more like a superhero—who used his super ability all the time? We may think, "Well, wasn't Jesus God? And God doesn't have to struggle to make something happen; he just speaks the word and it's so, without any effort at all." So we reason:

"How could Jesus know the thoughts of others?" "Because he was God."

"How could Jesus resist temptation and live without sin?" "Because he was God."

"How could Jesus perform miracles?" "Because he was God."

"How could Jesus forgive his enemies while being tortured on the cross?" "Because he was God."

---

[2]Ibid., p. 101. Team Hoyt also illustrates the effects of our dependency on the Holy Spirit; Rick must depend on his dad to accomplish activities he couldn't do on his own.

At the popular level we may bandy around the phrase "What Would Jesus Do?" but down deep we may tend to let Jesus' deity overwhelm his humanity in the practical living out of daily life.[3] But I've been persuaded otherwise. The Bible indisputably shows us how human Jesus was. I wonder how I could have so misjudged Jesus' character and the heroic effort it took to live within human constraints. Jesus truly is our genuine example, a person who mainly lived in his humanity as you or I do.

There is sufficient scriptural evidence to show that Jesus was *both* fully God and fully human. We often ignore the latter, to the detriment of the formation of our character. Consider Alan Spence's explanation regarding our reluctance on this issue, even among some Christian scholars.

> The difficulty seems to lie in an inability to conceive of the incarnate Christ as "normative man." Although those who hold to his divine sonship are usually quick to affirm his true humanity, there has, nevertheless, been in the past an unwillingness to give due weight to the Gospel testimony to his growth in grace, wisdom and knowledge; to his continual need of divine comfort and empowering through the Holy Spirit; and consequently to the implication that as man he stood just as we do, a creature totally dependent on his God.[4]

In contrast to other chapters in this book, this one gives more space to discussing Jesus' example, and less space on application for our formation. The truth about Jesus' authentic human experience has great potential for impacting our personal formation journey, so it's worth giving such emphasis. The main point is that Jesus predominantly relied on the divine resources of the Father and the Holy Spirit to accomplish his messianic mission. There are two parts to the discussion: the first focuses on doctrinal teaching related to Jesus' messianic ministry, and the second presents the biblical evidence for Jesus' dependent lifestyle. As we delve into this matter—to honor our Lord's full human-

---

[3]Docetism was an ancient teaching the early church leaders opposed, for it affirmed that Jesus only seemed or appeared to be human, but really was not.

[4]Alan Spence, "Christ's Humanity and Ours: John Owen," in *Persons, Divine and Human*, ed. Christoph Schwöbel and Colin E. Gunton (Edinburgh: T & T Clark, 1991), p. 75.

ity—we must do so cautiously so as not to diminish his full deity.[5]

As you read the various ideas in the chapter, you may wish to note your internal processing of these ideas. This chapter may provide a firsthand experience of uncovering core worldview beliefs, some being affirmed and some being challenged. You may wish to pay attention to what feelings of agreement or hesitance surface as you engage the ideas presented, and to reflect on how your experience relates to the discussion of core worldview belief change in part one of the book.

As long as there is ambiguity or ambivalence about Jesus' authentic human experience, it will be difficult for believers to make much progress in responding to Jesus' invitation to "learn from me" (Mt 11:29) and to rely on the same divine resources Jesus did. I'm amazed at Team Hoyt—Dick and Rick are worthy of respect—but I believe Jesus is worthy of greater honor as the greatest hero.

The Theological Importance of Jesus' Authentic Human Experience

At a general level it is difficult to deny Jesus' humanity at the obvious points: He was embodied (e.g., he was thirsty, Mt 25:35; hungry, Mt 4:2; weary, Jn 4:6; and he died, Jn 19:30-34).[6] He experienced a full range of emotions (e.g., weeping, Lk 19:41; compassion, Mk 6:34; righteous anger, Mk 3:5; frustration, Mt 17:17; being troubled in spirit, Mt 26:37). Many who encountered him, especially the religious leaders, regarded Jesus as *nothing more than human*, not as some kind of alien or superhero from outer space. To paraphrase the Nazareth folk with whom he grew up, "It's just Jesus, no one special" (Mk 6:3). Furthermore, Jesus was tempted (Mt 4:1-11)—an experience which Scripture denies of God (Jas 1:13)—yet without sinning (Heb 4:15). Furthermore, Paul's comparison between Adam and Christ bears testimony to the humanity of Jesus (Rom 5:12-21; 1 Cor 15:20-22, 45-49). Regarding God's design of human nature, Bernard Ramm notes, "In the

---

[5]This study works with the canonical New Testament texts and within the basic boundary conditions for orthodox theological inquiry as set down by the Chalcedonian Definition (A.D. 451).

[6]I use the past tense, although Jesus still lives today with both divine and human natures.

very act of the creation the possibility of a future incarnation was made possible. If humankind is produced in the image of God then there is some of that image in God. Hence God can become incarnate."[7]

Yet adding on a human nature is not enough. Jesus also had to engage his humanity and *live a genuine human life,* facing and successfully emerging from genuine human struggles and temptations as we do. Jesus' human experience is essential to provide an example for believers today. But more important, this feature is also necessary for Jesus to accomplish two unique messianic priestly functions; that is, a predominantly genuine human experience is required for Jesus (a) to offer a humanly sinless life as a substitution for us (Rom 5:18-19; 8:3; 2 Cor 5:21; 1 Pet 2:22-24) and (b) to become our humanly sympathetic high priest (Heb 2:10-17; 4:15-16; 5:8-10). "In bringing many sons and daughters to glory, it was fitting that God, for whom and through whom everything exists, should make the pioneer of their salvation perfect through what he suffered" (Heb 2:10). "Son though he was, he learned obedience from what he suffered and, once made perfect, he became the source of eternal salvation for all who obey him and was designated by God to be high priest in the order of Melchizedek" (Heb 5:8-10).

William Lane explains,

> In [Hebrews] 2:10 and 5:9 the emphasis falls on Jesus' perfecting through sufferings. Read against this background, the perfect passive participle of v 28 implies that a *life-time of human experience* punctuated by testing, humiliation, and the affliction of death is now behind Jesus. . . . The verb *teleioun,* "to perfect," is accordingly best understood in a dynamic sense as referring to *the whole process* by which Jesus was personally prepared and vocationally qualified for his continuing ministry in the presence of God.[8]

Thomas Oden, summarizing a consensus of historical Christian teach-

---

[7]Bernard Ramm, *An Evangelical Christology* (Nashville: Thomas Nelson, 1985), p. 53. Furthermore, Ramm explains, "In the humanity of Jesus Christ God has revealed what it is to be a true person. Hence a Christian anthropology can be constructed only from a Christology" (p. 77).
[8]William L. Lane, *Hebrews 1–8,* Word Biblical Commentary 47A (Dallas: Word, 1991), pp. 195-96 (emphasis added).

ings, also affirms this point. "A necessary part of Jesus' mediatorial role was that, like us, he struggled against sin and temptation. He voluntarily entered into that human (all-too-human) arena of genuine temptation, so as to become victorious over sin."[9] Bruce Demarest concurs, "The ground of justification, in the first place, is Christ's *virtuous life*."[10] If during his first coming Jesus did *not* engage daily existence in his humanity as his predominant mode of living, then serious conflicts arise with these key biblical teachings. Thus, the purpose of Jesus' human life involved much more than being an example.

Divine Ability for Jesus' Life and Ministry

Before determining the particulars of Jesus' example for us, we must first address a prior question: What does Scripture teach about Jesus living an authentic human life that qualifies him for his messianic ministry of becoming a substitutionary atonement and a sympathetic high priest? As was mentioned before, if Jesus mainly engaged his own *divine* ability rather than his human ability for his life and ministry, then Jesus did not enter into the normal human experience—which would contradict other scriptural teaching. Further, if this was the case, then we humans *cannot* possibly follow Jesus' example. As William Barry admits, "If Jesus is superhuman, then I can admire him, but I do not have to take seriously his call to emulate him. I can never be a superhuman being."[11]

To pursue this line of inquiry we'll need to ask regarding Jesus' messianic life and ministry—particularly the supernatural aspects—whose *divine ability* was mainly involved? (1) Was it Jesus' own divine ability? (2) Was Jesus dependent on the Father's and the Spirit's divine ability? or (3) Was it some combination of these? Five logical options are possible.[12]

---

[9]Thomas Oden, *The Word of Life* (1992; reprint, Peabody, Mass.: Prince, 1998), p. 244.

[10]Bruce Demarest, *The Cross and Salvation* (Wheaton, Ill.: Crossway, 1997), p. 369.

[11]William Barry, *Letting God Come Close* (Chicago: Jesuit Way, 2001), p. 111.

[12]In presenting these five options, I will make the following two assumptions: (1) Jesus' human ability is unnecessary and unused on those occasions when he's using his own divine ability. On these occasions, Jesus cannot be an example for mere humans like us. I will argue that Jesus rarely or infrequently used his own divine ability. (2) When Jesus depended on the Father's and

Regarding Jesus' messianic life and ministry:

Option A: Jesus *exclusively* used his own divine ability, *never* depending on the divine resources of the Father and Holy Spirit and *never* using his human ability.

Option B: Jesus *predominantly* used his own divine ability, *infrequently* depending on the divine resources of the Father and Holy Spirit and infrequently using his human ability.

Option C: Jesus used his own divine ability *about half the time* (not using his human ability), and for *the other half* he depended on the divine resources of the Father and Holy Spirit (on these occasions he used his human ability), thus balancing/alternating an equal use of both abilities.

Option D: Jesus *infrequently* used his own divine ability, and *predominantly* depended on the divine resources of the Father and Holy Spirit and also predominantly used his human ability.

Option E: Jesus *never* used his own divine ability and *exclusively* depended on the divine resources of the Father and Holy Spirit while he exclusively used his human ability.

Which options deserve further consideration? The Scripture provides clear evidence of some form of dependence on the Father (Jn 5:19-20; 14:10) and on the Holy Spirit (Mt 12:28; Lk 4:1, 14), so option A (no dependence on the Father or the Spirit) can be eliminated. Option B (mostly living from his divine ability) is problematic with minimal opportunity for sufficient authentic human experience to qualify Jesus to become a sympathetic high priest, or a genuinely human sinless offering to atone for sins. So option B can be eliminated. Option C (half and half use of divine and human abilities) might be possible, but we only get half a lifetime of authentic human experience. Is that sufficient for his priestly functions? Probably not. Overuse of his divine ability minimizes his roles as a fully sinless human offering and a sympathetic priest with extensive, lifelike human experience. So option C

---

the Spirit's divine ability for life and ministry, then Jesus did *not* use his own divine ability but rather used his human ability. On these occasions, Jesus did engage an authentic human experience to qualify him for his messianic priestly role and also as an example for us in matters common to our humanity.

does not offer a strong contribution. Option E (never using his own divine ability) may be problematic since the Gospels seem to indicate Jesus used his divine ability on a few occasions—for example, perhaps manifesting his glory in the transfiguration (Mt 17:2; Mk 9:3; Lk 9:29). I believe such instances are the exception, not the rule. (I postpone treatment of Jesus' miracles to a later discussion.)

I think option D is, thus, the most viable—Jesus infrequently used his own divine ability, and predominantly depended on divine resources of the Father and Holy Spirit and also predominantly used his human ability. Such dependence by Jesus would be then the *norm* of his life on earth. This option permits sufficient human experience for Jesus to qualify as a sympathetic high priest and a genuinely human sinless sacrifice. Let's consider the scriptural evidence to support this option.

Scriptural Evidence for Jesus' Dependency on God for Life and Ministry

That Jesus predominantly lived within his humanity while depending on God is developed from biblical evidence within three categories.

a. Jesus depended on the Father.

b. Jesus exercised his own faith and trust in God.

c. Jesus depended on the Holy Spirit.

I present scriptural passages that represent *explicit* support as well as those in which we can infer the point with *implicit* support. The verses identified as implicit evidence *include* his actions of dependence and also assume the principle that Jesus practiced what he preached. That is, in any teaching to his disciples to rely on available divine resources, Jesus is sharing the results of his own personal dependence pattern while living in his humanity. The relevant passages will be listed at the beginning of each section for further study. Only a few key passages will be discussed.

Jesus' Dependence on the Father
Explicit: John 5:19-20, 30; 8:28-29, 42; 11:41-42; 12:27-28, 49-50; 14:10, 24, 31; 15:9-10; 16:32; 17:7-8; 18:11.

Implicit: Being sent by the Father: John 7:28-29; 17:18; looking up to heaven: Matthew 14:19 (Mk 6:41; Lk 9:16); Mark 7:34; John 17:1; in Gethsemane: Matthew 26:39-42 (Mk 14:36; Lk 22:42); at arrest: Matthew 26:52-54; on the cross: Luke 23:34, 46.

Mainly in the Gospel of John, there are multiple occurrences of Jesus' own declaration of his complete dependence on the Father. "Don't you believe that I am in the Father, and that the Father is in me? The words I say to you are not just my own. *Rather, it is the Father, living in me, who is doing his work*" (Jn 14:10 NIV, emphasis added). New Testament scholar D. A. Carson comments on John 17:7: "The strange way of putting the last point—that everything you have given me comes from you . . . carefully emphasizes Jesus' dependence upon his Father."[13]

Jesus Exercised Faith and Trust in God

Explicit: Hebrews 12:1-6.

Implicit: Matthew 6:30 (Lk 12:28); Matthew 8:26; 14:31; 16:8; 17:20; Mark 9:23; Luke 8:39; 17:6. Possibly, Paul's use of *pistis Christou* ("faith *of* Christ") in Romans 3:22, 26; Galatians 2:16 (2x); 2:20; 3:22; Ephesians 3:12; Philippians 3:9.[14]

We learn that Jesus himself expressed faith and trust in God the Father during his earthly sojourn. That Jesus experienced his own faith in God did not cross the minds of some translators of Hebrews 12:2, so they inserted "our" in the text where there is none in the Greek manuscripts: "looking to Jesus the pioneer and perfecter of *our* faith" (NRSV; so also KJV, NIV and NET Bible). Commentators now approach Hebrews 12:2 with fresh eyes. William Lane explains the verse "Fixing our eyes

---

[13]D. A. Carson, *The Gospel According to John*, Pillar New Testament Commentary (Grand Rapids: Eerdmans, 1991), pp. 559-60.

[14]The matter concerns how the Greek phrase *pistis Christou* should be translated. It appears seven times by Paul—Romans 3:22, 26; Galatians 2:16 [2x]; 2:20; 3:22; Ephesians 3:12; and Philippians 3:9. Some commentators recognize the legitimacy of the phrase as a subjective genitive, that is, "faith [or faithfulness] *of* Jesus," meaning Jesus himself experienced faith in God, rather than an objective genitive ("faith in Christ"). Daniel Wallace summarizes the grammatical options in *An Exegetical Syntax of the New Testament* (Grand Rapids: Zondervan, 1996), pp. 115-16, and sides with the subjective genitive view, with which I agree. For further treatment of this important issue see Richard B. Hays, *The Faith of Jesus Christ*, 2nd ed. (Grand Rapids: Eerdmans, 2001); Hays has been a key scholar in offering support for this subjective genitive view.

on Jesus, the author and perfecter of faith" (NASB):

> The poignant description as a whole points to Jesus as the perfect em-
> bodiment of faith, who exercised faith heroically. By bringing faith to
> complete expression, he enabled others to follow his example. The
> phrase reiterates and makes explicit what was affirmed with a quotation
> from Scripture in [Hebrews] 2:13, that Jesus in his earthly life was the
> perfect exemplar of trust in God.[15]

In the Gospel account of the healing of the demonized son, some
commentators suggest that Jesus' reply to the father's request in Mark
9:23 is both a challenge to the father and a testimony of his own life of
faith in God: "And Jesus said to him, 'If you are able?' All things are
possible to him who believes" (NASB). Sharyn Dowd explains, "Jesus is
not merely an example to be imitated, but a leader to be followed. It is
likely, then, that 'the one who believes' in 9:23 is deliberately ambigu-
ous. Jesus has faith and he calls the father to have faith."[16] O'Collins
agrees, "[Jesus] speaks about faith as an insider, one who knows personally what the life of faith is and wants to share it with others (see 2 Cor
4:13)."[17]

If Jesus was such an insider as a person of faith himself, then when
he criticizes the disciples for their lack of faith (e.g., Mt 6:30 [cf. Lk
12:28]; 8:26; 14:31; 16:8; 17:20; *oligopistoi* "little faiths"), he is actually
speaking as one who experientially knows what he is talking about.
Could we look to Jesus' own early developmental experience of faith
and trust in God when he learned that even small trust in God can accomplish great things? "If you have faith as small as a mustard seed, you
can. . ." (Mt 17:20; Lk 17:6; cf. Mk 11:12; 1 Cor 13:2). Ian Wallis con-
cludes his monograph on the faith of Jesus,

> It is the conviction of the present author that interest in Jesus' faith was
> an unfortunate and unnecessary casualty of early Christological con-
> troversy, in which its significance was determined more in terms of

---

[15]Lane, *Hebrews 1–8,* p. 412.

[16]Sharyn Dowd, *Prayer, Power, and the Problem of Suffering: Mark 11:22-25 in the Context of Markan Theology,* Society of Biblical Literature Dissertation Series 105 (Atlanta: Scholars Press, 1986), p. 111.

[17]Gerald O'Collins, *Christology* (Oxford: Oxford University Press, 1995), p. 261.

what it conceded to rival positions rather than of what it contributed to our knowledge of God and humanity of Jesus Christ. . . . Certainly, Jesus' faith does seem to provide a point of departure for Christology which is rooted in common human experience and which explores his theological significance through reflection upon his human being in relation to God.[18]

Finally, we come to Jesus' dependence on the Spirit.

Jesus' Dependence on the Spirit

Scripture shows that the Holy Spirit empowered Jesus so that he could live predominantly in his humanity. The evidence mainly comes from the Synoptic gospels: Matthew, Mark and Luke (verses in parentheses are parallel passages). Discussion of the Holy Spirit's involvement in Jesus' birth, childhood and baptism is postponed till later in the chapter.

From Jesus' own words—Explicit: Matthew 12:28 (Lk 11:20); Luke 4:16-21; 23:46.

From Jesus' own words—Implicit: Matthew 10:19-20 (Mk 13:11; Lk 12:11-12); Mark 3:28-30 (Mt 12:31-32; Lk 12:10); Matthew 26:41 (Mk 14:38); John 7:37-38; "power": Luke 8:46 (Mk 5:30).

Other explicit support: Baptism: Matthew 3:16 (Mk 1:10; Lk 3:22); temptation: Matthew 4:1 (Mk 1:12; Lk 4:1); Lk 1:14; 10:21; John 3:34; Acts 1:2; 10:38; Hebrews 9:14.

Other implicit support: Great Commission, Matthew 28:19; parallel between John the Baptist (Lk 1:15, 80) and Jesus (Lk 1:35, 2:40); "power": Luke 5:17; 6:19; 24:49; Acts 1:8; by crowd: Luke 4:36.

A few explicit references from Jesus himself offer significant support for his dependence on the Spirit. Near the beginning of his public ministry, Jesus is the guest synagogue speaker in his hometown of Nazareth (Lk 4:16-21). He startles his hearers when after reading a prophetic passage from Isaiah 61:1-2 he states, "Today this Scripture has been fulfilled in your hearing" (Lk 4:17). Darrell Bock explains

---

[18]Ian Wallis, *The Faith of Jesus Christ in Early Christian Traditions*, Society for New Testament Studies 84 (Cambridge: Cambridge University Press, 1995), p. 221.

that Jesus thus announces "himself to be the bearer of . . . God's new age of salvation" being the one who has received the "anointing with God's Spirit."[19]

Later in his ministry, Jesus makes an explicit declaration about relying on the Spirit for his exorcisms: "But if it is by the Spirit of God that I cast out demons, then the kingdom of God has come upon you" (Mt 12:28).[20] George Beasley-Murray notes that this saying "gives Jesus' own explanation of his exorcisms: they are performed not by his own ability but by the ability of God, i.e., by the Spirit of God, and since the defeat of the evil power is a feature of the end time, they show that the kingdom of God has appeared in his activity."[21]

Finally, a saying that may be the most telling of Jesus' relation to the Spirit is "The Spirit indeed is willing, but the flesh is weak" (Mt 26:41; Mk 14:38 KJV). Here Jesus makes a contrast between relying on divine ability of the Holy *Spirit* and solely relying on human resources ("flesh"), which can never stand alone against the assaults of Satan. Jesus elsewhere made similar contrasts between the divine sphere and human sphere (Jn 3:6; 6:63), which have Old Testament precedent in Isaiah 31:1-3, contrasting an Egyptian alliance ("flesh") against relying on the Lord God ("Spirit"; see also Ps 51:11-12). Is not Jesus giving the three disciples the secret to his own victory in the garden? William Lane comments on Mark 14:38,

> The "willing spirit" which stands in opposition to the weak flesh is not a better part of man but God's Spirit who strives against human weakness. The expression is borrowed from Ps. 51:12, where it stands in parallel with God's Holy Spirit who qualifies a man to speak with boldness before sinners. Spiritual wakefulness and prayer in full dependence upon divine help provide the only adequate preparation for crisis (cf. [Mk] 13:11). Jesus prepared for his own intense trial through vigilance

---

[19]Darrell Bock, *Luke 1:1–9:50,* Baker Exegetical Commentary on the New Testament (Grand Rapids: Baker, 1994), p. 407.

[20]Note that Jesus employs the plural "demons," indicating this deliverance as well as others was done by the power of the Holy Spirit.

[21]G. R. Beasley-Murray, "Jesus and the Spirit," in *Melanges Bibliques en homage au R. P. Beda Rigaux,* ed. A. Deschamps and A. de Hallelaneux (Gembloux, Belgium: Duculot, 1970), p. 471.

and prayer, and thus gave to the disciples and to the Church the model for the proper resistance of eschatological temptation.[22]

Jesus' comment here furnishes a clear inference of his own dependence on the Holy Spirit and of the implications as a teaching for all believers for all times.

The explicit and implicit biblical data offer sufficient cumulative evidence of Jesus' authentic human experience, empowered by the Father's and Spirit's divine resources for his life and ministry. In 1991 Gerald Hawthorne published a full book on the topic. "Without denying the reality of the incarnation, or that God became a man, it is the purpose of this book, nevertheless, to argue for the reality of Jesus' humanness and that as such he was not aided to rise above and conquer temptations *as God*, but rather as a man whose will was set to do the will of God."[23] Before moving to the section on Jesus' example for us, we'll address a few additional questions.

Questions Related to Jesus' Dual Natures

Let's consider five particular issues that need some explanation as we ponder Jesus' two natures and his dependence on the Holy Spirit.

Jesus' temptability as the God-man. A particular difficulty of Jesus' dual nature is how it can be the case that Jesus was genuinely tempted (Heb 2:18, 4:15; life examples narrated in the Gospels, e.g., Mt 4:1-11; 16:23; 26:38-46), despite the fact that God cannot be tempted by evil (Jas 1:13). Part of the explanation comes by clarifying how Jesus did not rely on his divine ability to resist temptation so as not to sin. Bruce Ware offers a helpful analogy on this point.[24] Imagine a man who wishes to swim across the English Channel from England to France. After much training, he hires a boat to go alongside to rescue him in case he is overcome with weariness or cramps. Being nearby, the crew

---

[22]William Lane, *The Gospel According to Mark*, New International Commentary on the New Testament (Grand Rapids: Eerdmans, 1974), pp. 520-21.

[23]Gerald Hawthorne, *The Presence and the Power: The Significance of the Holy Spirit in the Life and Ministry of Jesus* (Dallas: Word, 1991), p. 96 n. 94. Hawthorne's book was a key factor in launching me on my own continuing investigation of Jesus' humanity and example.

[24]Bruce Ware, "The Man Christ Jesus," *Journal of the Evangelical Theological Society* 53, no. 1 (March 2010): 5-18 (the swimmer analogy appears on pp. 15-16).

in the boat would not permit him to drown. On the day of the swim, he launches out, perseveres against the cold water, the waves, the weather, and triumphantly reaches the other shore. So we ask: Why *could* the swimmer not have drowned? Because of the boat. But why *did* the swimmer not drown? Because he swam and finished his course. Accordingly, why *could* Jesus not have sinned? Because of his deity. But why *did* Jesus not sin? Because he resisted the temptations in his humanity, relying on God's powerful grace. The answers to these two questions must be kept distinct.

Another part of the issue involves explaining that if Jesus knew he was God—which he did—and God cannot sin, why did he need to struggle against temptations? That Jesus actually fought against temptation is clear from Scripture, particularly in Gethsemane ("his sweat was like drops of blood," Lk 22:44; I don't think anyone would view that struggle in Gethsemane as just an amazing dramatic performance worthy of an Academy Award). Resolving the temptability issue requires more space than can be allotted here, but let me suggest one possible resolution.

We can affirm that Jesus could not actually sin (called "impeccability")—that this was not a *metaphysical* possibility. Yet we can affirm that Jesus' temptability was an *epistemic* possibility.[25] This means that, within Jesus' own understanding and perception of reality during his state of humiliation, although Jesus knew he was God, he was *not certain* that his divine nature would override his human nature to prevent him from sinning. Due to this uncertainty he struggled in his humanity against temptation. When we know a fact, it can be with varying degrees of certainty. For example, although I rarely have problems with my word processing software program or the computer, I still back up the various drafts of this chapter I'm writing almost all the time. I'd rather spend the extra effort and time on doing backups than be sorry to have to reconstruct the work I've already written. This

---

[25] Thomas Morris, *The Logic of God Incarnate* (Ithaca, N.Y.: Cornell University Press, 1986), pp. 147-48. Millard Erickson is not persuaded by this point and takes the option that Jesus could have actually sinned, but the implication he suggests for how the Father would have prevented that event seems problematic. See Erickson, *The Word Became Flesh* (Grand Rapids: Baker, 1991), pp. 561-64.

is not a perfect example, but you get the idea. When we have some measure of uncertainty, we'll do activities we wouldn't do if we were 100 percent certain. If I could be 100 percent assured that my software program and computer would never fail, I'd be wasting my time doing all these backups.

We could postulate that the Father and the Holy Spirit never offered a definitive response to Jesus' question on that particular theological matter. Thus Jesus, with some uncertainty, chose to face the temptations as if he might be able to sin. Furthermore, due to his formed heart of holiness, Jesus was much more painfully aware of the evil attacking him than we are. And he resisted every temptation, requiring greater intentionality in effort and reliance on divine help (Heb 12:3-4), and lived a sinless life in his humanity. Thomas Oden notes, "Jesus' moral excellence, like all human moral excellence, grew through choices of will."[26]

Veiling of divine attributes. For Jesus to live predominantly within his humanity during his first coming—having a genuine human experience as we know it—required a "veiling" of his divine ability and glory (e.g., Jn 17:5), particularly the three omni's: his omnipotence, omniscience and omnipresence. John Calvin notes,

> Rather, although Christ could justly have shown forth his divinity, he manifested himself as but a lowly and despised man. For, to exhort us to submission by his example, he showed that although he was God and could have set forth his glory directly to the world he gave up his right and voluntarily "emptied himself." He took the image of a servant, and content with such lowness, allowed his divinity to be hidden behind a "veil of flesh."[27]

The concept of concealment or veiling can be inferred in Gospel passages indicating Jesus' distinctly human limitations (e.g., Mt 4:2; Lk 2:40; Jn 4:6) and is stated explicitly in Philippians 2:5-11. According to Ben Witherington, the verb "emptied himself" *(ekenōsen)* in Philippians 2:7 indicates that the vessel

---

[26]Oden, *Word of Life*, p. 235.
[27]John Calvin, *Institutes of the Christian Religion*, ed. John T. McNeil, trans. Ford Lewis Battles (Philadelphia: Westminster Press, 1960), 1:476 [2.13.2].

must have some content to it, and it is not adequate to say Christ did not subtract anything since in fact he added a human nature. The latter is true enough, but the text says that he did empty himself or strip himself. What it does not tell us explicitly is of what he emptied himself. The contrast between vv. 6b and 7a is very suggestive; that is, Christ set aside his rightful divine prerogatives or status. This does not mean he set aside his divine nature, but it does indicate some sort of self-limitation, some sort of setting aside of divine rights or privileges.[28]

Although Jesus was God, his deity was veiled—a humble act of service for us as God—permitting him to experience a normal human life with its attendant weaknesses (Heb 2:17-18).

This leads to a discussion of the role of the Holy Spirit in Jesus' life prior to his baptism. Since the Scripture only explicitly identifies the Holy Spirit at Jesus' birth (Mt 1:18, 20; Lk 1:35) and his baptism (Mt 3:16; Mk 1:10; Lk 3:22; Jn 1:32-33), some infer that Jesus was basically on his own during the thirty years of his childhood and young adult years without any divine mentoring by the Holy Spirit. Yet if we compare the birth and childhood accounts of John the Baptist and Jesus that Luke offers, we can make an important inference.

If John the Baptist, the forerunner of the Messiah, was filled with the Spirit while in the womb (Lk 1:15, 17), would not that be the case for the Messiah himself, whose birth was caused directly by the Spirit (Mt 1:20; Lk 1:35)? Furthermore, we note two key terms used of the boy Jesus: a reference to "wisdom" (*sophia*, Lk 2:40, 52) and Jesus' "understanding" *(sunesis)* of Scripture, which amazed the temple teachers (Lk 2:49). These two characteristics are specifically identified with the Messiah through the ministry of the Spirit in Isaiah 11:2, "The Spirit of the LORD will rest on Him, / The spirit of wisdom and understanding [LXX, *pneuma sophias kai suneseōs*], / The spirit of counsel and strength, / The spirit of knowledge and the fear of the LORD" (NASB). Sinclair Ferguson notes,

---

[28]Ben Witherington, *Friendship and Finances in Philippi* (Valley Forge, Penn.: Trinity Press International, 1994), p. 66.

There is a continuing ministry of the Spirit in the life of Jesus ("filled," *pleroumenon*, in Lk. 2:40 indicates experience which was progressive as well as passive). We may assume, from Luke's comment that Jesus "increased in wisdom and stature, and in favour with God and man" (Lk. 2:52 RSV), that he gave expression to the appropriate fruit of the Spirit at each period of his human development.[29]

Luke's phrasing of Jesus' growth is similar to the account of the prophet Samuel as a child (1 Sam 2:26), the only Old Testament record of a young child who heard God speak to him (1 Sam 3:2-19). Would it not be the case that Jesus' teaching, "Truly I tell you, whoever does not receive the kingdom of God as a little *child* will never enter it" (Lk 18:17), is based on his own experience of being a child who was aware of "the grace of God" (Lk 2:40) and grew "in favor with God" (Lk 2:52)?

Gerald Hawthorne offers a summary of the matter: "The Spirit who was present and active in the conception of Jesus, in his boyhood and youth, throughout all of his adult ministry, in his death and resurrection, was what might be called—dare I say it?—the 'Holy Synapse' by which the truly human Jesus was made aware, made conscious, of the fact that he *was* indeed the Unique Son of God."[30] The important event of Jesus' baptism in which the Spirit rested on him (Mt 3:16; Mk 1:10; Lk 3:22; Jn 1:32-33) was not Jesus' first encounter with the Spirit, but rather it was a commissioning with the Father's blessing for his public ministry. Jesus' dependence on the Spirit from his birth through his death and resurrection confirms the scriptural teaching about Jesus' veiling.

Furthermore, additional factors also argue for the Holy Spirit's continuous participation in Jesus' life from birth onward, throughout Jesus' whole life. First, Luke informs us that Jesus, at age twelve, already had the knowledge and conviction of his special relationship with the Father (Lk 2:49). This would not be possible without the Father's involvement and, I would add, the Spirit's participation as Jesus' tutor. Second, the Spirit's participation throughout the whole of Jesus' life is required for his example for believers, including children and young adults. If

---

[29]Sinclair B. Ferguson, *The Holy Spirit* (Downers Grove, Ill.: InterVarsity Press, 1996), p. 44.
[30]Hawthorne, *Presence and the Power*, p. 215.

Paul's admonition about being "filled with the Spirit" (Eph 5:18) is also for children, then Jesus also offers these younger ones an example of depending on the Spirit.

Finally, the Holy Spirit's participation in Jesus' life from birth may help us understand *how* this unusual veiling was accomplished. For example, for Jesus to be ignorant in his humanity, he would need to block out, intentionally and consciously, his own access to his divine consciousness in which he is omniscient. Yet rather than Jesus monitoring his own veiling during his lifetime, could it be that the Holy Spirit performed this ongoing veiling work, which the Son had agreed to prior to the incarnation? Accordingly, the Holy Spirit would function as a divine, dynamic firewall that coordinated Jesus' two natures within Jesus' one person, what is called the hypostatic union. With this kind of moment-by-moment restriction accomplished by the Spirit, Jesus could live fully within his humanity, experiencing the finite characteristics of human nature that were incompatible with his infinite divine nature.[31]

For example, the Holy Spirit would be able to conceal Jesus' divine consciousness and divine knowledge from Jesus' awareness, perhaps in a way like the experience of a dormant subconscious. Thus Jesus could move through the normal stages of human development and consciousness formation from infant, to child, to young adult, to adulthood, learning the usual ways, but also being tutored by the Holy Spirit and the Father.

To summarize, from Jesus' birth onward the Holy Spirit indwelt and filled Jesus during his private years as well as during his years of public ministry. The Spirit also uniquely participated in monitoring the Son's veiling of his divine ability and knowledge, so that Jesus could predominantly live a human life that is in common with us. We now return to other questions of Jesus' dual natures.

Miracles. A third issue regarding Jesus' dual natures is how Jesus could perform miracles if he infrequently used his own divine ability.[32]

---

[31]Along these lines, if Jesus delegated the veiling responsibility to the Holy Spirit, he could also have temporarily delegated to the other members of the Trinity his usual divine duties, such as sustaining the universe (Col 1:17; Heb 1:3).

[32]Oliver Crisp conveys the scholarly consensus in labeling the view that Jesus performed his miracles by the power of the Spirit—the view held by John Owen and that is being presented

Both the Old Testament and New Testament record miracles done by mere humans—not in their own human ability, but sourced in the ability of God, similar to those Jesus performed; for example, (a) raising the dead (2 Kings 4:8-37; Acts 9:36-42), (b) curing a leper (2 Kings 5:1-15), (c) healing the lame (Acts 3:1-10), (d) making an axe head float on water (2 Kings 6:4-7), (e) multiplying food (2 Kings 4:42-44), (f) walking on water for a brief time (Mt 14:28-30) and (g) healing the sick and casting out demons by means of Paul's handkerchief and clothes (Acts 19:11-12). Specifically Jesus says that he casts out demons "by the Spirit of God" (Mt 12:28). If this is the case, then other miracles Jesus performed could all be accomplished by the Spirit. Jesus need never use his divine ability to perform any miracle. There is good Scriptural support for this claim.

If Jesus' miracles cannot be used as evidence for his deity, what Scriptural evidence can be used to support his deity? Although this chapter proposes that each miracle is done by the ability of the Spirit, the cumulative effect of these varied evidences still points to Jesus' deity: Jesus receiving worship (e.g., Mt 28:9, 16; Jn 20:28), his self-claims (e.g., Mt 22:42-45; Jn 8:58-59), the use of "Lord" (e.g., Lk 2:11; Jn 20:28) and the testimony of Gospel writers (Jn 1:1, 18). Despite the veiling of Jesus' deity during the incarnation, there is sufficient manifestation of his divine person that still shines through clearly, for, as Jesus teaches, "Whoever has seen me has seen the Father" (Jn 14:9). Furthermore, we need to keep in mind the evidence for his unique and distinctive messianic mission as the God-Man, which also includes the cumulative effect of his miracles (e.g., Mt 11:3-5; Lk 4:18).

Unique to Messiah? Fourth, is the Holy Spirit's ministry unique to Jesus as the Anointed One/Messiah, or does the Holy Spirit also empower Jesus to live his earthly life in a manner similar to how the Spirit works with believers? May I suggest a "yes" to both questions? Although the same Spirit that indwelt Jesus indwells all believers, Jesus did have a greater measure of the Spirit (Jn 3:34), due to his unique role as the divine-human Messiah, which could include the Spirit's participation in

---

in this chapter—as the "non-conventional view on this matter." Crisp, *Divinity and Humanity* (Cambridge: Cambridge University Press, 2007), p. 25.

Jesus' unique veiling of his divine abilities. It may also be that Jesus' complete dependence on the Father and his life of holiness permitted a greater flow of the Spirit's empowerment for life and ministry. Oden notes, "His baptism not only signaled the public beginning of his messianic vocation, but also provided him with all spiritual gifts necessary to fulfill his mission."[33] Yet, as will be discussed next, our missional task is not to be a messiah like Jesus, but to enter into more of kingdom life and ministry to the degree we are available and ready. Our honest prayer can be that of the man in Mark 9: "I do believe, help me overcome my unbelief!" (Mk 9:24). Jesus teaches that it is possible to grow in greater dependence on God so we can emulate more and more of his life and ministry (e.g., Mk 11:22-25; Jn 13:12-17; 14:12-14).

An example in everything he did? Finally, since Jesus was fully divine and fully human, the Anointed One, the God-Man, he must also acknowledge that he was not *merely* human—he was more than human. Thus, Jesus was not an example for *everything* that he did. We'll need to make some distinctions to help us appreciate Jesus' wider scope of activities and identify virtues and practices from Jesus we can imitate. The following five categories or factors, clustered within three groupings, can help us in our study of Jesus' life to attend to matters that we (A) cannot or (B) need not emulate, and (C) what we can emulate.[34]

A. Cannot emulate:

Factor #1: Jesus' life related to being God (e.g., receiving worship, claims of deity)

Factor #2: Jesus' life related to being Messiah, the God-Man (e.g., atoning for sins through crucifixion, calling twelve disciples to leave all and follow only him)

B. Need not emulate:

Factor #3: Jesus' life related to situational matters of time and culture (e.g., eating kosher food or being seated while teaching)

---

[33]Oden, *Word of Life*, p. 281.

[34]The development of my analysis of Jesus' non-example was stimulated from the article by Marguerite Shuster, "The Use and Misuse of the Idea of the Imitation of Christ," *Ex Auditu* 14 (1998): 70-81.

Factor #4: Jesus' life related to non-normative, temporal limitations imposed by his messianic mission (e.g., little association with non-Jewish persons, limited geographic travel in Palestine)

C. Need to emulate:

Factor #5: Jesus' life related to being our example in aspects of our common humanity as regenerated members of God's family (e.g., humility, forgiving from the heart)

This range of categories needs to be kept in mind in any study of Jesus' life, particularly for our purposes to discern Jesus' example for believers today. In the next chapter I'll offer some specific suggestions for factor #5, for what virtues and practices Jesus does exemplify for us to imitate and follow.

As we conclude this section regarding questions about Jesus' dual nature, it's worth quoting a summary statement from John McKinley's recent scholarly study of Jesus' impeccability, temptation and sinlessness.

> Because Jesus has redeemed his people from slavery to sin and sent them the Holy Spirit, believers stand in nearly the same relation to temptation as Jesus had with the same empowering grace available to enable their faithful obedience to God. Thus, the empowering grace that was effective for his victories over temptation seems to be the same help of the Holy Spirit that is promised for believers. The Holy Spirit's role in the hypostatic union enabled God the Son to enter temptation as a man because he was kept from knowing for certain he was immune to sin. God's provision of aid for Jesus allowed him to experience temptation in a way that constituted him empathetic for others who must struggle in the same human terms that he did. The model of his life for others is as a peer, not merely as the ideal because he limited himself to the resources that God likewise makes available to Jesus' followers. His empathy is credible because the transcendent security of his sinlessness was inevitable but not automatic. Jesus had to fight sin on the same basis that we do.[35]

---

[35]John McKinley, *Tempted For Us: Theological Models and the Practical Relevance of Christ's Impeccability and Temptation* (Milton Keynes, U.K.: Paternoster, 2009), p. 315.

Having established that Jesus' human experience was authentic, that he lived predominantly in his human ability, what can we learn from Jesus' example for life and ministry for believers today? Let's consider one key exemplary implication: how the Holy Spirit can enable us in a similar way today. As was mentioned at the beginning of the chapter, the key linkage and transition between Jesus' life and ours is the empowering ministry of the Holy Spirit (Acts 1:3-8).[36]

The Holy Spirit as Divine Mentor and Partner

Sanctification and empowerment for ministry are the work of the Holy Spirit. As the divine agent of renewal in our life, the Spirit renders a comprehensive and pervasive ministry for believers. The New Testament records at least four significant areas in which the Spirit's assistance is needed for living well within God's kingdom:

a. empowerment in deepening our relationship with God ("fellowship of the Spirit," Phil 2:1; 2 Cor 13:14)

b. empowerment for Christlike living ("fruit of the Spirit," Gal 5:22)

c. empowerment for growing together into a healthy and mature Christian community ("the unity of the Spirit," Eph 4:3)

d. empowerment for ministry to others ("spiritual gifts," 1 Cor 12:1), and for evangelism ("filled with the Spirit and spoke the word of God boldly," Acts 4:31; cf. Acts 1:8)

Regarding the process of sanctification, although the Holy Spirit has promised its eventual completion (Rom 8:29-30), the believers' growth is never complete this side of death and heaven. Due to our general cluelessness (Mt 7:3), wouldn't it be great to have access to a wise counselor—any time, day or night—who is able, in love and grace, to point out our foibles and frailties, but in a confidential

---

[36]Regarding the role of the Spirit in the "already" aspects of the kingdom, Mark Saucy states, "The aims and means of the kingdom in the present age are none other than the aims and means of the Spirit. Thus, in the eschatological tension between the 'already' and the 'not yet,' it is biblical pneumatology [doctrine of the Holy Spirit] that will hold us from the poles of over-realized or under-realized eschatology." Saucy, "The Role of the Spirit in the Social Ethics of the Kingdom," *Journal of Evangelical Theological Society* 54, no. 10 (March 2011): 90-91.

manner? For this very purpose, the indwelling Spirit willingly mucks about in the cesspool of the unconscious and conscious aspects of our being to facilitate the transformation of our lives toward Christlikeness.

Despite the reality that God the Holy Spirit lives in every genuine believer forever (Jn 14:16), some of us simply ignore the Spirit throughout the day—as I did for much of my adult life. But now I can't ignore the New Testament evidence for the role of the Holy Spirit in Jesus' life, and the emphasis on the Spirit in Paul's letters: "Live by the Spirit, I say, and do not gratify the desires of the flesh" (Gal 5:16 NRSV). Perhaps exploring certain metaphors can help us gain a perspective about the kind of working relationship we can develop with the Spirit.

By combining two biblical word-pictures, the Spirit as wind and the believer as a soaring eagle (e.g., "they will soar on wings like eagles," Is 40:31), a dynamic image takes shape, depicting how supernatural assistance helps believers rise above human limitations. Eagles were made for soaring, having long wingspans with powerful feathers. They soar great distances for hours at a time when the wind carries them.

Consider a personal metaphor related to air travel, of a pilot and copilot flying the planes we often use to visit family or to meet for a business appointment. In many cases, it requires two pilots to commandeer these multimillion-dollar technological wonders through the friendly skies. Similarly, human life, a priceless and miraculous creation of God, was expressly designed from the beginning to be a "two-pilot" arrangement similar to an airplane. God has so fashioned human nature that both a human person *and* a Divine Person can occupy the pilot's quarters together (the Holy Spirit indwells us forever, Jn 14:16). Yet the Holy Spirit does not wish to become the senior pilot in this arrangement, although he is the superior expert. The Spirit is our Divine Mentor, our flight instructor as it were, to help us live our lives to the glory of God. We desperately need a copilot of greater power, of greater wisdom, to guide us in navigating through the turbulence toward the important destinations of life. The Divine Mentor goes with us wherever we go, and is always ready to offer counsel, encouragement and admonishment—if we are ready to listen and ask for formation grace.

Jesus' promise of "another helper" is just what we need. God the Spirit makes available to us all the resources to help us become the kind of persons who love God and serve him (2 Pet 1:3-4). Christian living is a cooperative or synergistic venture. Flying *solo* portends an accident waiting to happen. Most of us have learned this truth through countless "crashes" in our lives, the disasters of our own doing. Perhaps we could share more testimonies in our small group meetings and when we gather at church about the times God has shown up in our lives in amazing ways. Such stories would help remind us not to go it alone, but to keep asking for God's sustaining empowerment.

I've become convinced that we cannot move forward in formation in Jesus without the regular awakening ministry of the Holy Spirit in each of our lives. Calvin Miller notes, "Awakening is the act of coming out of sleep or lethargy so that we may infuse our lives with a greater, spirited vitality. We need to do this until such vitality becomes a way of life. The church should remain in a constant state of renewal. Our own personal awakenings must occur every morning of our lives."[37] God the Spirit can awaken us to our gaps and empower us to live more like Jesus, if we're open to listen.[38]

During a particularly long season of my life, on a daily basis I prayed the words of the apostle Paul's rich trinitarian prayer from Ephesians 3:14-21. It's a prayer that includes a reference to the Father, to Jesus and to the Holy Spirit. The two key requests are for believers to experience deeply *God's empowerment through the Holy Spirit* and to experience deeply *God's love through the love of the Son*—key resources that undergird heart flow change. Wouldn't God be more ready and willing to answer a prayer that was inspired from Scripture? I am continuing to

---

[37]Calvin Miller, *Loving God Up Close* (New York: Warner Faith, 2004), p. 111.
[38]For further guidance on developing a relationship with the Holy Spirit, see chapter six, "Communication: Hearing the God who Speaks," in my *Wasting Time with God* (Downers Grove, Ill.: InterVarsity Press, 2001), pp. 151-82; see also Dallas Willard, *Hearing God* (Downers Grove, Ill.: InterVarsity Press, 1999).

sense God's movements in sustaining my life and heart flow change. I encourage you to pray this prayer as well.

> For this reason I bow my knees before the Father, from whom every family in heaven and on earth takes its name. I pray that, according to the riches of his glory, he may grant that you may be strengthened in your inner being with power through his Spirit, and that Christ may dwell in your hearts through faith, as you are being rooted and grounded in love. I pray that you may have the power to comprehend, with all the saints, what is the breadth and length and height and depth [of the power of God],[39] and to know the love of Christ that surpasses knowledge, so that you may be filled with all the fullness of God.
>
> Now to him who by the power at work within us is able to accomplish abundantly far more than all we can ask or imagine, to him be glory in the church and in Christ Jesus to all generations, forever and ever. Amen. (Eph 3:14-21 NRSV)

Our attitude can be "I do believe, help me overcome my unbelief!" (Mk 9:24). Jesus teaches that it is possible to grow in greater dependence on God so we can emulate more and more of his life and ministry (e.g., Mk 11:22-25; Jn 13:12-17; 14:12-14).

In the next chapter we explore a third foundational divine resource for our formation journey, this time giving attention to God's Word and its essential role in helping us see reality—so that God's truth can liberate us from the lies that imprison us and can point us to particular virtues and practices we can imitate from Jesus' example.

AWAKE to gaps → ADMIT with honesty → ASK for formation grace → ACT, take a first step

Figure 5.1. Four-step framework

---

[39]There is no identified object in the Greek text related to the four dimensions mentioned. Most translations borrow the phrase "the love of Christ" from the next line and insert it as the object of this line. I am including the phrase "the power of God" as the object of this first line of request, based on the study of the passage by Clinton E. Arnold, *Ephesians,* Zondervan Exegetical Commentary Series (Grand Rapids: Zondervan, 2010), pp. 214-17.

Pause Button

As you practice taking thirty-second pauses throughout your day, consider using an old chorus, "Spirit of the Living God," as a prayer of invitation to the Holy Spirit to fill you afresh.[40] When evangelist D. L. Moody (d. 1899) was asked why he urged Christians to be continually filled by the Holy Spirit, he reportedly quipped, "I need a continual infilling because I leak!"

Key Points

1. We were not meant to live the Christian life solely on our own human resources—it's not possible to do well without divine help.

2. Learning to trust and rely on the divine mentor living within is not automatic. We will need to learn how to cooperate with the Holy Spirit, who awakens us to help reduce the willing-doing gap.

3. The Holy Spirit who indwells us forever (Jn 14:16) does not want to run our life for us, but to mentor/guide and partner/empower us so we can engage in a flourishing life in Jesus' kingdom.

4. Jesus lived an authentic human life, empowered by the divine resources of the Father and the Holy Spirit, in order to complete various tasks of his unique mission from God as Messiah, and also as an example for us.[41]

Reflection Questions

1. Regarding the discussion of Jesus' dependence on divine empowerment, some passages were discussed (others just listed). Which passages did you consider to be important in the discussion? Explain.

---

[40]"Spirit of the Living God" was written in 1926 by Daniel Iverson (1890-1977), a Presbyterian pastor, church planter and evangelist; lyrics available at <www.hymnary.org/hymn/PsH/424>.

[41]I provide more details on the study of Jesus' human example in "Learning from Jesus to Live in the Manner Jesus Would If He Were I: Biblical Grounding for Willard's Proposal Regarding Jesus' Humanity," *Journal of Spiritual Formation and Soul Care* 3, no. 2 (Fall 2010): 155-80; and in "Jesus' Example: Prototype of the Dependent, Spirit-filled Life," in *Jesus in Trinitarian Perspective*, ed. Fred Sanders and Klaus Issler (Nashville: B & H, 2007), pp. 189-225.

2. Which of your concerns regarding the claim that Jesus predominantly lived his life in his human ability were answered? For which particular concerns would you like to do more study and discussion?

3. To what extent does your church community include the third person of the Trinity, the Holy Spirit, in common discussion regarding living the Christian life? What practical next steps would be helpful to get to know the Holy Spirit more intimately?

6

Scripture

Divine Revelation of Reality
and a "Jesus" Lifestyle

Do not suppose that I came to undermine the authority of the OT scriptures,
and in particular the law of Moses. I did not come to set them aside but to
bring into reality that to which they pointed forward. I tell you truly: the
law, down to its smallest details, is as permanent as heaven and earth and
will never lose its significance; on the contrary, all that it points forward to
will in fact become a reality (and is now doing so in my ministry). So anyone
who treats even the most insignificant of the commandments of the law as of
no value and teaches other people to belittle them is an unworthy representa-
tive of the new regime, while anyone who takes them seriously in word and
deed will be a true member of God's kingdom.

But do not imagine that simply keeping all those rules will bring salvation.
For I tell you truly: it is only those whose righteousness of life goes far beyond
the old policy of literal rulekeeping which the scribes and Pharisees represent
who will prove to be God's true people in this era of fulfillment.

MATTHEW 5:17-20, R. T. FRANCE,
THE GOSPEL OF MATTHEW

. ℘ .

In this chapter, we focus on God's accurate representative of reality as revealed in the Scriptures. Jesus promises that practicing his teachings can form our character, resulting in a flourishing life, a life that withstands the storms that may come. We'll begin with a way to approach Scripture so that God's Word may affect both our head and our heart. Then we'll continue our study of Jesus' example, offering an initial list of exemplary characteristics we can imitate.

The Meditative Approach:
A Personal Moment with God

In his classic book on prayer, Andrew Murray proposes that we attend to God more personally as we read, study and meditate on Scripture.

> This hearing the voice of God is something more than the thoughtful study of the Word. One can study and gain knowledge of the Word having little real fellowship with the living God. But there is also a reading of the Word, in the very presence of the Father and under the leading of the Spirit, in which the Word comes to us in living power from God Himself. It is to us the very voice of the Father, a real, personal fellowship with Himself. The living voice of God enters the heart, bringing blessing and strength, and awakening the response of a living faith that reaches back to the heart of God.[1]

One way Scripture becomes more personal for me is through meditation. For example, I was studying and meditating on Mark 10:13-16, in which Jesus blesses the children, for about a month. Based on my meditation, I began putting words together for a poem, looking at the event through the eyes of a child. The writing and revising process took about two more months. As you read the following poem, imagine being there in the village in Jesus' day, as a child might be.

Wow

Why are all the older people going over there?
I'm playing with my friends and winning a game,

---

[1]Andrew Murray, *With Christ in the School of Prayer* (New Kensington, Penn.: Whitaker House, 1981/1887), p. 164.

But they're all running off to join the crowd, leaving me alone.
It's not fair; I'm winning. Finally, I decide to go too.

Wandering through the crowd to see what's going on, I see *Him*.
He's sitting in the marketplace talking, and everyone's listening.
Some kids and a couple of parents holding babies walk toward Him.
Hey, that's Zac—he's always ahead of everyone—walking right up to
    Him.

But some men get up, yelling at them, blocking the way.
Zac's being pushed back; he trips and falls. Ouch!
I'd never do that! Zac's always getting into trouble.
Even He gets up and starts yelling. Boy, I'm glad I didn't go up there.

But He pushes past the men, kneels down and picks Zac up, and hugs
    him.
Why doesn't He scold Zac? Why is He smiling at Zac?
That's not what's supposed to happen. If you get in trouble you get
    yelled at.
And He hugs all my friends, smiles at each one; and he's holding
    babies too. Wow.

And then . . . He looks at me, and I'm scared. Why is He looking at me?
But His eyes are different; they're sort of like smiling eyes.
He motions for me to come to Him; but I'm frozen—I can't move.

Just then a bird lands on His hand—a bird lands on His hand! Wow.
Smiling, He walks over to me, stroking the bird and speaking to it.
He kneels down next to me and asks if I want to pet the bird.

Wow, I've never done that before. Why doesn't it fly away?
I touch the bird, and it stays. I pet it. It feels so soft and warm and
    friendly.
"I better let it get on its way," He says, and lets it fly away.

Then, He hugs me, and I let Him. He's warm and friendly too. It feels
    so good.
I start to leave, but He holds me close and I begin to cry. He looks at
    me and says,
"Did you know God loves you, that you're special—you're special to
    God and Me?"

Wow. No one ever told me that before. It feels so good.

I feel so safe in His arms. He tickles me, and we laugh together.

As he prays for me, he says a blessing with His hand on my head.

   Wow.

As He's saying goodbye, I feel very sad. Now I want to stay with Him.

He gets up and walks toward those men. I watch Him.

Before they leave, He turns around and smiles and waves at me. Wow.

My meditation on this passage helped me to connect at an emotional level with Jesus' blessing the children.

It's helpful to recognize there are two complementary approaches when we come to Scripture—one I will call *analytical* Scripture reading and the other *meditative* Scripture reading. Taking Andrew Murray's comment to heart, I think it's good that believers engage regularly in both. The analytical mode for the reading and study of Scripture is highly honored in the scholarly evangelical tradition. The words *Bible study, exegesis* and *hermeneutics* are associated with this approach in which we bring questions to the text and analyze it in order to gain knowledge of the truth. Analytical reading highlights the use of our God-given mind to master the public meaning of the God-given written text, an essential process to discern the objective truth of God's special revelation. We wrestle with the written Word to winnow out the author's intended meaning, resident in the text, to know the truth. We're on a mission to ply the text with questions until we discern the answers.

Yet meditative Scripture reading also offers a rich opportunity to visit with God. Meditative reading is of a different tone and texture and adds another dimension to how the Bible can impact our life. Here we patiently wait and listen for God to speak to us personally. Our purpose is not to master a certain portion of Scripture, but to read a few verses, slowly, meditatively, vocalizing each word, and monitoring our heart to sense God's movement to highlight a certain word or phrase or sentence for our attentive reflection and rumination. In meditative reading, we have no agenda; there is no hurry to read so many verses, to pose questions of the text, no need to control or direct our reading. We wish to be ready for God to speak to us personally. With David we invite God to expose the depth of our soul: "Search me, God, and know my heart; test me and know my anxious thoughts. See if there is any offensive way in me, and lead me in the way everlasting" (Ps 139:23-24). And with the child Samuel we open ourselves to God with submission: "Speak, for your servant is listening" (1 Sam 3:10).

I think we need both analytical and meditative approaches to Scripture if we wish to be fully responsive to God's transforming work in our lives through his Word. In the analytic approach, we wrestle with the text, with what the human and divine authors have written for us, to discern its *meaning* as it was originally understood by the hearers of that day. Then the *significance* of the text relates to the implications of the passage to a particular situation of the contemporary reader. So we study the passage following certain interpretative procedures to discern the author's intended meaning and purpose and how the readers received the text. Then, also by following certain helpful guidelines, we can respond to the message God has for us today for Christian formation and living.[2]

In the meditative approach to Scripture, we place ourselves in a context of openness to the mystery of God, with no real agenda, as he seeks to touch our lives in the deep places. For if we wish to seek a personal word from God, nowhere else can we be as certain of hearing God's voice as when we are listening to the very words of God in Scripture. This opportunity is possible because the Bible is the Word *of God*, not a word detached from God. We come to Scripture as a conversation *with* God. Scripture must always be studied within the context of a dynamic relationship with the divine author of Scripture, *the Holy Spirit who is personal.*

I prefer to engage these two approaches in a *cyclical* process, now employing an analytical mode, now pausing to engage the meditative mode, then again employing an analytical mode, and pausing again to engage

---

[2]For helpful guidelines on hearing God's message today when studying a particular Scripture passage, see Mark L. Strauss, "A Reflection," in *Four Views on Moving Beyond the Bible to Theology*, ed. Gary T. Meadows (Grand Rapids: Zondervan, 2009), pp. 293-98.

the meditative mode, and so on. Through such repetitive movement I seek understanding of truth and universal principles for living and to welcome God's penetrating and personal touch of my life. Both a *textual* focus and a *relational/personal* focus are necessary in our engagement with the Scriptures. Notice the connection between Hebrews 4:12 and 4:13: "[12] For the word of God is alive and active. Sharper than any double-edged sword, it penetrates even to dividing soul and spirit, joints and marrow; it judges the thoughts and attitudes of the heart. [13] Nothing in all creation is hidden from God's sight. Everything is uncovered and laid bare before the eyes of him to whom we must give account." William Lane explains, "In context, the force of v 13 is to assert that exposure to the word of Scripture entails exposure to God himself."[3] Gerhard Maier highlights this personal element: "The Bible is far more than a treasure trove of doctrinal truths. To view it [only] as a catalog of God's utterances would be to mistake its character. It is primarily communication of God—communication in the literal sense: God himself communes with us. He wants us to experience communion with him."[4]

As we come to God's Word, we are not just studying recorded history; we are engaged in a personal communication and communion with God. Furthermore, we are part of a larger community of saints, both living and now with God. Both the interpretation of the Word and formation by the Word must be seen as part and parcel of participation within this larger Christian community.

Applying Scripture Through a Participatory Meditation

Within the meditative approach we follow no real method. We simply become open to moments when God Himself *immediately* directs his Word suddenly to our attention. Sometimes the text seems to jump off the page and touch our hearts in a deep spot. Within this meditative approach, the key distinction is *how* the application arrives: we do not derive or devise the application from the passage; rather it is something that *comes to us*, from

---

[3]William L. Lane, *Hebrews 1–8*, Word Biblical Commentary 47A (Dallas: Word, 1991), p. 103.
[4]Gerhard Meier, *Biblical Hermeneutics*, trans. Robert Yarbrough (Wheaton, Ill.: Crossway, 1994), p. 55.

the text, directly from God the Spirit alone. The better we can sense the Spirit's moving in our hearts, the better we can discern a true case of this divine movement rather than our own human machinations.[5]

Participatory meditation is a means of the study and meditation of the Gospels in which readers can encounter Jesus in a personal way. When Jesus taught by parables, he expected his listeners to enter into the story and identify with the characters (e.g., Mt 21:45). The Bible is God's grand story involving real people living in a real world. How God interacted with people in the past is how he can also interact with us today. Jesus shows the way through the deep knowledge of Scripture that guided his life and ministry (e.g., Mk 12:10; Lk 4:21; Jn 19:28). The study and meditation of God's Word is the preeminent source of divine guidance.

After first studying a Gospel passage, we then transition to participatory meditation in which we see with new eyes how Jesus ministers to people then and, by application/implication, to us today. The poem at the beginning of the chapter illustrates how Scripture study can impact the heart. We become one of the persons at the event (e.g., a disciple, a parent, a child or a local observing the event). As we read the Bible story slowly, we enter the story ourselves, taking on a role. We ponder, how am I *experiencing* this event in that role? We include as many of our physical senses as we can: What do we see? hear? smell? taste? touch? We journal our thoughts, feelings and reflections. This includes some speculative imagination.

As I engage in meditative Scripture reading, although I am expectant, I am often *surprised* when a thought comes out of the blue, redirecting my focus from where it was to a new place of thought or feeling, toward a certain word, phrase or concept that God wanted me to ponder. For example, from the story of the four who lowered their friend through a roof for Jesus to heal him (Mk 2:1-5), I was prompted to consider, "Am I one who prays for my friends to that degree?" From Mark 1:35 ("Very early in the morning, while it was still dark, Jesus got up, left the house and went off to a solitary place, where he prayed"), I was prompted to wonder how

---

[5]For further discussion of the Spirit's ministry of illumination and guidance see my book *Wasting Time with God* (Downers Grove, Ill.: InterVarsity Press, 2001), chap. 6.

Jesus knew to awaken while it was still dark. Perhaps if the Father awakened him, might the Spirit do that for me? I experimented for a month or so, not setting my alarm clock, awaiting a divine summons so we could fellowship together. Each night, I asked him to wake me for our meeting. God was faithful and (most often) so was I. That personal touch provided significant encouragement for me in these special times together.

The purpose of participatory meditation is to get inside the biblical story so we can get inside our own story. To engage our affect, it's important to take a different approach than we normally do in study mode.

The Importance of Scripture
as an Essential Source of Knowledge

Through our study and meditation of Scripture we wish to have our core beliefs transformed by truth. Jesus claims he is The Truth. "I am the way and the truth and the life" (Jn 14:6). In the Bible, Jesus presents an account of reality, without spin or sound bites. Jesus wants our life perspectives to be aligned with the wisdom that he teaches. Through Scripture our worldview can become aligned with God's view of reality. God the Father tells Jesus' disciples—and us today—to listen to Jesus, to follow his life and teachings. "This is my Son, whom I love; with him I am well pleased. Listen to him!" (Mt 17:5; Mk 9:7; Lk 9:35).

The Bible claims to present God's truthful presentation about reality. There is a uniqueness about Scripture that gives it an exceptional status among other sources (e.g., natural sciences, social sciences, humanities) as a source of knowledge. According to philosopher Dallas Willard, the Bible is a reliable source of unique knowledge, not just for Christians but also for the public arena.

> My hope [in this book] is to enable intellectually serious people, Christians or not, to understand the *indispensable role of knowledge in faith and life*. I also want to make it clear that *there is a body of uniquely Christian knowledge*, one that is available to all who would appropriately seek it and receive it—again, whether Christian or not. Like all knowledge of any complexity and depth, that body of knowledge does not jump down one's throat, and no one can force it upon another. It has to be welcomed to be

possessed. . . . When understood and accepted as knowledge, it is objectively testable—again, in ways suitable to its subject matter—and it lays a foundation for action and character that is unequaled for human good.[6]

The Bible provides an exclusive set of truth claims about key matters of life and reality itself that we can find nowhere else.

A survey of Jesus' life reveals how steeped in Scripture he was. His Bible was the Old Testament and he knew it well.[7] The phrase "it is written" or some variation occurs more than twenty unique times on Jesus' lips. He was so familiar with Scripture he could stump the Ph.D. seminary professors of his day. During his final week, the religious leaders tried to catch Jesus with various puzzling theological questions. For example, when asked to name the foremost command in the Old Testament, Jesus identified two commandments. The "Ph.D." in the law agreed, affirming that to love God and to love one's neighbor "is more important than all burnt offerings and sacrifices" (Mk 12:33). Jesus ably answered their brainteasers and then he posed a riddle of his own in Matthew 22:45-46. Quoting Psalm 110:1, Jesus asked, If Messiah was a descendent of King David, thus lesser in status than David, why did David call Messiah "Lord" (thus implying Messiah's deity and humanity)? Jesus knew his Scriptures well.

Some time ago I was asking the Lord what topic it might be worthwhile for me to study. I was thinking perhaps some particular issue in spiritual formation, theology or philosophy of education, which are the areas in which I teach. I happened to be reading through and meditating on the Gospel of Luke and this verse jumped out at me: "Heaven and earth will pass away, but my words will never pass away" (Lk 21:33; also Mt 24:35; Mk 13:31). I got the point that I need to keep as my key focus Jesus' teachings and the rest of God's Word.

Although Scripture is a legitimate source of knowledge in this world,

---

[6]Dallas Willard, *Knowing Christ Today: Why We Can Trust Spiritual Knowledge* (New York: HarperOne, 2009), pp. 7-8.

[7]In addition to the tutoring of the Father and Spirit, I think Jesus studied and meditated on the various Old Testament character studies of successes and failures—of how to relate to God, how to flourish, how to engage with one's community and how to fulfill one's mission. Chuck Swindoll has developed a series of book studies on various Old Testament persons that may serve as a resource guide.

it is not an exhaustive source. Even the Bible directs us to learn wisdom from observing nature: "Go to the ant, you sluggard; consider its ways and be wise! It has no commander, no overseer or ruler, yet it stores its provision in summer and gathers its food at harvest" (Prov. 6:6-8). The apostle Paul explains that we may fill our minds with truth in all of its varied manifestations: "Whatever is true, whatever is noble, whatever is right, whatever is pure, whatever is lovely, whatever is admirable—if anything is excellent or praiseworthy—think about such things" (Phil 4:8). Yet Scripture, which is God-breathed (2 Tim 3:16-17), is *uniquely authoritative* for Christians as the true and certain presentation of reality and as the normative guide for Christian living and practice. We can trust it as the way to know God and to follow Jesus.

What Scripture Teaches
About Jesus' Human Example

Let's return to Jesus' human example and consider some guidelines for drawing out implications for Christian living. It's clear in Scripture that Jesus is our example.[8] After he washed the disciples' feet, he followed that demonstration with the teaching, "I have set you an example that you should do as I have done for you" (Jn 13:15). The last chapter presented the case that Jesus lived predominantly in his finite humanity, which he shared in common with us. Yet there are also features of Jesus' life we cannot emulate, or need not emulate. In the last chapter, at least five factors were identified to help us make the appropriate distinctions. Based on these five factors, three questions can be posed:

a. From Jesus' life and ministry, what are the particular virtues, practices and missional projects we *cannot* imitate because they relate to Jesus being God (Factor #1) and to Jesus being Messiah (Factor #2)?

b. From Jesus' life and ministry, what are the particular virtues, practices and missional projects we *need not* imitate because they relate to

---

[8]NT verses that support Jesus' example: *Jesus' own lips:* Matthew 20:26-28 (Mk 10:42-45; Lk 22:24-27); Luke 6:40; John 13:13-15, 34-35; 15:12-13. *Pauline Epistles:* Romans 6:11; 15:3, 7; 2 Corinthians 1:5; 4:6; 11:1; Ephesians 5:2; 5:25, 29; Philippians 2:4-11; 3:17; 1 Thessalonians 1:6; 2 Thessalonians 3:7-9; 1 Timothy 1:16. *General Epistles:* 1 Pet 2:21-23; 4:1; 5:3; Hebrews 4:15; 12:2-3; 1 John 2:6; 3:3, 16.

Jesus' historical and cultural situation (Factor #3) or to the non-obligatory aspects of Jesus' messianic mission (Factor #4)?

c. From Jesus' life and ministry, what are the particular virtues, practices and missional projects we *can* imitate because they relate to his common humanity with us within God's kingdom family and purposes (Factor #5)?

Since our interest is in Jesus' example for us, we'll focus only on item *c*. Regarding this third question, I suggest some additional matters to help guide the inquiry.

Six Themes from Jesus' Sermon on the Mount

As we examine the particulars of Jesus' example, using a normative framework will help us avoid identifying gleanings that fit solely within our customary perspectives. For such a guide, I recommend Jesus' Sermon on the Mount (Mt 5–7), regarded as a summary of his major teachings, suggesting a wide range of important arenas for living like Jesus. Below I've synthesized this sermon into six broad themes, ordered by appearance in the sermon and associated a summarizing word beginning with the letter *c* for each theme.[9]

1. *Missional participation (calling):* Jesus' disciples distinctively impact the world (Mt 5:11-16).

2. *Scriptural saturation (catechesis):* Jesus' disciples respect, practice and teach the complete Word of God as the standard and guide for life (Mt 5:17-20 [7:24-27]).

3. *Inner heart formation (character):* Jesus' disciples eagerly seek Christlike *inner* heart wholeness through transformation by the Holy Spirit from the inside out, rather than focusing on external religious behavioral conformity and rule keeping (Mt 5:21-48).

4. *Seeking God above all (communion):* Jesus' disciples seek first after God and God's kingdom priorities, trusting in God for his love and

---

[9]Klaus Issler, "Six Themes to Guide Spiritual Formation Ministry Based on Jesus' Sermon on the Mount," *Christian Education Journal* 7, no. 2 (Fall 2010): 366-88. The principles are based on the Sermon, but edited to include Jesus' broader teaching.

commendation and his provision for our needs (Mt 6:1-34).

5. *Relational formation as Jesus' church (community):* Jesus' disciples respect and care for one another as Jesus' new family, in compassion, forgiveness and love (Mt 7:1-12).

6. *Two kingdoms discernment (cosmic conflict):* Jesus' disciples discern and avoid the false and foolish ways of Satan's kingdom and desire and increasingly practice the righteous and wise ways of God's kingdom (Mt 7:13-27).

These broad themes may provide balance and breadth as we consider Jesus' example.

Exemplary Practices and Character

Now that we have some breadth—a range of various themes—we need an analytical tool that permits some exploration of depth for our inquiry. I suggest we consider the two categories of "practices"—what Jesus did ("doing," lifestyle routines)—and "character"—inner heart qualities that are explicitly stated or that we can infer from Jesus' deeds ("being," personal qualities he acquired during his human life).

To keep track of these various features, I'll assign the letter A to the six themes mentioned above from the Sermon on the Mount. B will be assigned to "practices," and C to "character." Then, for each of these two categories of "practices" and "character" I suggest three subcategories to help in further analysis as listed below:

A. Aligning practices with six themes from the Sermon on the Mount (listed above).

B. "Doing"—regarding Jesus' practices or lifestyle routines, what he did, what we can imitate from his:

   1. *character-affirming practices* (e.g., use of Scripture in response to temptation, Mt 4:4-10; freedom to weep, Jn 11:35)

   2. *relational practices* (e.g., praising Abba, Mt 11:25-26; depending on the Spirit, Mt 11:28)

   3. *kingdom/missional practices* (e.g., customarily attended praise/study gatherings, Lk 4:16; intercessory prayer, Lk 22:32)

C. "Being"—regarding Jesus' character, his inner heart, what we can imitate from his:

1. *virtues* (e.g., humility, Mt 11:29; serving heart, Mk 10:45)

2. *relational "in"-dwelling* (focusing on significant persons who have become internalized or represented within ourselves [cf. Jn 17:21-23; Phil 1:7], e.g., identification with Abba, Jn 14:9-10; affection for his disciples, Jn 13:1)

3. *knowledge and competencies* (these can be separated from virtues, yet have an important role in one's character, e.g., Scripture knowledge, Mt 22:43-45; self-awareness of inner emotional states, Mk 14:33-34)

Combining these various considerations mentioned above into a framework, I suggest in table 6.1 an initial list of exemplary characteristics from Jesus' life as one way to explore this important issue. Column A lists the relevant six themes from the Sermon on the Mount, aligned where they seem to connect with the practices in column B. Table 6.2 lists items from category C. The exemplary items listed under the various subtopics in categories B and C are suggestive and are not meant to be strictly, mutually-exclusive classifications. The dotted lines indicate the overlapping nature of many of these characteristics. (We'll explore six of Jesus' exemplary practices in the final two chapters.)

This initial list can stimulate further study of Jesus' exemplary life, and indicate possible areas for personal formation. A follow-up inquiry might be, what particular virtues and practices from Jesus' life and ministry are repeated or amplified in the rest of the New Testament? For example, Peter reinforces being an example of non-coercive leadership, using the same phrase Jesus did: "Be shepherds of God's flock that is under your care, serving as overseers . . . not *lording it over* those entrusted to you, but being examples to the flock" (1 Pet 5:2-3, emphasis added; cf. Mt 20:25, 28). Paul shines light on the Son's humility to come to earth and "empty himself" (Phil 2:7 NASB; 2 Cor 8:9) as an example of unselfish love for others.

Yet our search in the rest of the New Testament is to understand how the Spirit inspired these writers to present the range of virtues

Table 6.1. An Initial List of Exemplary Practices from Jesus' Life

A. Sermon on the Mount Themes	B. Jesus' Exemplary Practices/Lifestyle Routines (Doing)
	Kingdom/Missional Practices (task)
1. Missional Participation	Acted to enlarge the kingdom of God
	Witnessed God's good works
	Spoke the truth in love
	Customarily participated in community gatherings of believers for praise and study
	Did various acts of service
	Engaged in intercessory prayer and expected answered prayer
	Cared generously for the needy
6. Two Kingdoms Discernment	Confronted evil, Satan (& religious leaders); acted to decrease the kingdom of Satan; engaged in spiritual warfare
	Character-Affirming Practices (Being)
2. Scriptural Saturation	Use of Scripture, study, meditation
3. Inner Heart Formation	Response to suffering/resisted temptation
	Fasted
	Gave alms
	Freedom to weep, to be joyful
	Relational Practices (Relating)
4. Seeking God	*Cultivated friendship with Abba*
	Regular prayer, communication, listening
	Praise, thanksgiving
	Depended on and empowered by Father and Spirit
5. Relational Formation	*Committed to God's family*
	Cultivated friendship with disciples, friends; fellowshiped with various believers
	Prayed for unity of believers; peacemaking; mediated conflict
	Welcomed others
	Noticed those around him
	Gracious to others
	Hospitable

and practices for Christian living. The purpose is *not* to confirm or disconfirm Jesus' example or teaching, for it seems to me that Jesus' exemplary life and ministry *trumps* other Scripture on the matter of exemplary Christian virtues and practices. Since Jesus is central to our sanctification, to Christian ethics, then the primary reference point for Christian living is Jesus' own life and ministry. If we discern an exemplary feature in Jesus' life and ministry that is not mentioned in the rest of the New Testament, that should not disqualify it. The Gospel record of Jesus' life and ministry should be regarded as having credibility of its own.

As mentioned previously, the kingdom of God was a central theme in Jesus' teaching. Commenting on Romans 14:17, "For the kingdom of God is not a matter of eating and drinking, but of righteousness, peace and joy in the Holy Spirit," James Dunn notes that the apostle Paul uses the term *kingdom* only 14 times but *Spirit* more than 110 times, whereas the Synoptic Gospels use *kingdom* 105 times and *Spirit* only 13 times."The Spirit, indeed, [is] the first installment of the inheritance which is the kingdom."[10]

Table 6.2.

C. An Initial List of Jesus' Exemplary Inner Heart (Being)		
Virtues	**Relational "In"-Dwelling**	**Knowledge and Competencies**
Integrity, love, joy, peace, patience, kindness, goodness, faithfulness, gentleness, self-control (Gal 5:22-23), humility, serving heart, self-giving sacrifice, compassionate, gracious, forgiving, truthful, courageous, loves good, aversion to evil, promise-keeping	*With Abba:* love, loyalty, trust, dependence, affection (trusting God for basic material needs; trusting God in suffering) *With disciples/close friends:* love, loyalty, trust, unity, affection	Scripture knowledge Self-aware of internal emotional states Discernment of good and evil, of two kingdoms

---

[10]James Dunn, *Romans 9–16*, Word Biblical Commentary 38B (Dallas: Word, 1988), p. 822.

The Importance of Truth Encounters

To conclude his Sermon on the Mount, Jesus presented the parable of the two builders, in which two models of house foundations are contrasted: the strong one on the rock, and the weak one on sand (Mt 7:24-27; Lk 6:47-49). Here Jesus offers a promise—a rock-solid guarantee if you will—that if we put into practice his teaching—building our lives ("houses") on this strong foundation of his teachings ("the rock")—we will withstand all the storms of this life. When Scripture becomes embedded within our hearts, it is life-giving, life-sustaining and life-empowering. Based on Jesus' teaching on hypocrisy (Mt 7:21-23), Donald Hagner notes that "the ultimate test of [knowing] the truth is in [lifestyle] deeds, not claims or pretensions."[11]

Encountering truth—being confronted by reality—is an important means to facilitate the formation of deeply held worldview beliefs. That's why studying and meditating on Scripture is a key part of the change process. God can use a variety of means to facilitate the dislodging of false worldview beliefs and nurture a process of heart flow formation. The challenge, then, is attending to what kind of heart responses we are cultivating so we can welcome truth when it comes our way. Encounters with truth can facilitate embracing new true worldview beliefs, affirming current true worldview beliefs, and also correcting false worldview beliefs. But this is only possible if we have a responsive heart.

At times learning the truth may be troubling since we'll have to admit we've been wrong. In addition, our arrogance may urge us to dismiss the truth and delay or even forestall the learning process. I'm embarrassed to admit my own deep heart attitudes have not always trusted God, which surely has hindered my teaching ministry. After almost twenty years of being a pastor and seminary professor, in my mid-forties God the Spirit showed up on my first extended spiritual retreat and convicted me of self-righteousness. I sensed God directing me to read from Romans 1. On my knees with my Bible open on my bed, I suddenly was overwhelmed with the powerful convicting force

---

[11]Donald Hagner, *Matthew 1–13*, Word Biblical Commentary 33A (Dallas: Word, 1993), p. 184.

of the Holy Spirit as I read the words: "arrogant, boastful, unloving, unmerciful" (Rom 1:30-31 NASB)—verses on the vices of unbelievers! I broke down and cried from the inner conviction of these sinful attitudes—gaps that were news to me. My wife, Beth, was aware of them but I couldn't receive such a message from her at that time. It required a sudden and vivid encounter to jar me awake. That event began an intentional process of inviting God's heart-tenderizing ministry in my soul. From a human perspective, I probably would've remained the same kind of self-righteous person had I not gone on that retreat, opening the way for this gracious "woodshed experience." The Spirit can use a variety of means to jolt us so we can hear truth at deep levels if we're receptive.

Growing in Prayer

Consider the matter of intercessory prayer, a practice of Jesus. In the past I had little expectation that God would answer prayer. Then I was challenged by Wayne Grudem's comment, "If we were really convinced that prayer changes the way God acts, and that God does bring about remarkable changes in the world in response to prayer, as Scripture repeatedly teaches that he does, then we would pray much more than we do. If we pray little, it is probably because we do not really believe that prayer accomplishes much at all."[12] That was me. So I'm on a quest to explore such possibilities.

I admit I'm as reluctant as the next person, but Jesus' life and teachings about prayer urge me onward in this quest. "Very truly I tell you, all who have faith in me will do the works I have been doing, and they will do even greater things than these, because I am going to the Father" (John 14:12). In response to this promise, evangelical commentators use words such as *staggering, breathtaking, startling, astonishing.* I don't have a good explanation of what Jesus means by "greater things," but I do know it means a greater measure of kingdom power is available than I'm currently experiencing. On Matthew 7:7-8 ("Ask, seek, knock"), R. T. France comments:

---

[12]Wayne Grudem, *Systematic Theology* (Grand Rapids: Zondervan, 1994), p. 377.

For all that necessary caution [not everything we would like to have is granted], there is an openness about vv. 7-8 which invites not merely a resigned acceptance of what the Father gives, but a willingness to explore *the extent of his generosity,* secure in the knowledge that only what is "good" will be given, so that mistakes in prayer through human short-sightedness will not rebound on those praying.[13]

Why not explore "the extent of [God's] generosity"?

As A. W. Tozer (d. 1963) noted, "True faith is never found alone; it is always accompanied by expectations. The man who believes the promises of God expects to see them fulfilled. Where there is no expectation there is no faith."[14] Over the past eight years or so, my expectations about God's involvement in our world have increased a bit, but it's a slow process since changing deep core beliefs take time. I've benefitted from taking courses on intercessory prayer, and also joining with experienced intercessors in praying for others. Carson's simple point bears true: "Christians learn to pray by listening to those around them."[15]

I'm also encouraged by stories of answered prayer, like Ken Eldred's. Ken, CEO of Living Stones Foundation (www.lsfoundation .org), remembers "three very unusual beacons or spikes on the daily sales chart" as an early answer to prayer and a specific confirmation that "I was right where God wanted me."[16] Five years into his business career, Eldred committed his life to Jesus. Soon after, in 1975, Eldred and a business partner launched a mail-order catalog, and same-day-shipping business to service computer needs of larger corporations—a concept Eldred sensed God had directed them to. At the time, the only option was to buy direct from computer manufacturers in which "12 weeks was a good delivery window."[17] Daily sales, critical to survival with same-day shipping, grew to $2,000 per day, but then began to go south.

---

[13]R. T. France, *The Gospel of Matthew,* The New International Commentary on the New Testament (Grand Rapids: Eerdmans, 2007), p. 279, emphasis added.

[14]A. W. Tozer, *God Tells the Man Who Cares* (Harrisburg, Penn.: Christian Publications, 1970), p. 37.

[15]D. A. Carson, *A Call to Spiritual Reformation* (Grand Rapids: Baker, 1992), p. 182.

[16]Ken Eldred, "The 'Calling' Myth," in *Our Souls at Work*, ed. Mark L. Russell (Boise, Idaho: Russell Media, 2010), p. 36.

[17]Ibid.

Cash-strapped, Ken desperately needed guidance from God. Did God really call him to this particular business, or did God have another in mind—or should Ken become a missionary, something he'd wrestled through earlier? Roberta, his wife, suggested they take God's perfect number seven and trust God for a $7,000 sales day—well beyond any best day they'd ever had! Further, so it wouldn't be a coincidence, they needed to pray for three of these special days. "I thought those numbers were nearly impossible and certainly outrageous. Not wanting to appear unspiritual, I agreed. We decided to light a candle and keep it burning for ten days while we prayed for three $7,000 days."[18] Although Eldred was still worried after five days of praying, by the tenth day, Sunday, he'd become convinced God would give them their answer, and so had Roberta.

On Monday, Eldred announced to his small staff to expect $7,000 sales that day, but they were skeptical. Sales were steady all day, which was unusual. After closing, the customer representative came into Eldred's office, having checked the figures twice on a ten-key calculator—it was a $7,000 sales day. The next two Mondays were the same. These spike days never occurred again, although annual sales eventually reached around $400 million (Inmac Corp merged with Micro-Warehouse in 1996). This early milestone confirmed for Eldred God's favor on his work in the business world, and that God answers specific prayer. God is trustworthy, yet each of us will need to learn that for ourselves experientially.

As an analogy, consider comparing intercessory prayer and an automatic door at a department store that opens through motion sensors. The doors only open as we get close and intend to walk through the door. When we stand fifteen feet away, nothing happens. To keep the analogy going, in some cases when we approach the door, it opens, and the prayer is answered, and there is great blessing and joy. In other cases, the door remains closed (it's locked) and we bang into it, which can be frustrating, discouraging, even embarrassing. This is similar to occasions when prayer doesn't seem to be answered right away. Let's

---

[18]Ibid., p. 34.

take the risk and pray for others with greater expectancy in both our attitudes and our words and see if the door will open this time (cf. Acts 12:11-16). Jesus guarantees it will open *sometimes*, for answered prayer is one way to bear fruit and glorify the Father (Jn 15:7-8). We have the opportunity to learn to become better pray-ers so that more answers to prayer are received than we're currently experiencing (Jas 5:12-18).[19]

Final Thoughts

Kingdom reality is what Jesus' life and teaching convey. Truth encounters—including the study of and meditation on Scripture—are important means to help transform our core worldview beliefs to match reality as Jesus can see it, so that our heart flow evidences more Jesus-like living. Jesus' life and ministry is a rich resource of virtues and practices for us to grow into. Consider these challenging words from the author of Hebrews:

> And let us run with perseverance the race marked out for us, fixing our eyes on Jesus, the "champion" and perfecter of faith. For the joy set before him he endured the cross, scorning its shame, and sat down at the right hand of the throne of God. Consider him who endured such opposition from sinners, so that you will not grow weary and lose heart. In your struggle against sin, you have not yet resisted to the point of shedding your blood (Heb 12:1-4).

We've come to the close of parts one and two of the book. We have gaps that hinder us from living more into the life of Jesus. Jesus' teaching is clearly optimistic about the potential to become more like him. Chapters one through three suggested a framework and process for helping us reduce our gaps. Yet we cannot do this in our own power. Part two focused on three essential divine resources to make our formation journey effective: our Abba's unconditional love offers us a safe context in which to admit our gaps (chapter four), the Holy Spirit is ready to awaken us to our gaps and empower us within our formation (chapter

---

[19]As one means to stretch your God confidence, see my *In Search of a Confident Faith: Overcoming Barriers to Trust in God*, with J. P. Moreland (Downers Grove, Ill.: InterVarsity Press, 2008), and the classic by Andrew Murray, *With Christ in the School of Prayer*.

five), and God's Word of truth uniquely presents knowledge about reality, so that as we align our perspectives with those truths, we can enter more into abundant living, following Jesus' example (this chapter).

In the final two chapters (part three), we'll explore two areas in which the Christian community experience evidences some obvious gaps: our relationships (chapter seven), and our attitudes about money and work (chapter eight). We'll suggest some relevant exemplary practices from Jesus' life for each area.

Pause Button

As you practice taking thirty-second pauses throughout your day, consider using the Jesus Prayer as a prayer and as a way to meditate on your relationship with Jesus. These ten words, used by Christians for centuries, are an adaptation from Matthew 20:30 and Mark 10:47. The prayer conveys good theology, a good request and a humble posture.

Lord Jesus Christ, Son of God, have mercy on me.

In the "Awake, Admit, Ask and Act" box below, to remind us to avoid the disconnected gap, I've added the phrase "ABIDING in Abba, Jesus, Holy Spirit" as a "relational activity" that undergirds the whole process of formation.[20]

AWAKE to gaps → ADMIT with honesty → ASK for formation grace → ACT, take a first step
ABIDING in Abba, Jesus, Holy Spirit

Figure 6.1.

Key Points

1. The more our deeply held worldview beliefs become aligned with Jesus' worldview—becoming anchored in reality—the more we can

---

[20]We have trinitarian support for our formation. Scripture teaches that *each* person of the Trinity abides in us: God the Father (e.g., Jn 14:23; 1 Jn 4:15), God the Son (e.g., Jn 14:23; 15:4) and God the Spirit (e.g., Jn 14:16-17). It seems to me that God is gracious and desires a closer relationship with us, and is not so concerned with which person of the Trinity we speak to. That we connect with God is the more important matter.

enter into kingdom living now. Truth encounters are a key means to dislodge false beliefs, and immersing oneself in Scripture is an essential encounter with truth since it offers unique knowledge to be found in no other source of knowledge.

2. We can count on Jesus' life and word to represent reality. Tables 6.1 and 6.2 summarize an initial list of exemplary practices and character qualities from Jesus' life.

3. One method to hear God's Word is participatory meditation: Take on the role of one person in the biblical story and see/feel the events through that person's perspective.

4. Jesus was steeped in Scripture—it marked his words and his deeds—and he learned much wisdom from it.

Reflection Questions

1. Ponder Dallas Willard's quotation that the Bible is a legitimate source of knowledge and should be regarded as such, whether in a university setting or on a national news program. Where is there resistance to that idea in the public arena? What unique knowledge does Scripture offer?

2. Select one of the two tables from the chapter (6.1 or 6.2) and evaluate how compatible the items listed are with Jesus' life and teaching. What editing and adaptations would you suggest? What reason or support comes to mind for this editing/adapting?

3. As you read the meditative poem, what impact did it have on you? Perhaps try out this participatory meditation approach with these Gospel episodes. Why not take about a month to focus on one passage and see how God might speak to you?

a. Jesus heals blind Bartimaeus (Mk 10:46-52)

b. Jesus affirms the woman who washed his feet (Lk 7:36-50)

c. Jesus affirms Zacchaeus' repentance (Lk 19:1-10)

PART THREE

FOLLOWING JESUS DAILY
IN OUR GAPS

7

Three Exemplary
Jesus Practices
About Relationships

Don't pick on people, jump on their failures, criticize their faults—
unless, of course, you want the same treatment. That critical spirit has
a way of boomeranging. . . . Here is a simple, rule-of-thumb guide for
behavior: Ask yourself what you want people to do for you,
then grab the initiative and do it for them. Add up God's
Law and Prophets and this is what you get.

MATTHEW 7:1-2, 12 *THE MESSAGE*

· ℮ ·

Part one identified the gap problem and a transformation process for becoming more like Jesus. In part two, three essential dynamic divine resources were explored, since we can't do any formation in our own power. Now in the remaining two chapters of the book I highlight two particular gaps within the Christian community to raise our awareness in light of Jesus' example and teaching, and suggest some exemplary practices from Jesus' life.

Our Reputation as Christians

Philip Yancey opens his book *What's So Amazing About Grace?* with reflections from a single mother who was a prostitute told to him by a friend. Yancy's friend had offered her a listening ear as she poured out her heart, sobbing with anguish, about the terrible mess she was in. She was even renting out her two-year-old daughter for sex, since this made more money than she could. At one point, Yancey's friend had wondered why she didn't go to a church for help, so he asked her about it. "I will never forget the look of pure, naive shock that crossed her face. 'Church!' she cried. 'Why would I ever go there? I was already feeling terrible about myself. They'd just make me feel worse.'"[1]

Only a decade ago, the Barna Group published a report titled "Christianity Has a Strong Positive Image Despite Fewer Active Participants." But times have changed and a new generation of young adults are expressing negative views of the Christian church, a number of them having had hurtful encounters with churches or Christians, as revealed in a recent Barna survey. David Kinnaman and Gabe Lyons note, "In our national surveys we found the three most common perceptions of present-day Christianity are antihomosexual (an image held by 91 percent of young outsiders), judgmental (87 percent), and hypocritical (85 percent)."[2]

An initial reaction might be, does it matter what "the world" thinks of Christians? Christian teaching on morality will not be well received by those with an atheistic, naturalistic worldview. Being perceived as judgmental could be viewed as people just reacting to Christian truth, yet that single mother's perception also points to a judgmental aspect that is ungracious. What this research information calls for is not defensiveness, but weeping and confession before our God. Furthermore, we cannot easily sidestep claims of hypocrisy and being ungracious. Taking the higher moral ground above others and being wrapped in self-righteousness and moral arrogance is what hypocrisy is all about.

I know about those vices as an insider. Subtle forms of self-righteousness and moral arrogance emanated from my character, covered over in an acceptable churchianity form. I "should have" known better,

---

[1]Philip Yancey, *What's So Amazing About Grace?* (Grand Rapids: Zondervan, 1997), p. 11.
[2]Dave Kinnaman and Gabe Lyons, *unChristian: What a New Generation Really Thinks About Christianity . . . and Why It Matters* (Grand Rapids: Baker, 2007), pp. 181-82.

having studied a lot about God, having been a pastor and a seminary professor, but I was unaware nonetheless about a deep layer of pride, as I've mentioned earlier in the book. Since that "divine woodshed" experience, I'm a bit more sensitized to when my own arrogance and self-righteousness arise, or to that of others when abuses occur. Kinnaman and Lyons explain,

> The primary reason outsiders feel hostile toward Christians, and especially conservative Christians, is not because of any specific theological perspective. What they react negatively to is our "swagger," how we go about things and the sense of self-importance we project. Outsiders say that Christians possess bark—and bite. Christians may not normally operate in attack mode, but it happens frequently enough that others have learned to watch their step around us.[3]

Confronting the Pharisee Within

We can be so petty with each other—even about things like whether or not it's okay to have a jar of peanut butter in the house. Overseas in a country where this particular American food was not available, a missionary couple had peanut butter mailed to them for their young family to enjoy. Yet these shipments went against the religious spirit of other missionaries, who "fasted" from peanut butter as a badge of holiness and sacrifice. The pressure to conform to this pettiness eventually became unbearable, so that the missionary couple left for the United States without planning to return to the mission field.[4] How sad, how petty.

Remember the Pharisee who presented a litany of acts of (self) righteousness to justify himself before God (Lk 18:11-12)? Brennan Manning recounts a similar testimony.

> At a prayer meeting I attended, a man in his mid-sixties was the first to speak: "I just want to thank God that I have nothing to repent of today." His wife groaned. What he meant was he had not embezzled, blasphemed, fornicated, or fractured any of the Ten Commandments. He

---

[3]Ibid., p. 26.
[4]Chuck Swindoll, *The Grace Awakening* (Dallas: Word, 1990), pp. 93-94.

had distanced himself from idolatry, drunkenness, sexual irresponsibility, and similar things; yet, he had never broken through into what Paul calls the inner freedom of the children of God.[5]

Manning counsels, "To deny the Pharisee within [each of us] is lethal. It is imperative that we befriend him, dialogue with him, inquire why we must look to sources outside the Kingdom for peace and happiness."[6]

Pastor and theologian Basil of Caesarea (d. 379) admitted that this was a problem during theological debates in the early church, in how Christian pastors and theologians treated each other. "Those who judge the erring are merciless and bitter, while those judging the upright are unfair and hostile. This evil is so firmly rooted in us that we have become more brutish than the beasts: At least they herd together with their own kindred, but we reserve our most savage warfare for the members of our own household."[7] Accordingly, Dallas Willard explains, "Christians are routinely taught by example and word that it is more important to be right . . . than it is to be Christlike. In fact, being right licenses you to be mean, and, indeed *requires* you to be mean—righteously mean, of course."[8]

Consider this situation. Imagine you are seated at a coffee shop and you recognize, together at another table, a pastor and a Christian business leader from your city. Suddenly you hear the word *damn* and see the business leader jumping up, trying to avoid more hot coffee spilling on his lap. What's your first reaction? Empathy for the physical pain he's experiencing? Or shock and dismay that such language came from his lips? Our first reactions tell us what's in our heart.

Now change the situation. You hear the word *damn* and notice this time it's the pastor muttering that exclamation. He's got hot coffee spilling on his lap. What's your first reaction? I imagine some of us would be more uptight about the language than the physical pain

[5]Brennan Manning, *Abba's Child* (Colorado Springs: NavPress, 1994), p. 86.
[6]Ibid.
[7]Basil of Caesarea, *On the Holy Spirit*, p. 117, cited in Graham Cole, *He Who Gives Life* (Wheaton, Ill.: Crossway, 2007), p. 248.
[8]Dallas Willard, *Renovation of the Heart: Putting on the Character of Christ* (Colorado Springs: NavPress, 2002), p. 238.

prompting the language. The *unChristian* research offers us some honest feedback. We need more of God's grace for each other to become more like Jesus.

Jesus' Mission for Us

We've got more than a public relations problem—we're off-course on the mission Jesus calls us to. Jesus has begun a new family: "Whoever does the will of my Father in heaven is my brother and sister and mother" (Mt 12:50). Near the end of his ministry, Jesus proposed to the twelve disciples a "new command" to "love one another" (Jn 13:34). The new standard of love involved Jesus' own example—"as I have loved you" (Jn 13:34; 15:12; see also Jn 13:1; 15:9). Furthermore, "by this everyone will know that you are my disciples, if you love one another" (Jn 13:35).

Based on his study of this "surrogate kinship" or family community that Jesus instituted, Joseph Hellerman notes,

> The strong-group outlook of the New Testament church meant that the early Christians did not sharply distinguish between commitment to God and commitment to God's family. . . . For the early Christians, loyalty to God found its tangible daily expression in unswerving loyalty to God's group, the family of surrogate siblings who called Him "Father." . . . [For Jesus] family served as the primary locus of relational loyalty for persons in the strong-group social matrix of the New Testament world.[9]

This new family relationship is why we notice the extensive use of the term *brother* (implying sibling relationships including sister) by both Jesus (e.g., Mt 5:22; 18:15) and Paul (e.g., Rom 14:10; 1 Cor 6:6). All Christians have been adopted as members into this new family. Jesus invites us to live as brothers and sisters, who evidence our family heritage from the Father by being merciful (Lk 6:36) and loving (Mt 5:43-48).

In this chapter we'll explore three kinds of practices from Jesus'

---

[9]Joseph Hellerman, *When the Church Was a Family* (Nashville: B & H Academic, 2009), pp. 73-75.

teachings and life example to help us grow toward greater family unity: forgiving one another, peacemaking in conflict and developing closer friendships as part of building community. Following each section, some prayer projects will be suggested to ponder ways to practice Jesus' teaching and example.

Practice 1: Forgiving One Another

Political philosopher Hannah Arendt (d. 1975), in *The Human Condition*, her most influential work, claimed that "the discoverer of the role of forgiveness in the realm of human affairs was Jesus of Nazareth."[10] Yale philosopher Nicholas Wolsterstorff agrees with Arendt that "the origin of forgiveness as a component of our moral culture is the words and deeds of Jesus."[11] Although forgiveness is mentioned occasionally in nonreligious antiquity, it is not a main component there as it is with Jesus. Both Arendt and Wolterstorff agree that Jesus moved beyond Old Testament values, teaching his disciples to forgive those who had done evil against them. To learn more about forgiveness, we must look to Jesus.

The journey toward forgiving another involves much more than a simplistic decision to "forgive and forget." Along the way God engages us in a tenderizing transformation process within our hearts as we respond in trust even though we still feel the pain of suffering. And then we're able to give away healing grace freely to others. This important theme takes a prominent place in the prayer Jesus taught his disciples, which has been prayed by Jesus' followers daily around the world for centuries: "And forgive us our trespasses, as we forgive those who trespass against us" (Mt 6:12).[12]

Did Jesus need to forgive others? Consider how Jesus had to practice what he preached about forgiving others. The political and religious

---

[10]Hannah Arendt, *The Human Condition* (Garden City, N.Y.: Doubleday Anchor, 1959), pp. 212-19.

[11]Nicholas Wolterstorff, "Jesus and Forgiveness," in *Jesus and Philosophy*, ed. Paul K. Moser (Cambridge: Cambridge University Press, 2009), p. 195. Wolterstorff affirms that forgiveness was a key component of Jesus' *religious* message, and that it was partially rooted in the Hebrew Scriptures, not discovered within his close-knit community of followers as Arendt asserted.

[12]*The Book of Common Prayer* (New York: Oxford University, 2008), p. 54.

leaders didn't perceive Jesus as someone of consequence, but merely a
messianic pretender worthy of their ridicule. They accused him of being
demon-possessed (Mt 12:24; Jn 7:20); tried to trap him in order to
falsely accuse him (Mt 21:23-46; 22:15-40), even of blasphemy (Mt
26:65-66). Filled with rage because Jesus pointed out the gaps between
their teaching and their practice, they wanted to kill him (Mt 12:14;
26:4; Mk 14:1; Jn 11:53). Imagine living your life when such death
threats were common knowledge (Jn 7:19, 25; 8:37, 40). The fickle
crowd on one day could hail him as messianic king (Lk 19:38) and
scream for his crucifixion and death by the end of that same week (Mt
27:20-23).

Despite all, Jesus' heart of grace is evident as he weeps over Jerusalem: "As he approached Jerusalem and saw the city, he wept over it and
said, 'If you, even you, had only known on this day what would bring
you peace—but now it is hidden from your eyes'" (Lk 19:41-42). Jesus'
own natural brothers didn't regard him as anyone special (Jn 7:3-5).
Even his disciples frustrated him now and then (Mk 8:17-18; 9:19-19).

Pondering Jesus' abuse during his trial and crucifixion is sickening:
he was blindfolded and they spat in his face; he was slapped, beaten
with fists by the religious leaders (Mt 26:67; Mk 14:65), flogged and
scourged by professional Roman soldiers (Mt 27:6; Jn 19:1) and eventually crucified, an excruciatingly slow and humiliating form of death.
Yet on the cross we hear the most remarkable expression of forgiveness
in the midst of such torture. "Father, forgive them, for they do not
know what they are doing" (Lk 23:33-34).

Does Jesus genuinely understand what he is asking us to do when he
teaches, "Whenever you stand praying, forgive, if you have anything
against anyone, so that your Father who is in heaven will also forgive
you your transgressions" (Mk 11:25 NASB)? I think so. Isaiah 53:3 captures it well: "He was despised and rejected by others, a man of suffering, and familiar with pain."

Comparing God's forgiving and our forgiving. Jesus desires that we
realize the great gift of God's forgiveness as the basis for extending
such grace to others, as depicted in the parable of the king and his two
servants (Mt 18:23-35). The day of reckoning had come for all who

owed money to the king. Pay up or go to jail. One servant owed an amount that was impossible to ever repay in his lifetime (ten thousand talents; one talent was half a lifetime's wages—equivalent to millions of dollars today). The king demanded he pay or he and his family would be sold to get some monetary return. The servant fell on his knees and begged for mercy. Taking pity on him, the king canceled the full debt and released him! Yet that servant couldn't forgive a fellow slave who owed him the equivalent of seven thousand dollars today (one hundred denarii; a day's wage was one denarius, and one talent equaled roughly six thousand denarii), and had him thrown in jail. But word got back to the king about this sad state of affairs.

The king called in that unforgiving slave and lectured him about his hypocrisy. "'You wicked servant,' he said, 'I canceled all that debt of yours because you begged me to. Shouldn't you have had mercy on your fellow servant just as I had on you?'" (Mt 18:32-33). The point? "This is how my heavenly Father will treat each of you unless you forgive a brother or sister *from your heart*" (Mt 18:35, emphasis added). This final saying of Jesus is astonishing since it's directed toward believers. He urges us to pass on this gracious release to others.

Mike Wilkins, my dean of faculty at Talbot School of Theology, shares how God helped him forgive a stepfather who had brought much grief and pain to his family when he was a child. Before he became a Christian, Mike's attitude resembled the bumper sticker "I don't get mad, I get even." While Mike was serving in Vietnam, his anger brought him to make a vow that he would kill his stepfather on first sight "to make him pay for what he had done to our family."[13] Soon he returned to the United States and about a year later Mike came into a saving relationship with Jesus Christ. Four years later, when Mike was married and had a little girl, his stepfather showed up at their door. They invited him in. While chatting politely Mike remembered the vow he had made. Mike shares what happened as he confronted his stepfather.

---

[13]Michael Wilkins, *Matthew*, NIV Application Commentary (Grand Rapids: Zondervan, 2004), pp. 636-37.

"I made a vow in Vietnam that the first time I saw you, I would kill you. Today is that day." I will never forget the look of terror that came over his face. He started to sweat and slide down the couch. I went on, "But I now know that I'm no better a person than you. God has forgiven me. And if he can forgive a sinner like me, I can forgive you. I will not allow you to hurt my family again, so don't think that this is made out of weakness. Rather I forgive you because I have been forgiven." I was probably as shocked as he was. I had not thought about saying those words of forgiveness, but they came easily. I was deeply aware of the mercy and forgiveness that God had extended to me.[14]

Only Jesus' grace can soften our edges, making it possible for us to enter into the pain of others and become agents of Jesus' compassion to others.

A process of forgiving. For more particular guidance on the practical steps of forgiveness, my first choice is Robert Enright's *Forgiveness is a Choice*, published by the American Psychological Association.[15] Enright is a well-established social science researcher and a Christian. What is involved in forgiving? As the result of their pioneering research over many years, Enright and his team propose various phases, both in giving forgiveness and wanting to receive forgiveness.

First, we are acknowledging that the offense was unfair and will always continue to be unfair. Second, we have a moral right to be angry; it is fair to cling to our view that people do not have a right to hurt us. We have a right to respect. Third, forgiveness requires giving up something to which we have a right—namely our anger or resentment. Forgiving is an act of mercy toward an offender, someone who does not necessarily deserve our mercy. . . . In spite of everything that the offender has done, we are willing to treat him or her as a member of the human community.[16]

The paradox of forgiveness, according to Enright, is that "as we reach out to the one who hurt us, we are the ones who heal."[17]

---

[14]Ibid., p. 637.
[15]Robert Enright, *Forgiveness Is a Choice* (Washington, D.C.: American Psychological Association, 2001). For Enright's challenging journey to research this topic, see Gary Thomas, "The Forgiveness Factor," *Christianity Today*, February 10, 2000, pp. 38-45.
[16]Enright, *Forgiveness*, pp. 25-26.
[17]Ibid., p. 75.

Forgiving another starts at a point in time. Yet forgiveness is not a one-time event, because it's also a journey into our inner healing. Forgiving difficult and deep emotional hurts involves a process that may require the uncovering over time of various layers of wounds, of grief, but also of self-righteousness and pride. We may have resolved the matter of forgiveness at one level, but then something prompts us to return to the situation and various hurtful feelings suddenly surface again.

On April 19, 1995, when the Alfred P. Murrah Federal Building in Oklahoma City was bombed, Chuck Douglas was one of the first police officers to arrive at the scene. Sadly this tragedy moved Chuck into deeper personal crisis—more drinking, angry tirades, depression—worsening his already strained separation from his wife. But some grace awakening within Chuck propelled him to work on his marriage. He urged Melissa to attend a Family Life marriage conference. She only agreed thinking what she learned there might help her next marriage. The seminar instructors were Tim Muelhoff, a Biola University professor, and his wife Noreen. Tim shares, "Noreen and Melissa connected right away and Noreen carefully explained to her the Gospel. Melissa listened intently and accepted Christ in the lobby of the hotel."[18]

God was also awakening Chuck's heart. After the final session, they drove to Melissa's mother's house where Melissa was staying. When Melissa was seated on the couch, Chuck made a confession. "'If this marriage is going to work,' he began, 'I need to come clean.'" He revealed he had engaged in a number of affairs. Overwhelmed with nausea by this information, Melissa ran to the bathroom, shutting herself inside. "God, I've been a Christian for 48 hours. I can't do this!" Later, Melissa shared what happened. "The only way I can explain what happened next is to say that I was flooded with an understanding of how much God had forgiven me. . . . Everything, forgiven. Now in this moment, the Lord was asking me to take a piece of that forgiveness and give it to my husband. As I walked back from the bathroom into the living room I made the decision to pass on to him God's forgiveness." God's grace continued to flow into their individual lives and their mar-

[18]Tim Muelhoff, "Perseverance and Answered Prayer," *The [Biola University] Chimes*, November 12, 2009, p. A4.

riage grew strong. Tim shares, "Chuck eventually left law enforcement and decided to come on staff with Family Life and today is in charge of the Oklahoma marriage conference—the very conference that saved his marriage."[19]

The way we respond to each circumstance requiring grace and forgiveness may vary. For example, the more difficult challenge is when there's continuing contact with someone who has hurt us and may continue to do so. What do we do about such a toxic relationship? We may need to move in what appears to be two contrasting directions at the same time, holding them in a continuing tension. While we can welcome God's work in us toward forgiveness of someone, we may also need grace to develop and manage appropriate boundaries with them in order to minimize any further intentional wounding on their part. Extending this complex form of grace involves a delicate dance, yet we can rely on God and our close Christian mentors and friends to help us navigate these troubled waters.[20]

Even for an action that unintentionally causes harm, it seems fitting to seek forgiveness if we become aware of the harm. That's what Richard Mouw, president of Fuller Seminary, chose to do. He pulled into a parking space and soon became aware of his mistake from the honking that followed. "The driver had obviously been waiting for the spot, and I had simply pulled in without noticing. She kept at the honking for several seconds, then gave me the middle finger and searched for another spot."[21] Mouw looked for her and apologized.

When we make a choice to be open to forgiveness and ask God for help, God will empower us to move our hearts in a good direction. And we need Christian community around us.[22]

---

[19]Ibid.

[20]For a helpful resource on setting relational limits, see Henry Cloud and John Townsend, *Boundaries: When to Say Yes, When to Say No to Take Control of Your Life* (Grand Rapids: Zondervan, 1992).

[21]Richard Mouw, *Uncommon Decency* (Downers Grove, Ill.: InterVarsity Press, 2010), p. 182.

[22]At a corporate level, do we provide a safe place for lamentation before God? Paul encourages us to "mourn with those who mourn" (Rom 12:8). By conducting a periodic lament service we could create a public forum where believers could mirror the thoughts and feelings of persons like Job and Jeremiah, and bare their souls in the midst of a loving and caring community.

Forgiveness prayer projects.

1. Pray/meditate on Jesus' parables about forgiveness (Mt 18:21-35; Lk 7:36-50). Ponder, what are my current attitudes and heart responses about God's forgiveness to me?

2. Consider doing the "glad, sad, mad, dreads and dreams" exercise from chapter two, and notice if any personal relationship conflicts or relationship conflicts among others close to you surface under "sad," "mad" or "dreads." Attend to your coping strategies in dealing with hurtful situations. Do you tend to distance yourself from feelings of anger and injustice? Or do you tend to become overly aggressive in response to these feelings? How harmful to you and others might these coping strategies be? Perhaps read this section on forgiveness again, and talk with God about these matters as God works in your heart.

3. If you're aware of a personal relationship conflict or one among others close to you, take this situation to God and ask for guidance in what to pray about, and if God may lead you to seek counsel from a trusted mentor and take a next step.

Practice 2: Peacemaking in Conflict

Mediation and reconciliation. From behind the front door, Frank yelled, "I have a bat, and I'll hit anyone who comes in."[23] Five Christian adults— four brothers and a sister—were fighting about the farm they inherited at the recent death of their mother. The complication was that the farmhouse was the only home Frank had ever lived in. He had cared for their mother after their father had passed away. In the will, a trust had been established to care for Frank since he had a disability that meant he had to stay home all his life, but all five adult children equally owned the farm. With a pastor's counsel, the three brothers and sister decided to let Christian love permeate their decision making, resulting in a win-win outcome for all concerned. Three weeks later, the extended family gathered at a local restaurant and honored Frank for his care of their mother

---

[23]Ken Sande, *The Peacemaker: A Biblical Guide to Resolving Personal Conflict*, 3rd ed. (Grand Rapids: Baker, 2004), p. 17.

over the past ten years. (Frank reluctantly left the house to come to this event.) They presented Frank with a plaque, and also with a signed agreement by the brothers and sister. Frank could live in the farmhouse for the rest of his life. A buyer was willing to purchase the farm land without the house. Frank was overcome with joy and relief. Older brother Joe, making the presentation, gave a physical demonstration of his reconciliation with Frank by hugging him.

Jesus' key teaching on servanthood and humility occurred on the occasions of strife among his disciples as they argued about who among them was the greatest (Mk 9:34; Lk 22:44). Has your pride and arrogance ever taken over your words and actions? Sadly, it's a common experience for us all. Demanding our own way and coercive manipulation are common practices in the world. James 3:14-15 says, "if you harbor bitter envy and selfish ambition in your hearts . . . such 'wisdom' is . . . of the devil" (NIV).

We need to gain Jesus' perspective on what may seem hopeless to us: "With human beings this is impossible, but with God all things are possible" (Mt 19:26). Jesus teaches a better way, a way of love, of keeping the concerns of others in mind as we work on our own goals in cooperation with others.

> The kings of the Gentiles lord it over them; and those who exercise authority over them call themselves Benefactors. But you are not to be like that. Instead, the greatest among you should be like the youngest, and the one who rules like the one who serves. For who is greater, the one who is at the table or the one who serves? Is it not the one who is at the table? But I am among you as one who serves. (Lk 22:25-27; cf. Mt 20:25-28; 1 Pet 5:2)

Jesus desires that we expend the extra effort to work toward unity. In chapter one I mentioned one of the hyperbolic illustrations Jesus gave to his Galilean listeners to demonstrate this kind of concerted intentionality: if, while making an offering in Jerusalem, they became awakened to a conflict, they should immediately go the eighty miles back to their village in Galilee (usually by foot), resolve the matter and then return the eighty miles to continue making their offering at the temple (Mt 5:23-24). Jesus himself worked through his own conflict with

Peter, first praying for him, then telling him the truth that (a) Peter would deny him and (b) Jesus had already prayed for Peter's strength prior to the three denials (Lk 22:31-34, 61). Finally Jesus initiated some personal follow-up meetings to reconcile their relationship (Lk 24:34; 1 Cor 15:5; Jn 21:15-22). Jesus is the "Lord of peace" (2 Thess 3:16; cf. Isa 9:6; Eph 2:14-17), the mediator par excellence (1 Tim 2:5). Jesus' example, teachings and empowerment through the Spirit can break through any conflict to bring about his deep peace upon his followers (Jn 14:27; Eph 2:18-22; Col 3:15).

For many years Ken Sande, a lawyer, along with his staff at Peacemakers (established 1982), have successfully used a four-step process to help Christians in varying situations, both in the United States and overseas, to resolve conflicts and reconcile relationships. It's simple to list these steps, yet the process requires time, persistence and prayer to help believers work through disagreements such as business dealings, neighbor disputes, marital strife and family inheritance issues.

1. *Glorify God* (1 Cor 10:31): How can I please and honor God in this situation?

2. *Get the log out of your eye* (Mt 7:5): How can I show Jesus' work in me by taking responsibility for my contribution to this conflict?

3. *Gently restore* (Gal 6:1): How can I lovingly serve others by helping them take responsibility for their contribution to this conflict?

4. *Go and be reconciled* (Mt 5:24): How can I demonstrate the forgiveness of God and encourage a reasonable solution to this conflict?[24]

Sande notes, "I have used these four principles in hundreds of conflicts over the past two decades and I have yet to encounter a situation in which they did not provide practical and effective guidance."[25]

Sande proposes the possible responses to conflict, ranging from *escape responses* (suicide, flight, denial) to *peacemaking responses* (overlook, reconciliation, mediation, arbitration, accountability) and finally to *attack responses* (assault, litigation, murder).[26] He explains that when using

---

[24]Ibid., pp. 12-13, 38.
[25]Ibid., p. 38.
[26]Ibid., pp. 22-29.

either escape or attack responses, the eventual result is that you "KYRG: kiss your relationship good-bye."[27] We need to reframe our view of conflict. Valuing relationships is an important priority throughout the process for brothers and sisters in Jesus' family. Sande notes that 1 Corinthians 10:31–11:1 "presents a radical view of conflict: It encourages us to look at conflict as an opportunity to glorify God, serve others, and grow to be like Christ."[28]

After almost a year of wrangling and bitter verbal fighting regarding the construction of a new house (including a lawsuit and a counter lawsuit), Bill (the builder) and Steve (the new home owner)—two prominent Christian businessmen—had made little progress to resolve the conflict. Then, reluctantly following one attorney's advice, they submitted their dispute to a Christian conciliation panel (consisting of a builder, a businessman and Sande as the attorney). The panel inspected the home and noticed some deficiencies, but Steve and Bill continued to pass on the blame and disagreed about a resolution. The two were challenged to study a list of Bible passages and to pray about their own contribution to the dispute.

And heaven was able to break in. The builder, Bill, recognized his actions weren't pleasing to God, nor to his family and others as a way Jesus would want him to deal with the conflict. At the next meeting, Bill owned up to his contributions to the problem—the defects in construction and his attitude of bad reactions to Steve's concerns. Bill also suggested how he'd like to fix the defects and a way to avoid this problem in the future through a checklist system. In response, Steve's heart melted as well, and he owned his part—tending to be a perfectionist and not doing a good job of talking with Bill about the problem. They offered each other forgiveness and made an agreement on future repairs and costs. Bill also apologized to Steve's wife. Even Bill's attorney marveled at the turnabout. In a private conversation with Sande after the meeting, he shared,

---

[27]Ibid., p. 28.
[28]Ibid., p. 31. In *The Peacemaker*, Sande provides detailed guidelines for moving through conflict to resolution, illustrated in various case studies. Appendix D clarifies factors that apply from 1 Corinthians 6:1-8 to be discerned and decided before going to court to resolve a dispute, whether filling a lawsuit or being sued.

What happened over there yesterday? I've watched those two fight for over a year, and I know how bitter they were. But when Bill came in to talk with me this morning, his attitude was completely changed. He said God had helped him to see his faults in the situation, and he explained the repairs he is going to make. When I pointed out what Steve had done wrong, Bill came to his defense! I've never seen anything like this.[29]

Peacemaker Ministries has many accounts of Christians in difficult circumstances who, after being persuaded to pursue a resolution while valuing relationships, see their patience and humility rewarded in situations like this.[30] Becoming a peacemaker requires the formation of our heart, as Miroslav Volf clarifies:

[It] has to do with *creation of the kind of social agents that are shaped by the values of God's kingdom and therefore capable of participating in the project of social transformation.* [31]

The Spirit enters the citadel of the self, de-centers the self by fashioning it in the image of the self-giving Christ, and frees its will so it can resist the power of exclusion in the power of the Spirit of embrace. It is in the citadel of the fragile self that the new world of embrace is first created (2 Corinthians 5:17).[32]

Peacemakers are blessed (Jas 3:18).

In his book, Sande offers suggestions in appendix F for pastors on how to transform church culture from one of disbelief about resolving conflicts within the church to one of a desire to resolve them within the church. An important component is developing a ministry of trained mediation teams who can engage with believers regarding disputes— within families, between families, between leaders and between business partners (e.g., Mt 18:15-35).[33]

---

[29]Ken Sande, *The Peacemaker*, 2nd ed. (Grand Rapids: Baker, 1997), pp. 14-15.

[30]See <www.peacemaker.net>.

[31]Miroslav Volf, *Exclusion and Embrace* (Nashville: Abingdon, 1996), p. 118 (emphasis in original). Volf employs the key concepts of exclusion (separation, cutting off from) and embrace (open hospitality). For a case study of peacemaking and reconciliation on a national scale, see Desmond Tutu, *No Future Without Forgiveness* (New York: Doubleday, 1999).

[32]Volf, *Exclusion and Embrace*, p. 92.

[33]Regarding domestic violence and child abuse, a different initial response is needed—not mediation, but immediate protection and advocacy to provide physical and emotional safety for the abused. Information and resources are available from Peace and Safety in the Christian

Peacemaking prayer projects.

1. Meditate on Matthew 5:23-24, Romans 12:18 and 14:19 and ponder, Lord, am I in conflict with someone? What is my part of the problem? What would you suggest be my next step?

2. Lord, am I aware of someone close to me in conflict? How can I pray for them? Is there a step I could take in this to be helpful? Where is there a place at our church where conflicts can be resolved? How can I pray for that ministry and for the teams involved at our church? Is there a step I could take to contribute to such a peacemaking ministry at our church?

3. How can I pray for matters of peacemaking, reconciliation and unity that affect the Christian church's witness to the world? Is there a step I could take to contribute toward Christian unity in some particular arena?[34]

William Spohn suggests one means toward local church unity is the regular practice of and participation in the Lord's Supper/Communion. In both scriptural accounts of this practice, matters of disunity and division among the believers were evident (Lk 22:20-34; 1 Cor 11:17-34). Spohn notes, "Forgiveness and solidarity are not minor aspects of the Eucharist that are dispensed with in a hasty opening penitential rite or taking up the offering. They are necessary components of the practice of the Lord's Supper."[35]

Turning from the arenas of forgiveness and peacemaking, we briefly consider how deepening Christian friendship plays an important role in growing family unity among Christians.

Home (PASCH) <www.peaceandsafety.com>. For further reading, see Nancy Nason-Clark et al., ed., *Responding to Abuse in Christian Homes* (Eugene, Ore.: Wipf & Stock, 2011); Albert Roberts, ed., *Handbook of Domestic Violence Intervention Strategies: Policies, Programs, and Legal Remedies* (New York: Oxford University Press, 2002); and Edward Kubany, Mari McCaig and Janet Laconsay, *Healing the Trauma of Domestic Violence: A Workbook for Women* (Oakland, Calif.: New Harbinger, 2004). Such situations may also be an arena of spiritual warfare. For a helpful resource, see Clinton Arnold, *Three Crucial Questions About Spiritual Warfare* (Grand Rapids: Baker, 1997).

[34]For example, one arena may be racial relations and unity. See John Perkins, *With Justice for All* (Ventura, Calif.: Regal, 2011). One disconcerting case of apparent discrimination regarding women in ministry is available at <www.ruthtucker.net>.

[35]William Spohn, *Go and Do Likewise: Jesus and Ethics* (New York: Continuum, 2000), p. 169.

Practice 3: Developing Closer Friendships
to Build Community

Focusing on friendships. How do we go about developing a positive
sense of relational community that provides a nurturing context for
forgiveness and mediation? God crafted our humanity, especially as
indwelt by the Holy Spirit, for the potential of a profound relational
intimacy and mutual indwelling with others and with God (Jn 17:21-
23). Various factors are involved, but it's more than just showing up at
group meetings. Even participating in group activities will not grow
the kind of deep community Jesus talks about. An important missing
ingredient in our strategy for community building is valuing close
friendships. There's an important relational distinction between a *group*
(i.e., three or more persons) and a *dyad* (i.e., a relationship between two
persons). A group includes various dyads (e.g., the Trinity, parents and
children, a sports team). The key glue of any healthy community is that
various sets of close friendships—of dyads—are interspersed throughout the group, providing an existing relational connectedness—a relational leavening—that can permeate the whole and draw others toward
unity. Was it due to this insight that within the twelve disciples, Jesus
had selected two sets of brothers (Peter and Andrew, Mt 4:18; James
and John, Mt 4:21)—involving already-existing close relationships—to
help "jump start" these individuals toward becoming a community?
Furthermore it is interesting to note that it was within this already in-
timate circle of brothers and fishing partners (Lk 5:10) that Jesus developed particularly close friendships.

Consider the following account from a Christian leader who was
awakened to the need for such dyad friendships:

> After nearly nine years as missionaries, my wife and I returned to our
> sending church, a large church in the US, in which we had been deeply
> involved in the life of the church in numerous leadership, board, and
> ministry capacities for many years. We anticipated a warm welcome by
> all these friends we'd left nearly a decade ago. We saw some familiar
> faces in the crowd but quickly realized we only knew these people as a
> crowd, the sum of our church relationships was what we did in groups.

How different from our experience on the mission field. We were frequently in one another's homes. Our ministry was more one on one and deeply personal. It didn't take long to discover that our connection to that group overseas was deeper and stronger because we knew the stories of individuals within the group. We had personal friendships that went deeper than anything we'd ever experienced in America. Leaving that group was gut-wrenching because of the life connections we had with the individuals within the group.

Our sending church now felt unfriendly and impenetrable; conversations superficial and deeply unsatisfying. We noticed that people would come and go within the group without anyone noticing their absence. We found ourselves dealing again with committees according to policies, procedures and protocol, not individual needs and situations.

After several weeks of frustration, we left that church and began attending a smaller church. Each week, people introduced themselves to us, asked us questions about ourselves, and drew us in with their genuine care—it was overwhelming. We quickly realized that our relationship with this church was not based solely on our interactions with the *group*, but with *individuals* within the group. Friendships—dyads—were forming. When we missed a Sunday, someone missed us.

Among the multiple factors involved here, we're convinced the most significant was the personal touch. We have genuine relationships with people and not just committees or teams. As a result, we sense our community is stronger, our fellowship deeper, our commitment more lasting than ever. Certainly it's a church we love and appreciate, but more than that, we feel that we have significant relationships with individuals that has deepened our connection to the group as a whole.[36]

Healthy communities have at their core many sets of close friendships. At first glance, the concept of friendship doesn't seem to be emphasized in the New Testament. Yet we can piece together some helpful insights and examples from the Old Testament (e.g., Prov 17:17; 27:10; David and Jonathan, 1 Sam 18:1-4). In the New Testament, key relational terms are used such as *koinoia* (fellowship, Acts 2:42; 1 Jn 1:3) and Paul's use of classic Greek terms for friendship (e.g., Phil 2:2).[37] And

---

[36]Ken Thompson (not real name), personal communication, September 27, 2007.
[37]For further study see John T. Fitzgerald, ed., *Friendship, Flattery, and Frankness of Speech,*

Jesus' own example underscores the goodness of close friendships. In his role as head of the Church, Jesus invited twelve disciples to be "with him" (Mk 3:14), spending a couple of years in daily living together. Within the twelve, Jesus had an inner circle of *deep friends:* Peter, James and John. Occasionally Jesus took along only these three, including at his time of testing in Gethsemane (Mk 14:33). John became the closest friend of Jesus, known as the one "whom Jesus loved" (Jn 13:23; 19:26; 20:2; 21:7, 20). Also, "Jesus loved Martha and her sister and Lazarus" (Jn 11:5). When he passed through Bethany near Jerusalem, Jesus often stayed with the sisters Martha and Mary and their brother Lazarus, the one whom Jesus eventually raised from the dead. Martha felt so comfortable in her friendship with Jesus she felt free to order him around (Lk 10:40)!

In light of Jesus' own practice of having friends, Jesus isn't prohibiting friendship love altogether in Matthew 5:46, "For if you love those who love you, what reward do you have?" Rather, Jesus only condemns an *exclusive* focus on friendship love as the totality of one's sphere of relationships. As we cultivate deeper friendships, let's also expand our range of hospitality and generosity beyond our friendships, to those who may be unlovable, to those who can't always repay our love. Those regarded by others as scandalous "sinners" enjoyed being around Jesus, and he enjoyed being with them (Lk 15:1-2).[38]

In fact our close friendship relationships actually provide a context in which to grow into that kind of love to share with others. With close friends we have the opportunity to practice the various "one another" passages (e.g., be devoted to one another, Rom 12:10; be patient, bear-

---

Supplements to Novum Testamentum 82 (Leiden: Brill, 1966).

[38]Let me make a brief comment about Jesus' harsh tones and words to and about the religious leaders (e.g., Mt 23:1-39). Jesus' role as Messiah (also along the lines of an OT prophet) included bringing about radical reform for a national-political entity—represented by these leaders—that no longer fulfilled its distinct, historical mediatorial role. That was Jesus' *unique* commission and not exemplary for us. Since God is now directing his affairs through a transnational, nonpolitical entity, his church, I believe we have no basis for adopting Jesus' unique prophetic commission today. If we claim we're following Jesus by speaking harshly to a supposedly hard-hearted fellow believer "as Jesus did," and we find it so *easy* to do so, do we wonder whether our desire to do this particular "Jesus practice" is more about our agenda than Jesus' agenda? I don't think we have any license to be ungracious to those within or without the family of God just because someone disagrees with various points in our theology (Eph 4:25-32).

ing with one another, Col 3:12-13; submit to one another, Eph 5:21). Gilbert Meilander explains, "Attachment to friends is a school in which we are trained for that greater [heavenly] community. . . . Life is a journey, a pilgrimage toward that community in which friends love one another in God and time no longer inflicts its wounds on friendship. Along the way, friendship is a school, training us in the meaning and enactment of love."[39] Thus, friendship is a great reward in its own right, an end in itself, yet it also serves as the crucial means to expand our loving—to reach beyond our circle of comfort—a school of love.

I've already admitted I'm a recovering loner. At times I think I can make it on my own. Of course, I don't actually think these thoughts. But these deep core beliefs, acquired over a lifetime, compel me *not* to depend on others (or God for that matter). I'd rather do it myself, thank you. Our culture tends toward a radical individualism. The Bible affirms an emphasis on both the individual and the community, but our Western bias is that individual concerns and rights more often then not trump community and relational concerns. We don't value relationships as much as other parts of the world due to our radical individualism and to our overly task-oriented busyness. As Stephen Covey reminded us, "How many people on their deathbed wish they'd spent more time at the office?"[40] Rather, end-of-life regrets are about relationships that were not valued enough. I'm growing in my relational competencies and appreciating the goodness of friendships.

For example, I've observed in myself that my "righteous anger" arises due to some perceived injustice (against me or a friend) but sometimes moves easily into plain anger and being judgmental. When I notice this movement, if I can consider Jesus' compassion and mercy for the offender—and that I'm no "innocent lamb"—it's much easier to be grace-filled with that person (in person or in thought). Recently I was at a coffee shop with a friend who was venting some frustrations about his business partner. I mentioned this practical insight. He called me the

---

[39]Gilbert Meilander, *Friendship: A Study in Theological Ethics* (Notre Dame, Ind.: University of Notre Dame, 1985), p. 66.

[40]Stephen Covey et al., *First Things First* (New York: Free Press, 2003), p. 17.

next day to share his victory of being more gracious to his colleague. I was encouraged as well.

Two key words sum up close friendship. *Confession* represents the side of transparent self-disclosure, a willingness to share with another who is in confidence one's own weaknesses and besetting sins (Jas 5:16). On the other hand, *candor* represents the freedom to speak the truth into another's life for their good, offering feedback about another's blind spots or "planks in the eye" of which they are unaware (Mt 7:3-5). I remember when my friend J. P. Moreland initiated a conversation with me several years ago to brainstorm ways to move into a better financial situation. I felt awkward and embarrassed at first having to admit making some bad financial decisions, but I greatly appreciated his willingness to broach the subject. Much good came from that conversation. He's been a faithful companion, by my side as a compassionate encourager and in my face on occasions requiring some honest talk. It's risky to speak this kind of tough love, yet it's a significant gift from a close friend. "Faithful are the wounds of a friend" (Prov 27:6 NASB).[41]

Jesus prays for our unity, which testifies to the world that Jesus is Messiah (Jn 17:21-23). This quest toward family unity will require us to deepen relationships with our close Christian friends.[42]

Friendship prayer projects.

1. Ponder, what qualities of being a friend am I cultivating in my character (e.g., humility, compassion, serving heart), and what kind of friendship practices do I regularly engage in with others (e.g., listening, encouraging, weeping with, laughing with)? What means are available to improve my relational competencies?

---

[41]When a need arises to discern the way forward regarding an important life decision, Parker Palmer suggests enlisting a handful of trusted friends for a "clearness committee." He explains that it's "a process in which the group refrains from giving you advice but spends three hours asking you honest, open questions to help you discover your own inner truth." *Let Your Life Speak* (San Francisco: Jossey-Bass, 2000), pp. 44-45.

[42]Although we can be gracious to those we have forgiven who have harmed us, we have no moral obligation to let them become close friends. In his classic work, Aelred of Rivaulx (d. 1167) makes an important distinction between Christian love (which is our due to all) and friendship love (which we voluntarily give to a few). "In the perfection of charity we love very many . . . but yet we do not admit these to the intimacy of our [close] friendship." *Spiritual Friendship*, trans. Mary Laker (Kalamazoo, Mich.: Cistercian, 1977), p. 74.

2. How comfortable am I regarding practicing *confession* and *candor* with close friends? Reflect on an occasion where one was being practiced. How did it go? What can be improved?[43]

3. Who are the close friends in my life? For example, which persons would be invited to

   a. a special birthday celebration?

   b. serve together on a short-term overseas mission project?

   c. spend a day at Disneyland, or shopping, or an evening for dinner and conversation?

   d. pray for a confidential prayer request?

   e. ask for a place to stay overnight if a sudden emergency arose and you couldn't get to your home?

   What are some steps to take toward deepening close friendships?

Final Thoughts

We are individuals who flourish best in community. Healthy communities nurture and respect the individuality of each of its members, work through the difficult process of forgiveness, and assist members in resolving conflicts and sustaining close friendships. In being formed to be more forgiving, we can be released from the prison of bitterness, a cancer of the soul that can destroy our life. We have been forgiven much. And we need God's empowering grace to pass that forgiveness on to others. If we don't keep moving into the process of forgiving, then we may be placing ourselves outside of God's blessing. "God opposes the proud, but gives grace to the humble" (1 Pet 5:5 NIV). As members of Jesus' family, God desires that we work toward unity.

In the final chapter of the book, we consider another gap that influences the Christian community, exploring how we can follow Jesus regarding our attitudes about money.

---

[43]For further reading on friendship see J. P. Moreland and Klaus Issler, *The Lost Virtue of Happiness* (Colorado Springs: NavPress, 2006), chap. 6, and my *Wasting Time with God* (Downers Grove, Ill.: InterVarsity Press, 2001), chap. 2.

Grace

Grace . . . What an empowering gift to receive from another,
    Affirmation, forgiveness, a smile, a touch, a knowing silence.
    But . . . difficult to give to another—or to myself.

I'm right! And must demand it be written just so.
    Pride arises within, I just can't lose!
I want revenge! This isn't fair!
    They must suffer for my pain.
I'm afraid! I need to protect myself,
    By controlling and managing others to make it safe (and get my
    way).

I'm such a sinner, these aren't "Jesus" ways.
    Can I ever be good enough?
    God must be disappointed or angry with me.

But Grace isn't about being Perfect or being Right, it's about being
    Family.
    We all fall short, yet God lavishes his Children with undeserved
    Grace,
    To live, to flourish, to work and play together, to get along.

Grace is our distinctive Family treasure, overflowing from God in us.
    Where Grace is there's civility, kindness, safety, even Love.
    Grace . . . What an empowering gift to grant a sister or brother.

©Klaus Issler, 2/2011

AWAKE to gaps → ADMIT with honesty → ASK for formation grace → ACT, take a first step
ABIDING in Abba, Jesus, Holy Spirit

Figure 7.1.

Key Points

1. Jesus is generally viewed as being a very gracious and forgiving person;
   yet his followers tend to be viewed mostly as judgmental and hypocritical. We can grow to become more gracious to others like Jesus is.

2. Jesus' parable of the king and two servants illustrates how much God has forgiven us to encourage us to work toward reconciliation with others (Mt 18:15-20) and extend this same grace of forgiveness to others (Mt 18:21-35).

3. Deepening our close Christians friendships not only offers us the opportunity to grow our ability to love others, but makes a significant contribution toward increasing Christian unity.

4. Jesus practices what he preaches: he is the Lord of peace, the mediator *par excellence*, reconciling us to God; he had the opportunity to forgive many during his earthly ministry; and he was deeply connected with some close friends and committed to participating regularly in a small group.

8

Three Exemplary
Jesus Practices
About Money and Work

You can't worship two gods at once. Loving one god, you'll end up
hating the other. Adoration of one feeds contempt for the other.
You can't worship God and Money both.

MATTHEW 6:24 *THE MESSAGE*

. ℘ .

Jesus regards our attitudes about money as very important in the formation of our character. "For where your treasure is, there will your
heart be also" (Mt 6:21; Lk 12:33). This verse comes next: "If your
eyes are *generous*, your whole body will be full of light. But if your eyes
are *stingy* [lit. 'evil eye'] your whole body will be full of darkness" (Mt
6:22-23; Lk 11:34, emphasis added).[1] R. T. France summarizes that
"One indication of a person's spiritual health is their generosity or lack
of it in the use of their material possessions."[2] When was the last time
we thought about our reputation regarding our possessions on loan
from God? Do we lean toward being more tightfisted or more open-

---

[1]Alternate translation, TNIV; so also R. T. France, *The Gospel of Matthew*, New International
Commentary on the New Testament (Grand Rapids: Eerdmans, 2007), pp. 261-62.
[2]Ibid., p. 262.

handed? It's ultimately God's money we're managing, so shouldn't it be easier to give away someone else's money? Loving God means developing a proper attitude about money, as noted in the verse at the beginning of the chapter.

This chapter's purpose is to explore Jesus' life and teaching on these matters and offer suggestions for our formation. Yet Jesus' teachings on money have been perceived as difficult to harmonize and difficult to discern the meaning of, reminding us of the challenges of interpretation raised in chapter one. Also, clarifying an understanding of a biblical view of *money* requires some idea about a biblical view of *work*. Consequently, the initial section of the chapter explores the subject of work, which in many cases is the means we engage to earn money for our material needs. Aspects of the discussion on work and money may seem new. I invite readers to work through the whole chapter before drawing preliminary conclusions. Perhaps record the questions that come to mind and note which items were addressed and which items need further study.

Due to space limits, I'll focus on the potentially good aspects of the topic as related to our formation. Andrew Perriman notes, "We cannot ignore the fact that wealth is a positive resource. It is a hazardous resource, certainly, but within a redeemed community there should be the wisdom and grace available to handle wealth responsibly."[3] Only brief comments are mentioned about the dangers of money. On that issue, please consult relevant sources cited in the notes.[4]

---

[3] Andrew Perriman, ed., *Faith, Health and Prosperity* (Carlisle, U.K.: Paternoster, 2003), p. 223, Report of the Evangelical Alliance [U.K.] Commissions on Unity and Truth Among Evangelicals.

[4] Among Christian scholars there are divergent views regarding a Christian perspective about money and business. Of course, there are common agreements, such as affirming the dangers of wealth, the importance for Christians to be generous givers, and the great need to care for and seek justice for the poor, locally and globally (see the "Oxford Declaration on Christian Faith and Economics," Jan. 1990; first published in *Transformation* 7, no. 2 [April/June 1990]: 1-8). Yet major differences remain among Christian leaders on these matters, as is the case with other Christian doctrines.

One common view is championed by Ron Sider (*Rich Christians in an Age of Hunger* [1977; reprint, Nashville: Thomas Nelson, 2005]). In this chapter I give voice to an alternative paradigm represented by the writings of, for example, John Schneider (*The Good of Affluence* [Grand Rapids: Eerdmans, 2002]), Wayne Grudem (*Business for the Glory of God* [Wheaton, Ill.: Crossway, 2003]), Kenman Wong and Scott Rae (*Business for the Common Good: A Christian Perspec-*

Part one (chapters one through three) of this book focused on our core worldview beliefs—how these can help us or hinder us from living more into the life of Jesus. Over the past seven years, I've experienced some perspective shifts regarding Jesus' view on money and work that have been liberating. From this journey, I've identified two particular gaps of my own for discussion later in the chapter: the "Sunday-Monday" gap and the "Money is worldly" gap. Some insights are helping me move forward, but I'm still on the way. This chapter has three major sections exploring the topics of work, money and giving. These particular areas relate to three exemplary practices from Jesus' own life: doing our work well, trusting in God's provision while wisely using money on loan from God, and giving generously.

Practice 1: Doing Our Work Well

Work is a permanent feature of humankind's design and destiny, not the result of the Fall into sin. Work was initiated in the Garden of Eden (Gen 1:28; 2:15), and it will continue into the next age, as we serve and reign with God forever (Rev 22:3, 5). Dallas Willard suggests some distinctions among four key terms helpful for this discussion (terms were displayed in concentric circles, the first term being in the smallest circle so that a later term incorporates and includes the previous term):

1. *Job*: What I am paid to do, how I earn my living

2. *Ministry*: That part of God's special work in my time that He has specifically allotted me

3. *Work*: The total amount of lasting goods that I will produce in my lifetime

4. *Life*: Me. My experience and who I am[5]

---

tive for the Marketplace [Downers Grove, Ill.: InterVarsity Press, 2011]), and Michael Novak (*Business as a Calling: Work and the Examined Life* [New York: Free Press, 1996]).

Differences are evident in biblical teaching about meeting the challenges of the poor. For example, Schneider emphasizes the great potential for good through the expansion of good business and wealth creation to benefit all in the world—including the poor—for God's kingdom purposes, whereas Sider gives greater emphasis to reducing use of the earth's resources and the redistribution of Christian wealth as the primary solution for addressing poverty.

[5]Dallas Willard, "Some Steps Toward Soul Rest in Eternal Living," Biola University Faculty Workshop, August 17, 2011.

Accordingly, when the term *work* is used in the following discussion, it includes a reference to our ministry and our job as well. Furthermore, there are an increasing number of academic contributions toward a theology of work for *all* believers in Christian thought. Two of these resources will be cited in the following section.[6]

Work's instrumental and intrinsic value. Darrell Cosden, summarizing his scholarly book-length treatment, proposes the following technical definition of work. Note that various factors are clustered around three particular dimensions.

> Human work is a transformative activity essentially consisting of dynamically interrelated instrumental, relational, and ontological dimensions: whereby, along with work being an end in itself *[ontological]*, the worker's and others' needs are providentially met; believers' sanctification is occasioned *[instrumental]*; and workers express, explore and develop their humanness while building up their natural, social and cultural environments thereby contributing protectively and productively to the order of this world and the one to come *[relational]*.[7]

Hints about these three dimensions are included in the definition: the *ontological* dimension comprises the transcendent, transformative and eternal value of work as an end itself—that work is greater than the sum of its parts—an activity that can be "permeated with the ethos of [God's] sabbath" (Gen 2:2; Heb 4:9-11);[8] the *instrumental* dimension involves both material sustenance needs connected with economic issues and personal spiritual formation/sanctification through work; and the *relational* dimension aligns with the opportunity for self-expression and flourishing as well as for broader societal development and matters of social justice.

Work is a continuing "community" endeavor, a fitting follow-up topic to the last chapter. Work is never accomplished solely as an individual performance, but requires the collaboration, coordination and

---

[6]For an ongoing project to study the Bible's teaching about work, see "Theology of Work" (www .theologyofwork.org). For example, see "Ecclesiastes and Work," which can be downloaded from their website. Another organization, The Acton Institute, promotes the integration of Judeo-Christian truths and business (www.acton.org).

[7]Darrell Cosden, *A Theology of Work* (Eugene, Ore.: Wipf & Stock, 2006 [2004]), pp. 178-79.

[8]Ibid., p. 184.

trust of many, such as suppliers, manufacturers, distributors and, of course, customers. Also, we cannot fail to mention resources from the material world and the dynamics of its physical laws that contribute to work—all provisions from God. Without these varied partnerships, work cannot be sustained.

As a blessing of the New Covenant, believers are indwelt and empowered by the Spirit to serve the common good in cooperation with God (Ezek 36:26-27; 2 Cor 3:6). Miroslav Volf proposes "work in the Spirit" as the foundation for a biblical theology of work, expanding the use and scope of our spiritual empowerments beyond the local church, rather than relying on the traditional concept of vocation. "All human work, however complicated or simple, is made possible by the operations of the Spirit of God in the working person; and all work whose nature and results reflect the values of the new creation is accomplished under the instruction and inspiration of the Spirit of God (see Is 28:24-29)."[9] Yet even those outside of God's family, being created in the image of God, are animated by God's power with the divine gifts of natural abilities. The point is that Jesus' followers have greater potential to work for the good of all as we partner with the Spirit.

Regardless of our occupation as plumber, trash collector, teacher, mechanic or pastor, we cooperate with God in doing good work. The apostle Paul uses the analogy of a physical body with many members, with implications for the division of labor: not all can be the eye; some will be the foot, knee or internal organs. "Those parts of the body that seem to be weaker are indispensable" (1 Cor 12:22). Each member, regardless of function, is important for the functioning of the body. "The whole body . . . grows and builds itself up in love, as each part does its work" (Eph 4:16). Of course, one motivation to work can be to make money to provide for material needs and share with others (Eph 4:28; 2 Thess 3:6-13). But there is more. Labor—as a permanent feature of our human design and destiny—also involves other instrumental *and* intrinsic values. If we wish to bring all of our life under the lordship of Jesus Christ, then our day job must be included too.

---

[9]Miroslav Volf, *Work in the Spirit* (1991; reprint, Eugene, Ore.: Wipf & Stock, 2001), p. 114.

Three job sectors. Our job tasks range across a wide spectrum, classified into three main working sectors: *public* (working for government), *private not-for-profit* (civic, moral and religious organizations that rely on donations for all or part of their operating budgets) and *private for-profit* (various small and large businesses in the marketplace). Table 8.1 provides estimates of these sectors' percentages in the 2010 U.S. total workforce. Musing on these differing percentages yields insight about two issues. First, some may wonder, with so much greed in the for-profit sector, how can Christians affirm business? Of course, a greater number of cases of greed and corruption will likely occur in the for-profit sector due to the vast majority of people working in this sector. Such evil also occurs routinely in other sectors since greed is a matter of the human heart (Mk 7:21-22), as reported somewhat regularly in the news. Second, one need not be a rocket scientist to recognize a basic economic principle: a much higher percentage of the workforce is essential in the business sector (currently around 80 percent) to sustain financial support for the continued existence of the other two sectors. Can Christians recognize how important good businesses are for creating the wealth that sustains charities and government services?

Table 8.1. Three Sectors of the United States Total Workforce—2010 Data

Private For-Profit Business	Private Not-for-Profit	Public Government
78.5% 109,094,000 in workforce	6.4% 8,968,000	15.1% 21,003,000

Total estimated workforce: 139,065,000 (www.bls.gov/cps).

Jesus and business. Do we realize that Jesus worked at a "secular" job for most of his young adult years? We might have expected a different career path and preparation for the one who would be Messiah. As was customary for boys in that day, Jesus was probably apprenticed alongside his father Joseph. His former neighbors knew Jesus by his previous trade: "Isn't this the *tektōn?*" (Mk 6:3; Mt 13:55). *Tektōn* has been rendered as "carpenter" since William Tyndale's English Bible translation (1526). Yet Ken Campbell suggests "builder" as a more accurate translation. "In the context of first-century Israel, the *tektōn* was a general craftsman who worked with stone, wood, and sometimes metal in large and small building projects."[10]

If apprenticed at the customary age of twelve, then Jesus spent at least eighteen years as a builder, six times as long as his public ministry (see table 8.2). Tradition suggests that his father Joseph died a few years prior to Jesus entering public ministry. During that time, then, Jesus headed up the family building business, implying Jesus' primary responsibility for financially supporting the family (Mt 13:55-56). Darrell Bock notes, "Only artisans or other craftspeople had the ancient equivalent of small, independent businesses. They constituted a minority of the labor force."[11] For Jesus' family to work in a trade indicates they were in the lower middle-income class of that day.[12]

Table 8.2. Jesus' Eighteen Years in the Building Trade

	Temple (12 yrs)	Baptism (30 yrs)	(33 yrs)
Phases:	Childhood	**Young Adulthood**	Later Adulthood
Years:	12 years	**18 years**	3 years
Occupation:		**Apprenticed, working as builder; probably headed family building business for a few years**	Public ministry as Messiah

Almost 50 percent of Jesus' parables have a "business setting" (see table 8.3). Perhaps some aspects of these stories had a personal connection. For example, when teaching on the cost of discipleship, Jesus mentions one should have the funds at the start to complete a tower (Lk 14:28). Might Jesus have built a tower for a customer but never have been fully paid?

---

[10]Ken M. Campbell, "What Was Jesus' Occupation?" *Journal of the Evangelical Theological Society* 48, no. 3 (September 2005): 512.

[11]Darrell Bock, *Studying the Historical Jesus* (Grand Rapids: Baker, 2002), p. 122.

[12]Walter Pilgrim, *Good News to the Poor* (Minneapolis: Augsburg, 1981), p. 46. Darrell Bock notes, "Fishing was a major industry in Galilee. [James and John] even had 'hired servants' (Mark 1:20), showing that they were among the closest thing to a middle class that existed at the time." *Jesus According to Scripture* (Grand Rapids: Baker, 2002), p. 98.

Table 8.3. Jesus' Parables Set Within Business-Related Contexts

Parable	Luke	Matthew	Mark
Two Builders	6:47-49	7:24-27	
Two Debtors	7:41-42		
Four Soils	8:5-8, 11-15	13:3-9, 18-23	4:3-9, 14-20
Rich Fool	12:16-21		
Faithful/Unfaithful Servants	12:42-46	24:45-51	
Barren Fig Tree	13:6-9		
Tower Builder	14:28-30		
Lost Sheep	15:4-7	18:12-14	
Unjust Manager	16:1-13		
Ten Minas	19:11-27		
Wicked Tenants	20:9-19	21:33-46	12:1-12
Wheat and Weeds		13:24-30, 36-43	
Field of Treasure		13:44	
Pearl of Great Price		13:45-46	
Unforgiven Debt		18:23-25	
Vineyard Workers		20:1-16	
Talents		25:14-30	

Can we conclude Jesus understands the business world as an insider? He probably worked as a subcontractor alongside other artisans, completing projects and handling finances—negotiating bids, purchasing supplies and contributing to family living expenses. For those many years Jesus worked with his hands in masonry and carpentry, in good and bad weather, getting paid and not getting paid. Jesus can identify with the ups and downs of a business workday. For a few years, he had responsibilities for day-to-day operations of running what we'd call a small business. And consider that this day job—where he spent a good part of his young adult years—contributed to Jesus' character formation to become the kind of person we read about in the Gospels.

Reflecting on the three-sector workforce framework (table 8.1), we can discern that Jesus affirmed each one. He implicitly acknowledged government has a legitimate role, by paying taxes himself (Mt 17:24-27; see also 22:21), by not requiring Zacchaeus as a chief tax collector to change his profession (Lk 19:2-10) and by including the tax collector

Matthew as one of the twelve disciples (Mt 9:9; 10:3; he wrote the
Gospel of Matthew). Regarding the private, not-for-profit sector, Jesus
lived on the donations of others during his three years of public ministry (Lk 8:3; Mk 15:41; Jn 12:6). Finally, Jesus worked in the for-profit
sector in the building trade. Similarly, the apostle Paul affirmed each
sector: he worked as a tentmaker (Acts 18:3), on occasion paying for his
companions' needs (Acts 20:33-35); he accepted financial support from
churches (2 Cor 11:7-9; Phil 4:15-16); and he relied on the benefits of
his Roman citizenship (Acts 16:37-38; 22:25-27), accepting government funding and personnel for his trip to Rome to receive Caesar's
judgment (Acts 25:10-12; 27:1-2).

Jesus quoted the common business proverb "workers deserve their
wages" (Lk 10:7; Mt 10:10) and extended the application to the not-for-
profit sector when he commissioned his disciples for their itinerant ministry. Since Jesus affirms the value of each of the three working sectors,
can we conclude that Christians are able to seek God's kingdom values
through a good job that seeks the common good within *any* sector?

Furthermore, Jesus acknowledged to the Father, "I glorified you on
earth by finishing the work that you gave me to do" (Jn 17:4). He carried out this messianic responsibility in such an excellent fashion that
the Father "exalted him to the highest place and gave him the name
that is above every name, that at the name of Jesus every knee should
bow, in heaven and on earth and under the earth, and every tongue
acknowledge that Jesus Christ is Lord, to the glory of God the Father"
(Phil 2:9-11). Amen! I think we can we infer from his messianic work
that Jesus also gave this same kind of excellence to his job as a builder.
Yet despite Jesus' own role in dignifying work in the business world,
Christianity generally has not had a favorable view of business.

The "Sunday-Monday" gap. What is the connection between our
worship of God on Sunday and "secular" job on Monday? Such "secular
Monday" labor has often been viewed primarily as a means of making
money to support "God's Sunday" ministry. Beyond that, there's a continuing concern about business among most clergy. David Miller explains, "Many business people are hungry to know how to integrate
their faith into work. Unfortunately, most clergy don't know how to

help these parishioners, and they often show benign neglect, or even outright hostility, toward the marketplace."[13]

As a card-carrying member of this group—having been a pastor and now a seminary professor—I became aware of my limiting core belief only late in life. Scott Rae and Kenman Wong note in their business ethics textbook, "The weight of historical Christian thought seems to lean against wholehearted participation in business."[14] From her study of sixty-five evangelical chief executive officers, Laura Nash reported that, "Many evangelical CEOs . . . felt that the clergy were unable to acknowledge the legitimacy of their roles as businesspeople or to see that the problems of business go beyond financial accountability."[15] Have we ever asked those employed in the for-profit sectors about their honest perceptions on this matter? I acknowledge that the church cooperates with the business sector in various ways, such as applying helpful business leadership principles. But these efforts do not address this deep-seated unease in "Christian culture" about business itself.

Several factors contribute to this long-standing disconnect. Christian philanthropist Ken Eldred notes, "The Church tends to have a skeptical view of the role of faith in business, and many in the Church have difficulty making the connection between the two. A subtle divide exists between the Church and business, between business schools and seminaries, and between realms considered sacred and secular."[16] On this last point, A. W. Tozer clarifies this underlying tension, writing about our relationship with God.

> One of the greatest hindrances to internal peace which the Christian encounters is the common habit of dividing our lives into two areas, the sacred and the secular. As these areas are conceived to exist apart from each other and to be morally and spiritually incompatible, and as we are compelled by necessities of living to be always crossing back and forth from the one to the other, our inner lives tend to break up so that we live

---

[13]"Scripture and the *Wall Street Journal*," an interview by Collin Hansen, *Christianity Today*, November 2007, p. 33.

[14]Scott Rae and Kenman Wong, *Beyond Integrity*, 2nd ed. (Grand Rapids: Zondervan, 2004), p. 73.

[15]Laura Nash, *Believers in Business* (Nashville: Thomas Nelson, 1994), pp. 279-80.

[16]Ken Eldred, *God Is at Work* (Ventura, Calif.: Regal, 2005), p. 269.

a divided instead of a unified life. . . . This is the old sacred-secular antithesis. Most Christians are caught in its trap.[17]

Yet this false dichotomy has become entrenched in an institutional way in the church. Isn't there an implied pecking order of value within our Christian culture about kinds of work? Persons called to "full-time Christian ministry" (missions, pastoring, teaching at a seminary) are often perceived as having greater value to God than those in roles without such a calling (e.g., business owner, plumber, homemaker). Sadly, such hierarchical valuing negatively impacts believers in business. John Beckett, chairman of R. W. Beckett, shares,

> For years, I thought my involvement in business was a second-class endeavor—necessary to put bread on the table, but somehow less noble than more sacred pursuits like being a minister or a missionary. The clear impression was that to truly serve God, one must leave business and go into "full-time Christian service." Over the years, I have met countless other business people who feel the same way.[18]

Geoffrey Bromiley bemoans the "unfortunate distinction between the laity and the clergy, or the secular and the sacred, or the secular and the religious, or the people and the Church, which has caused so much mischief in both doctrine and practice."[19] Can we affirm that all believers are called to full-time Christian ministry as we labor in different job sectors?

I'll summarize my key points about work before proposing some practical formational implications. This summary helps provide a background for our discussion of money in the next section.

Creation is good and thus physical matter is good. Work is normative for humans, part of our design and destiny. Work has eternal intrinsic value. All good labor is equally pleasing to God. There is no hierarchy of ultimate job valuations among the three sectors: for-profit, not-for-profit and public. Jesus affirmed work within each sector. A

---

[17]A. W. Tozer, *The Pursuit of God* (Harrisburg, Penn.: Christian Publications, 1948), p. 117.

[18]John Beckett, *Loving Monday* (Downers Grove, Ill.: InterVarsity Press, 1998), p. 69. Beckett was named Christian Businessman of the Year by the Christian Broadcasting Network (1999) and manufacturing Entrepreneur of the Year by Ernst & Young (2003).

[19]Geoffrey W. Bromiley, "Vocation," in *International Standard Bible Encyclopedia*, ed. Geoffrey W. Bromiley (Grand Rapids: Eerdmans, 1998), 4:995.

robust and substantial for-profit sector is required to sustain the not-for-profit and public sectors. Many of us earn money through our labor to meet our material needs and so we can share with others. Workers are worthy of their wages and businesses must make a profit so wages can be paid. Some jobs are more spectacular, others more mundane, and people may wish they could have done other kinds of work. Regardless, in doing good work, we each can cooperate with God for kingdom values and purposes, being empowered by the Spirit of God. We can infer, from our study in chapter five, that Jesus himself exemplified such daily living at his building job.

A formation approach to our job, our ministry, our work. Christians desire guidance for how to integrate their God life with their work life—especially those in the business sector. Ken Eldred suggests one integrative model that highlights a threefold Christian ministry focus at the office:

1. a ministry *at* work: pointing those around us to God

2. a ministry *of* work: serving and creating via work itself

3. a ministry *to* work: redeeming the practices, policies and structures of institutions[20]

Pointing others to God has been a traditional and important idea. Let's also expand our horizons to include the other two, of doing work well and also improving how work is done, regardless of our full- or part-time occupations as mother, as flight attendant or as nurse. Doing our work well and interacting well with those around us not only gets the job done, but can help Jesus' peace to dissolve the frustration and anxiety others may carry, improving the relational interactions that are part of our work.

For example, what happens when people notice our good actions? Bill Heatley, an IT professional, wanted to invite God to operate in and through him. Specifically one way to do this was by looking for ways to appreciate and support his fellow colleagues, providing space for God's love. Bill was involved in a project in which two departments were co-

---

[20]Ken Eldred, *The Integrated Life* (Montrose, Colo.: Manna, 2010), p. 107.

ordinating aspects of the project. His counterpart from the other department was a woman who was well prepared and "sweating the details," so he could anticipate a productive meeting for the project. The only problem was that these two groups had an eighteen-month history of feuding and Bill was new on the job. In light of this history Bill "did three simple things: I prayed for her. I thanked the management in another meeting, and I sent an email to her boss expressing my appreciation for her hard work."[21] The results were surprising—"the effect was immediate and beyond any reasonable explanations from my efforts."[22] Tension was eased and greater cooperation became evident between the two departments. As a result of this powerful experience, Heatley confessed, his God-confidence increased, encouraging him to look for more opportunities to make space for God at work.

We may not often see how doing good work may involve life-and-death circumstances. David Larsen shared with me how he greatly appreciated the smooth roads paved by the works department in Dallas, Texas. The pothole-free streets permitted an ambulance to transport his granddaughter, whose life was threatened by any major jostling, from one hospital to another without a mishap.[23] Each day we have the opportunity to cooperate with God the Holy Spirit, fulfilling our design and destiny at work. Pastoral responsibility for equipping "God's people for the works of service" (Eph 4:12) includes teaching the wide range of ministries Eldred noted above to help all of us be kingdom representatives at work.[24]

Work prayer projects. Consider these prayer projects as a way to emphasize a formation approach at work.

a. Reflect on Jesus' work as builder with stone and wood, probably for eighteen years of his life. Talk with Jesus about your reflections. Do any insights have implications for your work?

---

[21]Bill Heatley, *The Gift of Work* (Colorado Springs: NavPress, 2008), pp. 32-33.
[22]Ibid., p. 32.
[23]David Larsen, personal communication, June 30, 2011.
[24]For further study on work see Wong and Rae, *Business for the Common Good*. See Saddleback Church's website for an example of such an equipping emphasis, initiated by Helen Mitchell <www.saddleback.com/lake forest/adults/atwork>.

b. William Peel and Walter Latimer propose we first build a platform of credibility with fellow employees so they'll be more receptive to hearing about Jesus. We earn credibility to share the good news through developing a good track record in each of these three areas: *competency* (doing excellent work on the job), *character* (making wise job decisions of integrity) and *consideration* or *concern* (showing genuine mercy and compassion for our colleagues).[25] Consider the past month at work. Does a particular event or person come to mind that requires some further formational attention?

c. Envision yourself partnering with Jesus to do your work well, since Jesus is very interested in your job as part of his kingdom. Talk with Jesus about how it's going, your hopes, ways to do your work more excellently and new ideas to fulfill your company's overall mission.

Practice 2: Trusting God's Provision While Wisely Using Money on Loan from God

Jesus taught us proper attitudes about money through example and teaching. During Jesus' forty-day wilderness fast, he waited for God's provision of food rather than turning stones into bread (Mt 4:3-4, 11). From his teachings we infer that while Jesus was a builder, he practiced wise stewardship of his material resources. For example, in the parable of the talents, the servants were loaned money (1, 2 or 5 talents) in order to make a profit for the landowner (Mt 25:14-30). Jesus portrayed the landowner (representing either our Abba Father or himself as King) as someone who expected *more back* than what he'd loaned each servant. This required wise risk taking.

The Sermon on the Mount and money. The Sermon on the Mount (Mt 5–7) is regarded as a summary of Jesus' major teachings. One of the passages discussed in the next section, Matthew 6:19-34 (cf. Lk 12:22-34), represents about one-sixth of that sermon, indicating how important to Jesus our attitudes about money are. As you'll note, most of the biblical study in this section is based on Luke (including parallel

---

[25]William Peel and Walt Larimore, *Going Public with Your Faith* (Grand Rapids: Zondervan, 2004).

teaching in other Gospels) who includes the greatest portion of Jesus' teaching on money. According to Walter Pilgrim, "Luke's extensive discussion of wealth and poverty is addressed primarily to the rich."[26] Let me summarize Pilgrim's concept of the main message of Luke-Acts on this topic for the poor and the rich: The *poor* can be assured that God is for them, that hope can arise since all their needs will be bountifully met in the future kingdom and that, in the present, the renewed Christian community will care for their needs with compassion and justice. The *rich* need to be alerted to the dangers of the temptations of wealth and also to the call to discipleship in using their possessions with "a new standard of giving and sharing."[27]

Who can be considered "rich"? Perhaps anyone who's thrown away food he or she didn't eat?[28] Regardless of which group we fit in, Jesus' teaching offers important guidance for all.

In the passage on counting the cost of discipleship, Jesus uses the phrase "cannot be my disciple" three times (Lk 14:25-35, emphasis added):

> If anyone comes to me and does not hate father and mother, wife and children, brothers and sisters—yes, even life itself—such a person *cannot be my disciple*. (v. 26)

> And whoever does not carry their cross and follow me *cannot be my disciple*. (v. 27; Lk 9:23 adds "daily")

> In the same way, those of you who do not give up everything you have *cannot be my disciples*. (v. 33)

How shocking these strong words "hate father and mother" would be for a communitarian culture! It's obvious Jesus isn't literally commanding believers to hate family members, or to carry a large wooden cross of crucifixion around each day, or to divest all possessions. Rather, Jesus uses Semitic hyperbole to punctuate the point that our first priority above all must be Jesus. He believes we can easily become

---

[26]Pilgrim, *Good News*, p. 163.
[27]Ibid., pp. 160-66.
[28]You can go to <globalrichlist.com> and input your annual salary in dollars. You'll get a percentage of where your income places you in relation to the world's income, based on 2000 income data. The median global income is *$850 per year*.

distracted from serious discipleship in these arenas: family, self, money. Yet as believers we must be *ready* to experience losses within one or more arenas to be faithful to Jesus. We are challenged to cultivate a heart attitude of non-attachment about our possessions. What does that look like?

Jesus' teaching on money and discipleship. Consider a series of five themes that emerge from Jesus' Sermon on the Mount in Matthew 6:19-34 (parallel concepts in Lk 12:22-34):

1. Stop letting obsessive *worry* about material needs overwhelm us; it demonstrates a lack of trust in God ("little faiths," Mt 6:30; Lk 12:28). Through such paralyzing anxiety we become enslaved to money (Mt 6:24-25) and act like those outside God's family.

2. Grow our *trust* in God's provision for material needs. Nature offers a daily reminder: If God provides food for birds and beauty for flowers, God can provide for his more valuable children (Mt 6:26; Lk 12:26). Trusting in God frees us to pursue God's kingdom as a number one priority (Mt 6:32-33; Lk 12:30-31).

3. Be *thankful* to God for past provision of material needs. God already knows and cares about our material needs (Mt 6:32; Lk 12:30). Paul's prayer captures well these three particular themes: "Do not be anxious about anything, but in everything, by prayer and petition, with thanksgiving, present your requests to God. And the peace of God, which transcends all understanding, will guard your hearts and your minds in Christ Jesus" (Phil 4:6-7; Paul uses the same Greek word for "anxious/worry" as in Mt 6:25-34).

4. *Manage* wisely the finances God entrusts to our care, with an eye on the *future*. Jesus commands, "store up for yourselves treasures in heaven," (Mt 6:20), and "make yourselves purses . . . an unfailing treasure in heaven" (Lk 12:33 NRSV), giving our utmost attention and ambitions to what lasts for eternity. Jesus commands us to become a "faithful and wise manager" (Lk 12:42; 16:10-12). At death, we'll give an account for our use of God's material resources on loan to us, as illustrated in two parables (Mt 25:14-30; Lk 19:11-27; cf. Mt 12:36-37). To give a good account requires wise planning in this life.

5. *Give* generously to the needy from your material resources on loan from God. "Sell your possessions and give [alms] to the poor" (Lk 12:33; Mt 6:2-4). Jesus provides a basis for our giving now, "Do not be afraid, little flock, for your Father has been pleased to give you the kingdom" (Lk 12:32; Mt 25:34). With such a grand inheritance guaranteed—the new heavens and new earth involving both immaterial and material benefits—we can grow trust in God now for our own material needs and increase our generous sharing with the needy.

Paul's exhortation to wealthy Christians provides a reflection on these five themes—don't worry, trust, be thankful, manage, give—as well as a helpful summary of the apostolic teaching for believers with surplus wealth:

> Command those who are rich in this present world not to be arrogant nor to put their hope in wealth, which is so uncertain, but to put their hope in God, who richly provides us with everything for our enjoyment. Command them to do good, to be rich in good deeds, and to be generous and willing to share. In this way they will lay up treasure for themselves as a firm foundation for the coming age, so that they may take hold of the life that is truly life. (1 Tim 6:17-19)[29]

We are enjoined to trust God for our material needs, to enjoy creation and to be generous in giving to the needs of others. Believers need not divest themselves of their wealth. Yet God often uses a precarious financial situation as a reminder to increase our trust in him and not worry about our needs.

The "money is worldly" gap. I've heard Paul's saying about money commonly misquoted, that money itself is the root of all evil. Rather, "the *love* of money is *a* root of all kinds of evil" (1 Tim 6:10, emphasis added). Although I never consciously thought about it, in my underlying core worldview beliefs I think I regarded money to be basically "worldly"—of the material world, which meant someone in "full-time ministry" shouldn't give much thought to money. As I'll mention later,

---

[29]For some helpful reflections on this passage, see Rene Padilla, "Taking Hold of the Life That Is Truly Life," in *On Kingdom Business*, ed. Tetsunao Yamamori and Kenneth Eldred (Wheaton, Ill.: Crossway, 2003), pp. 310-14.

that had significant downsides (and I still worried about money but I wasn't aware of how anxious I was at the time). This incorrect idea is part of a larger viewpoint that matter is evil and that only the immaterial or spirit is good. Perhaps it was the case that I unknowingly misinterpreted Paul's exhortation, "Set your minds on things above, not on earthly things" (Col 3:2). David Garland identifies this potential pitfall, "We need to be careful to avoid injecting any potentially gnostic ideas that the world above is the pure realm and that the earthly dimension of our lives is somehow impure, evil, or useless. . . . Christians are not called to escape the world but to be obedient to God within it, allowing the transcendent dimension where Christ reigns to set the priorities for our lives."[30]

Gnosticism was a heretical view that "higher knowledge" was only accessible to the enlightened elite (*gnosis*, Greek for "knowledge"; it is mentioned in 1 Tim 6:20). For this group, matter was "intrinsically evil and the source from which all evil has arisen."[31] Yet in Colossians 3:2, Paul is making a contrast between our former non-Christian lifestyle (where we are oriented by "earthly things") with our new lifestyle in Christ (where we are oriented by "things above"), similar to the contrast Paul makes elsewhere between living by the "flesh" (living by our own human resources, particularly the Jewish laws and traditions) versus living by the Holy "Spirit" (Rom 8:1-17). And our eternal future is related to a very physical place. Life in the next age involves a material new earth (Rev 21–22), with glorified, resurrected physical bodies living in a physical world. So within a Christian understanding, spirit is good and so is physical matter, and money is simply an economic tool to use for good or ill.

But this particular money gap had negative consequences. I'm embarrassed to admit that I thought Jesus commanded us not to give much thought to financial planning. I wrongly assumed that were I to set specific financial goals and monitor my progress then I would be neces-

---

[30]David Garland, *Colossians, Philemon*, NIV Application Commentary (Grand Rapids: Zondervan, 1998), p. 214.

[31]A. M. Renwick, "Gnosticism," in *International Standard Bible Encyclopedia*, ed. Geoffrey W. Bromiley (Grand Rapids: Zondervan, 1992), 2:486.

sarily worrying about money. It seems throughout our thirty-five years of married life my wife, Beth, and I have had various seasons of financial pressure due to this inattention to financial planning. The study of Jesus' teaching that appears throughout this chapter has given me a better biblical perspective on the subject. Now I'm spending time setting and monitoring financial goals—without that false guilt—since I've realized how important handling finances is in God's plan.

Helpful resources are available for financial planning. The need is great. In December 2008, Barna Research reported that, due to the economic downturn, a large percentage of families had cut back giving to their church due to "serious financial debt."[32] Having considerable debt almost guarantees persistent worry—a distressed gap that often leads to a distracted gap. Perimeter Church in Atlanta began sponsoring Dave Ramsey's Financial Peace University seminars to help the congregation get a handle on finances. Two initial test groups took this training in 2009 and 2010 and eventually paid down $3 million in debt! Pastor Randy Pope concluded, "We watched the transformation in those people, . . . the way they learned to better steward their money, the way that stresses within marriages were relieved, and we decided to take this to the whole church."[33] Such a testimony affirms how good financial planning can be an important Christian formation practice.

And what about . . . ? The topic of money raises various questions. I will briefly address five key issues. First, there's a common belief about a direct cause-effect relation between wealth and poverty: as the rich get richer, the poor *necessarily* get poorer. This belief is usually portrayed as the proverbial pie. There are a limited number of pieces, so that if my piece is bigger, then necessarily other pieces must be smaller—winners imply losers. The underlying assumption is what is called a

[32]The Barna Group, "Churches Stand to Lose Several Billion Dollars in Lost Donations Due to Economic Downturn" (December 1, 2008) <www.barna.org/donorscause-articles/9-churches-stand-to-lose-several-billion-dollars-in-lost-donations-due-to-economic-downturn>.

[33]Quoted in Timothy Dalrymple, "Debtors' Helpers," *World*, March 26, 2011, p. 63. I've benefitted from the practical materials by Christian radio host Dave Ramsey; *The Total Money Makeover* (Nashville: Thomas Nelson, 2003) and the Financial Peace University DVD series are available at <www.daveramsey.com>. Another resource group is Crown Financial Ministries <www.crown.org>.

zero-sum or win-lose view of economics. This arrangement may have been the case prior to the Industrial Revolution, when wealth was largely based on owning land, and there were limited ways to acquire land—mostly through illegal and oppressive means. Yet today people can create wealth through a variety of good paths apart from owning land. The pie analogy doesn't represent the economics of today.

Despite evidence for this, sadly, many still hold the pie analogy as a core belief. This limiting perspective has debilitating effects on the community in two respects. Lawrence Harrison, a former USAID officer, clarifies that "The zero-sum worldview discourages initiative since anyone's gain is someone else's loss. [Furthermore] in many traditional societies . . . people who 'get ahead' are pulled back with a variety of sanctions, including redistribution of their wealth to the community."[34] Jesus' parable of the talents (Mt 25:14-20) and the minas (Lk 19:11-27) actually challenges this limited resources/zero-sum perspective—two servants doubled the master's money—and affirms some form of risk taking and market exchange. Contemporary economics includes the greatest potential of a win-win arrangement for all, as economist Charles Wheelan notes, "In theory, a world in which every individual was educated, healthy, and productive would be a world in which every person lived comfortably. . . . Economics tells us that there is no theoretical limit to how well we can live or how widely our wealth can spread."[35]

Theologian John Schneider affirms this optimistic note. Based on a study of the Garden of Eden, the Promised Land, the messianic banquet and Jesus' life, he argues that "it is a fundamental biblical theme that material prosperity (rightly understood) is the condition that God envisions for all human beings. . . . [Conditions of affluence in advanced societies] are good in the potential they have for human flourishing and, through it, the flourishing of the cosmos as God wills it to be."[36]

---

[34]Lawrence Harrison, *The Central Liberal Truth* (New York: Oxford University Press, 2006), pp. 40-41.

[35]Charles Wheelan, *Naked Economics* (New York: Norton, 2002), p. 115.

[36]John Schneider, *The Good of Affluence* (Grand Rapids: Eerdmans), p. 3. I agree with Schneider when he clearly disassociates his view from any type of "prosperity gospel" (pp. 4-5). Such a

Surely Jesus' lifestyle evidences enjoyment of life. Note the criticism "Here is a glutton and a drunkard" (Mt 11:19; Lk 7:34). Walter Pilgrim comments, "The Gospels as a whole recognize that possessions are both necessary and good gifts of God, a view that emerges in [Luke's] portrait of Jesus as well. . . . Luke's portrayal of Jesus' life depicts a person who rejoices in life and accepts the goodness of God's creation, including some of the things that only money can buy."[37]

Second, a related misconception is that earning a profit is itself an evil. Is it a background presumption that any for-profit venture is only about chasing "filthy lucre," the King James Version's term to convey "dishonest gain" (1 Tim 3:3; Tit 1:7, 11; 1 Pet 5:2)? This term became associated in some Christian circles to apply to *any* profit, dishonest or not. But without the possibility of earning some profit, there would be no motivation to launch a business, create more jobs or expand one's business to serve more people. Cofounder of Hewlett-Packard Dave Packard explains,

> I think many people assume, wrongly, that a company exists simply to make money. While this is an important result of a company's existence, we have to go deeper and find the real reasons for our being. As we investigate this, we inevitably come to the conclusion that a group of people get together and exist as an institution that we call a company so that they are able to accomplish something collectively that they could not separately—they make a contribution to society, a phrase which sounds trite but is fundamental.[38]

In the parable of the talents, Jesus has the master praising the profit earners and rebuking the one not earning a profit (Mt 25:21, 23, 26; Lk 19:13, 15; see also Prov 14:23; 31:18; Jas 4:13). We can imagine that Jesus, as a builder in Nazareth, earned a profit—an amount of money or bartered goods beyond costs of materials and other overhead—to contribute to meeting family needs.

---

view of a fully realized kingdom now doesn't fit with Jesus' teaching, for in a key "prosperity" passage, along with gaining material benefits we must also endure persecution (Mk 10:30).
[37]Pilgrim, *Good News*, p. 124.
[38]Dave Packard, cited in Charles Handy, "What's a Business For?" *Harvard Business Review*, December 2002, p. 54.

Third, what about the *inequality* of possessions? Some scholars argue that the Greek term *isotes* in 2 Corinthians 8:13-14 should be interpreted as "equality of possessions." Yet most commentators regard the two occurrences in these verses as identifying a principle of "fairness" (see Col 4:1) or doing one's "fair share," which becomes the motivation and ground of generous giving. Furthermore, within a win-win economic framework, inequalities will be normal and not necessarily evil. Jesus' parable of the talents implies that inequality is an ordinary aspect of life. Theologian Wayne Grudem is more blunt: "God has never had a goal of producing equality of possessions among people, and he will never do so. In the Year of Jubilee (Leviticus 25), agricultural land returned to its previous owner and debts were cancelled, but there was no equalizing of money or jewels or cattle or sheep, and houses inside walled cities did not revert to the previous owner (v. 30)."[39]

Fourth, what about the Old Testament prohibition against *usury*, charging interest on loaned money (Ex 22:5; Lev 25:35-37; Deut 23:19-20)? The main issue is abusive practice, particularly against the poor regarding their basic necessities of life. Business loans that don't impose such hardships are a different matter. In two parables Jesus affirms the use of such interest, when he has the master scold the lazy servant, "Why then didn't you put my money on deposit, so that when I came back, I could have collected it with interest?" (Lk 19:23; also Mt 25:27). Regarding the Old Testament passages, Grudem explains, "if we look at those passages [and related ones] in detail, and understand them in their proper historical context, they seem only to prohibit taking advantage of the poor in their poverty."[40] Jay Richards agrees, "The church didn't decide that usury was OK, however. Rather, it became much more precise in defining usury. Usury isn't charging interest on a loan to offset the risk of the loan and the cost of forgoing other uses for the money; it's unjustly charging someone for a loan by exploiting them when they're in dire straits. That's the work of loan sharks, not banks."[41] The final issue is addressed under the next header.

---

[39]Wayne Grudem, *Business for the Glory of God* (Wheaton, Ill.: Crossway, 2003), pp. 52-53.
[40]Ibid., p. 67.
[41]Jay W. Richards, *Money, Greed, and God* (New York: HarperOne, 2009), p. 144.

What about Jesus' command to sell all? Money is something we may feel guilty about, especially if we have more than what is necessary for basic living. Isn't Jesus' command to the rich young ruler the *normative* lifestyle model for *all* Christians, to give it all away? ("If you want to be perfect, go, sell your possessions and give to the poor, and you will have treasure in heaven. Then come, follow me" [Mt 19:21; Lk 18:22].)

Imagine Joe Christian giving up all he possesses and never again owning anything. To simplify the case, we'll assume he's single without dependents. Once all assets are distributed, what does Joe do next? How does he pay for food? Where does he go to sleep? One option is to arrange life as some homeless persons do and regularly cobble together leftover items from others for food, clothing and shelter. Or one could become attached to a wealthy patron who supplies all necessities in exchange for some good service as has been done in the past by artists or teachers of the patron's children.

Another option might be to join a covenant community in which Joe exchanges his labor for food, clothing and shelter. Of course the community, or persons in the community, will need to have access to (own/rent) a location for sleeping and living, and a means for earning regular income to sustain the community. The problem is that the matter of "possession" is just transferred from the individual to the community. Why shouldn't the command about giving up all possessions also apply to that community as well? I think it becomes obvious that giving up all one's possessions can only work for a few, if these few without possessions can rely on others who have possessions to help sustain their living. It's not an option for the majority.

What does Jesus intend with such absolutist statements? He wants to shock us into becoming aware of our worldview gaps. Jesus reminds us that we own nothing, that we have no genuine possessions, since all is on loan from God for us to manage wisely. The rich young ruler was not aware of his gap of idolatry, of putting his trust in wealth rather than in God. His negative response pointed out he was not yet willing to change. When we're confronted about our gaps, are we *willing to change?* Imagine you're the rich young ruler. How would you have responded to Jesus' challenge? Let's consider the following hypothetical positive response, although it may have taken some time to process this jarring challenge by Jesus.

> You're right, my money is my security. I'm ashamed. I've been an idolater. Oh Lord God, will you forgive me? Okay, Lord Jesus, I'm willing to do what you've commanded. It's going to take some time to liquidate all my assets, and it needs to be done very carefully. I've got a number of families who work for me and count on me for their livelihood. I want to make sure this process does no harm to them. I'll need to find them other employment.

Now there's room for wise guidance to take the next steps. Based on the tenor of Jesus' teaching about money, I suspect Jesus' purpose was to open up the young man's heart, not necessarily to give up all his money permanently. Continuing this hypothetical scenario, perhaps Jesus would have counseled him to become a wiser manager and generous giver of his possessions. Later, Jesus might have encouraged him to connect with Zacchaeus, another rich person who was experimenting with how to handle money entrusted to him (both probably lived in Judea; Mt 19:1; Lk 19:1). Jesus' absolutist statements jar us out of our complacency to awaken us to our gaps and help move us toward greater freedom and kingdom living.

Regarding Zacchaeus: without a specific command from Jesus, this chief tax collector volunteers to give away half of his wealth to the poor and to make a fourfold restitution for any fraud—an announcement Jesus praises as evidence of genuine salvation (Lk 19:8-10). Walter Pilgrim "regards the story of Zacchaeus as the most important . . . text [in Luke] on the subject of the right use of possessions. Luke intends this text as the paradigm par excellence for wealthy Christians in his community."[42]

Although Jesus required his own twelve disciples to travel without purse or extra clothes, yet at the Last Supper Jesus told them they'd need to return to their previous financial lifestyle. "'When I sent you without purse, bag or sandals, did you lack anything?' 'Nothing,' they answered. He said to them, *'But now* if you have a purse, take it, and

---

[42]Pilgrim, *Good News*, p. 129.

also a bag; and if you don't have a sword, sell your cloak and buy one'" (Lk 22:35-36, emphasis added). Bock explains this change, "Disciples are to engage the world, but [now] they will have to take care of themselves. . . . [in a manner of] readiness and self-sufficiency, not revenge" (the sword being a symbol of basic protection in that day).[43] In its early stages the Christian church was able to care spontaneously for the needs of the poor (Acts 2:44-45; 4:32). But as the church grew, caring for the needy required more intentionality and coordination on the part of leadership (Acts 6:1-6; 11:27-30).[44]

Jesus' point in his shock teaching on giving up all is for his followers to develop kingdom priorities and a view of themselves as stewards responsible for faithful use of the King's possessions. That's a lifelong challenge for us all.

More financial lifestyle options. Is it inherently evil to own much surplus wealth? Some have relied on the parable of the rich fool and Amos' judgment as biblical support for an affirmative response. I suspect that an underlying zero-sum economic framework plays an important role in that interpretation. The parable of the rich fool is not a condemnation of surplus wealth per se, but a judgment of a life which "is not rich toward God," with no compassion for the needy (Lk 12:21). Nolland clarifies, "The verse does not directly criticize the accumulation of wealth (though elsewhere Luke is insistent upon its dangers) but is content to emphasize the need to be rich in a Godward direction."[45] We see this view in Paul's advice to pastor Timothy for wealthy Christians: "Instruct those who are rich in this present world . . . to put their hope in God . . . to be rich in good deeds, and to be generous and willing to share" (1 Tim 6:17-18). Amos' prophetic judgment on the rich of his day conveys a similar point. "Woe to you who are complacent in Zion. . . . You drink wine by the bowlful and use the finest lotions, but

---

[43]Darrell Bock, *Luke 9:51–24:53*, Baker Exegetical Commentary on the New Testament (Grand Rapids: Baker, 1996), p. 1747.

[44]Some regard holding possessions as "common property" (Acts 4:32) as the norm for the church, yet Peter affirmed the personal right of private property (Acts 5:4) and Jesus affirmed it for the next age (Lk 16:11-12)—a delegated right, since God owns all. Peter's family still lived in a house (Mk 1:29; 9:33) although Peter had "left everything" (Mk 10:28).

[45]John Nolland, *Luke 9:21–18:34*, Word Biblical Commentary 35B (Dallas: Word, 1993), p. 687.

you do not grieve over the ruin of Joseph" (Amos 6:1, 6; see also Rev 3:17). Schneider notes, "Their whole spirituality expresses a lack of proper, sacred grief for the suffering around and about them."[46]

Can we affirm that there is a wide spectrum of financial lifestyles in which Christians can please God? Some may choose to retain and use more surplus wealth for kingdom purposes, others may retain some surplus, some may chose for a season to live dependently on others' financial support, and still others may choose to live with a minimum of surplus wealth. For an example of this last option, consider Christian author Evan Howard and his wife Cheri's testimony.

> After a season of study and exploration, we decided to commit ourselves to a standard of living resembling the United States' official definition of "poverty." We've kept to this standard pretty much all of our 33 years of marriage thus far. While some thought we're depriving ourselves, we've found it a wonderful life indeed. We have few financial obligations and no debt. We spend little on clothing and entertainment and enjoy a life of making music, reading stories, and growing food. Our two daughters were raised within this lifestyle and have chosen similar values for their own lives as adults. Over time we've grown to appreciate not only the strictly economic dimension of a life of simplicity, but also to seek to live into a life of humility and harmony with the earth. For us the choice to live simply has been a choice to live the richest life we could conceive.[47]

Believers, with the support of their Christian community, can discern what appropriate financial lifestyle to adopt, fitting their occupational calling—and being rich in serving God and caring for the needy. Furthermore, there are sufficient good role models from church history and contemporary life who have chosen differing financial lifestyle patterns along this continuum. Let's extend grace to each other to make voluntary choices about the matter without being judgmental. Why assume we know best how others should use their material resources on loan from God to them?

Money prayer projects. Consider the following prayer projects to

---

[46]Schneider, *Good of Affluence*, p. 105.
[47]Evan Howard, personal communication, March 14, 2011.

ponder further our attitudes about money.

a. Reread the section above regarding the five themes emerging from Jesus' teaching about money and meditate on Matthew 6:19-34 and Luke 12:22-34. Restate the five key themes in your own words as you journal and talk with God. Then meditate on 1 Timothy 6:17-19. Reflect on what comes to mind and any movements in your heart.

b. Meditate on Philippians 4:6-7 and bring to mind some recent worries about finances. Take each before the Lord. Become more intentional about reciting Philippians 4:6-7 as a prayer response when worry arises; attend to the resulting peace.

Finally, we come to the important theme of giving. More will be said about the poor and global poverty in this section.

Practice 3: Giving Generously

Sharing possessions to meet needs is a deeply held value and practice of the Christian church that stems from Jesus' life and teaching. For example, when Paul, the first missionary to the Gentiles, reminded the Ephesian church leaders about his own practice, he claimed to be following Jesus: "In everything I did, I showed you that by this kind of hard work we must help the weak, remembering the words the Lord Jesus himself said: 'It is more blessed to give than to receive'" (Acts 20:35). Although Jesus and his disciples lived on the financial support of others, Jesus directed some of these funds to be given to the needy (e.g., Jn 13:29). Jesus challenged the Pharisees who loved money (Lk 16:14-15) that a key spiritual practice for them to change their "inside" (i.e., heart) would be to give to the poor (Lk 11:39-41), to those who could not return the favor (Lk 14:13-14). Yet sadly it's possible to give without a pure heart, for example, when done for show (Mt 6:2-4; Acts 5:1-11) or done dutifully, without mercy or love (Mt 23:23; Lk 11:42). As we regularly engage in sincere giving, Jesus promises to honor our generosity (Lk 6:35, 38; Mt 6:4). Furthermore, ponder these familiar passages that exemplify giving (emphasis added): "For God so loved the world that he *gave* his one and only Son" (Jn 3:16), and "Christ loved the church and *gave* himself up for her to make her holy" (Eph 5:25-26).

To be generous requires one to have possessions to give. The Holy Spirit has granted some the spiritual empowerment of generous giving (Rom 12:8), which implies a special ability for earning, at least for some of this gifted group. May these generous givers stand out in their example to us, and help mentor the rest of us in generous giving. Financial planner James E. Hughes comments that "families learn more about long-term wealth preservation through giving than they do through spending or accumulating. Values discussions grow easily out of giving to others."[48]

In a chapter tucked near the end of *The Spirit of the Disciplines*, Dallas Willard discusses the influential use of wealth. He observes that the riches of the world will continue to exert their influence over society.

> Someone will control them [possessions], and the fact that *we* do not possess them does not mean that they [riches] will be better distributed. So to assume the responsibility for the right use and guidance of possessions through ownership is far more of a discipline of the spirit than poverty itself. Our possessions vastly extend the range over which God rules through *our* faith. Thus they make possible activities in God's power that are impossible without them.[49]

Willard poses the question, what if Christians directed how the world's wealth would be used to influence the marketplace and society? Willard believes that

> the idealization of nonpossession [that] had the effect of abandoning wealth to Satan and excluding those who control it from the service of God . . . [was a] terrible mistake. . . . [It behooves the church] to develop a ministry that prepares people for that [kind of] service. . . . Possession and right rule over material wealth is a spiritual service of the highest order.[50]

What are some ways to use surplus wealth for kingdom purposes? ***Generous giving and kingdom business.*** In 1991 Scott Lewis, CEO of Scott Machinery in California, became involved in financially sup-

---

[48]James E. Hughes, *Family Wealth*, rev. ed. (New York: Bloomberg, 2004), p. 33.
[49]Dallas Willard, *The Spirit of the Disciplines* (San Francisco: HarperSan Francisco, 1988), p. 202.
[50]Ibid., p. 203.

porting Campus Crusade's *Jesus Film* as an evangelistic tool, and personally participated in showing the film in Mexico and Albania. He was so excited about his experiences of seeing people come to know Jesus for the first time he decided to sell his business and become a missionary. But the planned sale began unraveling. So Lewis informed God that if the sale didn't go through, he would liquidate the assets and go overseas. One morning a couple of weeks before the planned shutdown of the business, Lewis woke up early, hearing the Lord say, "No, I don't want you to go to Albania, and I don't want you to get rid of the business. I want you to stay right here."[51]

At a conference a few months later, Scott and his wife heard Bill Bright (d. 2003), founder of Campus Crusade for Christ, make the challenge for twelve hundred people to give one million dollars to support the Jesus Film outreach around the world. The Lewises sensed God's encouragement, but they had no idea how this was possible. The past year they had given $17,000 total to charities. After the talk, Lewis met with Bright. "Sir, how do we do this? We don't have $1 million in our wildest dreams." After learning what Lewis had given last year Bright said, "'Good, but why don't you start the first of the year with a goal of, say, $50,000.' I said, 'Excuse me?' He said, 'Start with a goal of $50,000.' I said, 'Alright.' . . . He said, 'Watch what God does to your business. I bet you the next year you will be doubling that.'"[52] Lewis made the commitment and God provided in many remarkable ways to enable him to give over $50,000 in that next year. By 2001 they reached the cumulative giving goal of one million dollars, and haven't stopped yet.[53] Lewis is enthusiastic. "I am a missionary. I am using the skills and talents God gave me to do business for the purpose of making money to fund the fulfillment of the Great Commission. . . . We get a pile of money, and we go shopping—not down at the mall; we go shopping around the world to see where we can use this money to impact the kingdom of God."[54] This

---

[51]Scott Lewis, "Choosing to Give the Rest to the Lord," Generous Giving Conference, Atlanta, Ga., January 14-15, 1999; available at <http://library.generousgiving.org/articles/display.asp?id=3>.
[52]Ibid.
[53]Randy Alcorn, *The Treasure Principle* (Sisters, Ore.: Multnomah, 2001), p. 68.
[54]Lewis, "Choosing."

story and the next one reveal how businesses can be structured to do good and contribute to the kingdom blessing of others on earth.

Tom Chappell developed a business that also provided a way to give away money for good causes. In 1968 Tom gave up his corporate career in Philadelphia, and with his wife, Kate, moved to Maine to enter into a less stress-filled lifestyle. With five thousand dollars in 1974, they founded Tom's of Maine, a company committed to making environmentally friendly products, which became the leading maker of natural toothpaste. By 1981, the company was making $1.5 million in gross sales. The Chappells' first step into corporate philanthropy was a $25,000 donation for the purchase of curbside recycling bins in their hometown of Kennebunk. Later they implemented a new policy of corporate "tithing" at Tom's of Maine as "a commitment to distribute a proportion of our annual pre-tax profits to support education, the arts and humanities, environmental research and protection, and human-need projects such as shelters and programs for the handicapped. Our tithing began at five percent, soon went to seven and is now [1993] at ten percent."[55] Also, employees were permitted to spend 5 percent of their work time for paid volunteer community service.

In 2006, Colgate-Palmolive purchased an 84 percent controlling interest in the firm, allowing Tom's of Maine to function as a stand-alone unit, and Chappell remained on to lead that unit. Colgate-Palmolive agreed to continue Tom's of Maine's business philosophy and corporate philanthropy of giving away 10 percent of pretax profits. At the time of the purchase, annual sales at Tom's had reached about fifty million dollars. Here is a business that was structured to be successful and exemplary in serving customer's needs, treating employees with care and giving back to the community.

But you don't have to be a CEO of a national company to be generous. Despite a modest income as a U.S. postal worker, over his lifetime Thomas Cannon gave more than $140,000 (he died in 2005 at age seventy-nine).[56] Although Cannon grew up in poverty in a wooden

---

[55]Tom Chappell, *The Soul of Business* (New York: Bantam, 1993), p. 49.
[56]Sandra Waugaman and Thomas Cannon, *Poor Man's Philanthropist* (Richmond, Va.: Palari, 2004).

shack with no electricity or indoor plumbing, during the second half of his life he mailed out 140 gifts, usually as $1,000 checks, to deserving individuals whose story in the local newspaper inspired him as an example for others. Among the recipients were a Vietnam vet wheelchair marathoner, a woman with a brain tumor, a widow of an insurance agent killed in a robbery, and teenagers who saved a horse that might have drowned. Seminary professor Craig Blomberg with his family has been able to give away 50 percent of adjusted gross annual income for several years "without abandoning a lifestyle that surely qualifies as enjoying many good gifts that God has richly provided us."[57]

To whom are we morally obligated to give? Whom should we help? The parable of the good Samaritan (Lk 10:29-37) cannot imply that we must meet any need we're aware of. Reality reminds us we're finite with limited resources—we can't help everyone. For thoughtful and compassionate Christians who affirm the responsibility to care for the needy, John Schneider proposes the "principle of moral proximity" as one realistic approach. "For strong moral obligations to exist (the kind that have consequences like the ones Jesus describes), in addition to mere accessibility, the relationship between persons has to have the qualities of moral proximity."[58] We can recognize various concentric circles of concern for our care (e.g., Gal 6:10; 1 Tim 5: 8). Close relational proximity includes those with which we have ultimate *relationships*, our Christian community, immediate community of first order (including spouse, children and friends) and then extends to the broader Christian community: local community, state and nation. There is also a moral proximity within our particular *occupational callings* that can open opportunities beyond our locale.

> In terms of vocation, [our] primary focus will be on the people and various problems that arise within our proper response to it [our vocation, such as an attorney, a teacher or a business executive]. . . . In and through vocation, I believe that they [Christians in developed societies] indeed can [discern moral obligations for global issues], and that it often

---

[57]Craig Blomberg, "A Biblical Theology of Possessions," in *Revolution in Generosity*, ed. Wesley Wilmer (Chicago: Moody Press, 2008), p. 54.
[58]Schneider, *Good of Affluence*, p. 180.

happens that God calls certain people to ministries in places that are far away [other parts of the country or overseas] from their natural communities of obligation.[59]

Accordingly, there will be differences in application among believers. Schneider notes that

> moral proximity will often mean different things to different Christians. The general principle is the same, but it will mean one thing to an unmarried teacher, another to a banker with a large family, and quite another to a professional politician, stay-at-home mother, truck driver, garbage collector, or lonely artist.[60]

In our giving, sometimes we may be prompted to give extravagantly (Jn 12:1-6), and sometimes to give sacrificially (Mt 21:1-4). Kelly, a single mother living in public housing, gave away her much needed weekly laundry money to friend Lisa who had no money and no clean clothes for her kids.[61] Of course, giving can be done in other ways, not just with money, such as sharing our time and our skills as volunteers.

Giving and global poverty. Giving to address the needs of global poverty can be directed toward important relief efforts for basic needs and also toward long-term strategies. Christian leaders in development assistance are employing multiple paths toward societal and institutional solutions that can provide access to health, education, justice and jobs. John Perkins explains,

> To correct economic injustice, we must pursue a strategy of development—empowering people to become self-sufficient through the power of the gospel. Yes, the very lives of the victims of famine and war depend on our relief efforts. We dare not neglect those needs. But the greatest need is for development—to break the cycle of poverty, so that today's receivers become tomorrow's givers.[62]

---

[59]Ibid., p. 181.
[60]Ibid. For example, "relational tithing" could be an application of this principle, in which one covenants with others to pool funds for helping the poor in one's neighborhood. See Darin Petersen, "Relational Tithe: Wealth, Poverty & Communities of Faith" <www.relationaltithe.com>.
[61]Carol Genengels, "Mother's Day Gift," in *Stories for the Spirit-Filled Believer*, ed. Christine Bolley (Lancaster, Penn.: Starburst, 2001), pp. 279-81 (Kelly is not her real name).
[62]John Perkins, *With Justice for All*, 3rd ed. (Ventura, Calif.: Regal, 2007), pp. 12-13.

An initial focus that assists the poor regarding personal finances is to encourage saving as a starting point for capital accumulation through village Savings and Credit Associations (SCAs), such as were used by missionary pioneer William Carey (d. 1834) to empower women in India.[63] Another strategy to assist the entrepreneurial types is small loans (e.g., $50 to $1,000) from microfinance institutions (MFIs) offering access to seed money to start a business. Well-run MFIs' repayment rates can exceed 95 percent, according to Peter Greer, president of HOPE International, a Christian MFI.

Job creation is another important development goal and is one of the main purposes of the "Business as Mission" (BAM) movement, which *Christianity Today* labeled as "the next great wave of evangelization."[64] These overseas "kingdom business" ventures make a financial profit and facilitate the spreading of the gospel in difficult areas to reach. They create jobs in which employees then have funds to support the local economy and to give to their local church. Accordingly, larger companies have been launched through major capital investment, including outsourcing companies that do work for U.S. companies (remember talking to a credit card representative from India?).

It's encouraging to note that recent global economic growth is contributing to the reduction of those in extreme poverty (income less than $1.25 per day). Brookings Institute researchers Laurence Chandy and Goeffrey Gertz estimate that in 2005 there were 1.3 billion people living in extreme poverty, and that in 2010 the number was reduced to under 900 million. They project that by 2015 the number of those in extreme poverty will be lower than 600 million, which is "less than half the number regularly cited in describing the number of poor people in the world today. Poverty reduction of this magnitude is unparalleled in history: never before have so many people been lifted out of poverty over such a brief period of time."[65]

---

[63]Peter Greer and Phil Smith, *The Poor Will Be Glad* (Grand Rapids: Zondervan, 2009), p. 91.

[64]Joe Maxwell, "The Mission of Business," *Christianity Today*, November 2007, p. 24. See also Steve Rundle and Tom Steffen, *Great Commission Companies*, rev. ed. (Downers Grove, Ill.: InterVarsity Press, 2011); C. Neal Johnson, *Business as Mission* (Downers Grove, Ill.: InterVarsity Press, 2009); and <www.lausanne.org/issue-business-as-mission/overview.html>.

[65]Laurence Chandy and Goeffrey Gertz, "Poverty in Numbers: The Changing State of Global

Christian philanthropist Ken Eldred believes kingdom business strategies for missions have great potential and proposes that seminaries and business schools partner to "research and teach the philosophical, theological and practical aspects of Kingdom business. . . . Courses on relevant subjects will open many students' minds to the power and possibilities inherent in Kingdom business as a legitimate and effective missionary pursuit."[66] Randy Alcorn muses regarding his own seminary training, if Jesus taught "more about money than both heaven and hell," why hadn't he ever "had a single course on this subject in Bible college or seminary, though I'd had courses on subjects about which the Bible has a great deal less to say"?[67] If pastors receive such training, then churches could include in their venue of discipleship an emphasis on personal finance and business as mission.

Managing our affairs now with an eye on the future. If there is greater continuity than discontinuity between this life and the next age, then we'll need to avoid these two extreme viewpoints: "Engagement in this life is *all* that matters" and "Engagement in this life has *minimal* eternal value." We can have a flourishing life now, planted as kingdom seeds in this world (Mt 13:37-38) to let our light shine (Mt 5:14-16), and we have a grand life ahead of us, shining in God's future kingdom (Mt 13:43). Perhaps the following analogy captures a both/and perspective.

When I rent a movie, I enjoy watching the bonus features of behind-the-scenes information. For example, in the three Matrix movies (*The Matrix*, 1999; *The Matrix Reloaded*, 2003; *The Matrix Revolutions*, 2003), the main actors endured months of martial arts training for their future performances in the films. For the first movie, they underwent four months of rigorous instruction. For the next two movies, filmed at the same time, it was eight months of physical preparation, during which Carrie-Anne Moss ("Trinity") broke her leg. While these Ma-

---

Poverty from 2005 to 2015" (Washington, D.C.: The Brookings Institution, January 2011), p. 3. On the matter of addressing global poverty, John Schneider highlights the insightful analysis of Peruvian economist Hernando de Soto regarding barriers and the means to raise the living standards of the poor. Schneider, *Good of Affluence*, pp 211-20.

[66]Eldred, *God at Work*, p. 271.

[67]Randy Alcorn, *Money, Possessions, and Eternity*, rev. ed. (Carol Stream, Ill.: Tyndale House, 2003), p. 4.

trix actors were in training for future filming, they were still living their lives as normal humans. Their roles in the future films were guaranteed, but they still had to go through months-long preparation to fulfill their future roles in a maximum way.

How does our current use of our physical stuff on loan from God impact our next life in heaven? Jesus says, "So if you have not been trustworthy in handling worldly wealth, who will trust you with true riches? And if you have not been trustworthy with someone else's property, who will give you property of your own?" (Lk 16:11-12). If we faithfully manage money now, as a generous bonus, God grants us greater rewards in God's future kingdom—perhaps certain responsibilities (Mt 25:21, 23; Lk 19:17, 19) and material resources (Lk 16:11-12). Alcorn states the point more boldly: "God cares a great deal about our money—a great deal more than most of us imagine. . . . It's an index of our spiritual life. . . . How we view our money and possessions is of the utmost importance. What we do with our money will—and I choose these words deliberately—influence the very course of eternity."[68] And since we'll be living four hundred years from now, there's no urgency to finish our lifetime to-do or "bucket list" of dreams and adventures before we die. We can patiently postpone some items till the next age to make room for distinctive kingdom opportunities this side of heaven.

Our wise practice of managing and sharing our material possessions now blesses others, contributes to our own character formation and becomes one important basis for God's reward in eternity. I wish this teaching had been on my radar screen years ago.

I close with John Wesley's famous saying as edited by Dallas Willard: "*get* all you can; *save* all you can; freely *use* all you can within a properly disciplined spiritual life; and *control* all you can for the good of humankind and God's glory. *Giving* all you can would then naturally be part of an overall wise stewardship."[69]

Giving prayer projects. Consider the following suggestions for prayer projects.

---

[68] Alcorn, *Money*, pp. 4, 8, 11.
[69] Willard, *Spirit of the Disciplines*, p. 217.

a. Meditate on the stories of the young ruler (Mt 19:16-22) and Zacchaeus (Lk 19:1-10). Then conduct an imaginary garage sale of *all* your possessions. Reflect, where do I tend to be tightfisted and stingy? Where do I tend to be openhanded and generous? Seek God's guidance on forming a more generous heart.

b. Ponder the ideas and examples about giving that stood out to you. Does an action point come to mind? You may wish to learn more about Christian development efforts to address global poverty and consider giving to groups like HOPE International <www.hope international.org>, John Perkins' Foundation for Reconciliation and Development <www.jmpf.org> or Peacemakers <www.peacemakers .net>.

c. Consider how you might identify with the poor and needy of the world as a spiritual practice. This idea comes from Hebrews 13:3, "Remember those in prison as if you were together with them in prison, and those who are mistreated as if you yourselves were suffering." Of the ideas that come to mind, which one would you like to try out for a limited season? Furthermore, why not get closer and serve the poor with a group doing this on a regular basis?

AWAKE to gaps → ADMIT with honesty → ASK for formation grace → ACT, take a first step

ABIDING in Abba, Jesus, Holy Spirit

Figure 8.1.

Key Points

1. Jesus encourages us to grow our trust in and be grateful for God's provision for material needs, to plan wisely and manage our finances with an eye on the future, and to be generous in sharing our resources with the needy.

2. How we manage our money affects God's kingdom work now and also has implications for the responsibilities and rewards God provides for each of us in the next age. Since we are recipients of God's generos-

ity both now and in the next age, we can grow our hearts as generous givers, sharing our possessions with the needy who are nearby and far away. We will discern when and how and why we give.

3. Exploring Jesus' teaching about money and work can help us address a noticeable divide between church and business. Since probably 80 percent of Christians in this country work in the for-profit sector, it would be helpful for pastors and seminary professors to offer guidance on a theology of work and how to connect one's God life with one's job.

4. Since Jesus worked with his hands as a builder for at least eighteen years, he can genuinely identify with working people and the wide range of coordination needed to get the job done well. For a few years, Jesus was probably also the head of the family building business so he can identify with business owners in the challenges and joys of running a business.

Final Thoughts

To sum up, according to Jesus, "First clean the inside of the cup and dish, and then the outside also will be clean" (Mt 23:26). To be spiritually formed deeply within our inner life involves our participation in a formation process that is supervised and empowered by God the Holy Spirit, who indwells each believer forever. Furthermore, it's not an individual human effort on our part but is supported and sustained within grace-filled, loving relationships in community. This kind of radical change takes place in the depths of our soul: modifying our worldview beliefs into alignment with reality as it really is, and modifying our worldview desires and dispositions toward those that are good and worthy of praise. The Spirit's agenda is facilitating a growing intimacy with and dependence on our trinitarian God, rooted in a deep objective and experiential union with Jesus Christ. The outflow of such changes within our heart is a life that will resemble how Jesus might live your life or my life if he were you or me, living with our abilities and gifts, with our privileges and responsibilities, within the givens of our life circumstances.

Perhaps it would be helpful to go over the material again with a few others as a study project. False, settled, deeply held worldview beliefs take time to be transformed. And developing new core beliefs will require further persistence.

Listed below are the main ideas from each chapter to prompt reflection: Where do I want to go? What do I sense is God's next step for me? Be kind to yourself and consider just *one* area of focus. Invite the Holy Spirit to lead and empower, as you follow Jesus' life and teachings—Jesus, the greatest human hero and our Lord and Savior.

Part 1: A Process for Christian Character Formation

Chapter 1. Living into the life of Jesus is possible and realistic by putting aside an externally focused rule-keeping emphasis to Christian living and instead embracing Jesus' concentration on inner heart formation.

Chapter 2. We'll need to wake up to five broad categories of formation gaps identified by Jesus: disconnected, distressed, dismissive, discrepancy and distracted gaps (table 2.1). Attending to our gaps could be encapsulated in four steps: Awake, Admit, Ask and Act.

Chapter 3. Deep life change is a process (e.g., table 3.2) that involves engaging in relevant formation practices, sustained with divine formation grace. This is part of our kingdom priorities in the present age while God prepares us for living in the next age.

Part 2: Essential Divine Resources of Formation Grace

Chapter 4. When we flourish within our Abba's unconditional love, feeling safe and secure, it's easier to be transparent and admit our gaps to God and others.

Chapter 5. Formation can proceed when we're empowered and mentored by the Holy Spirit, just as Jesus was, living authentically in his humanity as an example for us, relying on the Holy Spirit.

Chapter 6. Formation requires our worldview beliefs to be aligned with reality; reality is uniquely and accurately presented in Scripture, which is inspired by God and which can dynamically impact our heads and hearts (tables 6.1 and 6.2 on Jesus' exemplary practices and virtues).

Part 3: Following Jesus Daily in Our Gaps

Chapter 7. Three exemplary Jesus practices about our relationships include forgiving others, peacemaking in conflicts and developing closer friendships.

Chapter 8. Three exemplary Jesus practices about money include doing our work well, trusting in God's provision while wisely using money on loan from God, and giving generously.

On the next page is a suggested prayer of recollection to use during a thirty-second pause-button break.

Additional resources (further reading, suggested movies) are located on my website: <www.klausissler.com>.

I Am a Breath of God

A Prayer of Recollection

To be read slowly;
pause to respond to the questions if you wish.

Now and then I pause, and listen to my breathing:
    Is it Slow? Quick? Easy? Labored? Congested?

And I ask, how do I feel, now, in my body?
    Relaxed? Tired? Tense? Bored? Weary?

Ruach, pneuma, wind, breath, spirit—
    I am a breath of God, an imaged, living being.

Breath, I invite you in, . . .* . . . fill me, refresh my body.

Spirit, I invite you in, . . .* . . . fill me, refresh my soul.

* take a breath if you wish
ruach, Hebrew (roo-ahk, with a soft "k" sound)
pneuma, Greek (noo-mah)

Acknowledgments

I've been working on this book for about five years, though in earnest the last three years. It's good to be at the end of this writing journey, and I'm glad to express my heartfelt thanks to many who assisted in various ways. My IVP editor, Gary Deddo, valued the book idea, encouraged me, and shepherded the book through the writing and editing phases, offering important suggestions and feedback. I appreciate Talbot School of Theology, Biola University, for sabbatical and research leaves and a climate that encourages research and writing. Thanks especially to deans Dennis Dirks and Mike Wilkins, and to Kevin Lawson, colleague and doctoral program director, for making these leaves possible.

Space prevents listing all of those who've given feedback on different parts of the book—thanks to you all. I will name those who read the whole manuscript: Mark Adler, Carol Amor, Ron Arko, Greg Campbell, Sundi Donovan, Orbe Eguizabal, Joe Gorra, Mary Guleserian, Evan Howard (of Evangelical Scholars in Christian Spirituality), John Israel, Ruth Issler, Keith Kettenring, John Kiemele, David Larsen, Jeff Lightner, David and Mary Norling, Bill Roth, and Jim Wilhoit. Students in two venues offered me the opportunity to teach the material and interact with their questions and suggestions: a Talbot doctoral seminar, January 2010, and early morning Sunday class at church, July 2010.

I'm grateful to the *Journal of Spiritual Formation and Soul Care* and the *Christian Education Journal* for permission to use material that was first published in each journal (these are cited in the book). I appreciate the assistance of Joe Gorra, Tom Kimber and Kevin Nguyen in locating sources, quotations and library books, and Flo Ebeling's help at Biola's interlibrary loan department. I'm sure some ideas in the book came from or were stimulated by Pastor Lance Pittluck's sermons (Anaheim Vineyard). Various people prayed for me in writing this book; especially I want to thank two dear women for this kind of prayerful undergirding: Chris Clelland and Ruth Issler (my mother).

One writes from both head and heart. I'd like to mention various mentors who have contributed to my journey: (academic) Howard Hendricks, Larry Richards, Warren Benson, Jim Dillon, Ted Ward and Dallas Willard; (life coaching) John Finch, Wilkie Au, David Lavenau, Chris Linamen and Bryan Van Dragt; (business) Greg Campbell and David Finkel (of Maui Mastermind). For more than three decades I've received loving encouragement from dear friends J. P. and Hope Moreland. Calvin Miller was gracious to write a foreword. Chip MacGregor, my agent, opened doors and offered encouragement throughout this project.

My wife, Beth, has been my special companion through this writing project—putting up with a bookworm and kindly reading every version of every chapter over these many years. We're both grateful for God's movement in our lives to bring us closer to him and closer to each other. Many thanks. Although the book is not inspired in the technical theological sense and manifests the frailty of a human author, the book is "inspired" in the popular sense that it could not have been written without divine empowerment, encouragement and insights from above that came along the way. Glory be to the Father, the Son and the Holy Spirit.

Name and Subject Index

accountability, 47

Acton Institute, 187n6

Adam (biblical figure), 96, 111

Adventures of Huckleberry Finn, The
(Twain), 66

Alcorn, Randy, 66, 67, 217, 218

altar calls, 53

Amos (prophet), 208-9

anger, 18, 74-75, 167, 179

anthropology, Christology and, 112n7

Arendt, Hannah, 164, 164n11

Arnold, Clinton E., 132n40

arrogance, 160-61

atonement, 113

attachment theory, 90-91

Barna Group, 160, 202

Barnabas (early church leader), 70, 108

Barry, William, 113

Barton, Ruth Haley, 78-79

Basil of Caesarea, 162

Beasley-Murray, George, 54, 119

Beckett, John, 194, 194n18

Benedict of Nursia, 79n33

Benner, David, 44, 57

Bible study: analytical reading and,
138-40; Gospels versus Epistles and,
19; Jesus and Old Testament and, 25;
knowledge versus belief and, 53;
meditative reading and, 136, 138-42;
relational/personal focus and, 140;
scriptural saturation and, 145, 148;
Scripture as source of knowledge and,
142-44, 156; textual focus and, 140;
truth encounters and, 155; willing-
doing gap and, 17; on work, 187n6

Blackburn, Simon, 29

Blomberg, Craig, 214

Bock, Darrell, 34, 119, 190, 190n12,
208

Book of Common Prayer, 79n33

boundaries, 169, 180n42

Bright, Bill, 212

Bromiley, Geoffrey, 194

Brookings Institution, 216-17

Brother Lawrence, 50

Browning, Elizabeth, 102

business as mission movement, 216, 217

busyness, distracted gap and, 47

Calvin, John, 122

Campbell, Ken, 189-90

Campus Crusade for Christ, 212

Cannon, Thomas, 213-14

Carey, William, 216

Carson, D. A., 116, 152

Chalcedonian Definition, 111n5

Chandy, Laurence, 216

change: altar calls and, 53; four-step
framework for, 54-55, 57, 72, 82, 104,
132, 155, 182, 219; in lives of
apostles, 33; priorities and, 80; as
realistic, 16-19; three-phase model of,
71-74; tipping point in, 72, 73-74;
Transtheoretical Model of, 71n20;
truthful feedback and, 57

Chapman, Gary, 89

Chappell, Kate, 213

Chappell, Tom, 213

character formation: abiding in Christ
and, 48-49; awakening by Holy Spirit
and, 131; behavioral results of, 23;
brothers and sisters in Christ and, 35;
change process in, 69-74; in children
versus adults, 23; cognitive and
affective elements of, 28, 28nn22-23;
computer analogy for, 29-30; core
beliefs and, 28; doing and being in,
146-47; effort and, 64-65; eternal
benefits of, 69; example of practice of,
74-75; four-step framework for,
54-55, 57, 72, 82, 104, 132, 155, 182,
219; friend qualities and, 180; grace
for, 221-22; inaccurate views about,
12; of Jesus, 60-63; for kingdom of
God, 63-64; lifestyle patterns and,
77-82; limits of, 33, 33n30; long-term
view of, 77, 82; process for, 221;
questions about, 32-34, 36; versus rule
keeping, 26-27, 27; spiritual practices

and, 75-77; suffering and, 63-64; three-phase change model and, 71-74; treasures for heaven and, 68-69; trinitarian support for, 155n20; work and, 195-96. *See also* formation gaps

child abuse, 174-75n33

childhood, character formation in, 60-62

Christian formation. *See* character formation

church and church community: Bible study and, 140; Christian activities and, 18; conflict resolution in, 174; friendship and, 176-81; God's love through, 102; pastoral equipping and, 196; pettiness within, 161; prophetic commission and, 178n38; relational formation in, 145, 148; reputation of, 160-61, 182; surrogate kinship in, 163-64; unity in, 175, 180, 183; work and, 187-88

Cloud, Henry, 76

Colgate-Palmolive, 213

Communion, 175

confession, 55-56, 180, 181

conflict, peacemaking and, 170-75, 173n28

contempt, anger and, 74-75

controlling tendencies, 30-31, 43-44

conversion. *See* regeneration

core beliefs: change over time in, 69-70, 75-77; discrepancy gap and, 42; dismissive gap and, 40; expectations of God's involvement and, 152; God-image and, 105; grace and, 56-57; individualism versus community and, 179; Jesus as teacher and, 51; lifestyle changes and, 220-22; living the truth and, 53; moral environment and, 29; profession versus lifestyle and, 42-43; questions about, 36; truth encounters and, 154; versus will power, 27-32

Cosden, Darrell, 187

Covey, Stephen, 179

Crabb, Larry, 24n10

creation, God's love and, 100

Crisp, Oliver, 126n33

David (psalmist), 55-56, 139

de Soto, Hernando, 217n65

Demarest, Bruce, 113

depression, God's love and, 101

DiClemente, Carlo, 71n20

discernment, 145-46, 148, 180n41

discipleship: cost of, 198-99; Jesus' centrality to, 21; money and, 199-210; rest and, 36

Divine Conspiracy, The (Willard), 74

divinity of Jesus. *See* dual natures of Jesus

docetism, 110n3

domestic violence, 174-75n33

Douglas, Chuck, 168-69

Douglas, Melissa, 168

Dowd, Sharyn, 117

dual natures of Jesus: authentic human experience and, 111-13; Christian anthropology and, 112n7; dependence on God the Father and, 115-16; dependence on the Holy Spirit and, 115, 118-20; divine ability and, 111-15, 113-14n12; docetism and, 110n3; faith in God and, 116-18, 116n14; formation journey and, 110; Holy Spirit as divine mentor and, 129-32; hypostatic union and, 125; Jesus as example and, 127-29; miracles and, 125-26, 126n33; study of, 110-11, 111n5, 120n23; temptation of Christ and, 120-22; uniqueness of Messiah and, 126-27, 133; veiling of divine attributes and, 122-26, 125nn31-32, 127

Dunn, James, 149

economic crisis of 2008, 27

Eden, Garden of, 96

effort: character formation and, 65, 73, 75-76; kingdom of God and, 64

Eldred, Ken, 152-53, 193, 195, 217

Eldred, Roberta, 152

emotions: distressed gap and, 50-51; listening to, 45-46, 170

empty-handed versus empty-hearted, 68

Enright, Robert, 167
Erickson, Millard, 121n25
ethics: core beliefs and, 28-29; Jesus'
   centrality to, 21, 26n19, 147, 149;
   virtue and, 26n19
evangelism, 196-97
Eve (biblical figure), 96
faith, 70, 151-52
Fall (of human kind), 63
Family Life marriage conferences,
   168-69
fellowship, 177
Ferguson, Sinclair, 123-24
Financial Peace University, 202
Finch, John, 102-3
forgiveness: asking for, 169; continuing
   harm and, 169; friendship and, 176,
   180n42; God's versus ours, 165-66;
   grace and, 64; healing and, 59; Jesus'
   example and, 15; Jesus' mission for us
   and, 164-70; lamentation and,
   169n22; Lord's Supper and, 175; in
   marriage, 168-69; prayer and, 170;
   process of, 167-69; prodigal son and,
   92-93; roots of, 164n11; of son for
   father, 166-67
Forgiveness Is a Choice (Enright), 167
formation gaps: admitting, 103-104;
   awareness of, 44-46, 57, 71-72, 75,
   131; confession and, 55-56;
   disconnected gap as, 48-50, 155;
   discrepancy gap as, 42-46; dismissive
   gap as, 39-42, 53; distracted gap as,
   46-48, 202; distressed gap as, 50-51,
   54, 57, 202; lifestyle patterns and, 79;
   money and, 186, 200-202;
   reinforcement of, 53; summary of,
   51-52, 56, 221; three-phase change
   model and, 74; time for addressing,
   65-67
Foster, Richard, 25, 76
Foundation for Reconciliation and
   Development, 219
France, R. T., 22-23, 35, 38-39n4,
   151-52, 184
free will, 101
friendship, 176-81, 180nn41-42, 183

Frost, Jack, 87
gaps. *See* formation gaps; willing-doing
   gap
Garden of Eden. *See* Eden, Garden of
Garden of Gethsemane. *See*
   Gethsemane, Garden of
Garland, David, 201
generosity: biblical examples of, 210-11;
   biblical exhortations and, 200;
   future-orientation and, 217-19; gifts
   as love language and, 89; God's, 151;
   kingdom purposes and, 185-86n4,
   211-14, 220; moral proximity and,
   214-15; prayer and, 219; relational
   tithing and, 215n60; spiritual health
   and, 184-85
Gertz, Goeffrey, 216
Gethsemane, Garden of, 50-51, 54,
   97-98
giving. *See* generosity
gnosticism, 201
God the Father: as Abba, 97-101,
   104-5, 148-49; abiding in, 145, 155;
   absence and presence of, 102;
   believers' dependence on, 127; Bible as
   Word of, 139; creation and, 100;
   generosity of, 151; greatness of, 96;
   image of, 94-97, 100, 105; Jesus'
   dependence on, 113-18, 127; love
   initiatives of, 101-3, 106; receiving
   love from, 98; rejection by, 99; as
   source of love, 91-95; voice of, 102,
   124. *See also* Holy Spirit; Jesus;
   Trinity
good deeds, heaven and, 69
grace: versus anger, 179-80; character
   formation and, 32-33, 221-22; of
   Christians for each other, 163;
   church's reputation and, 182;
   financial lifestyle options and,
   209-10; forgiveness and, 181;
   formation change and, 55, 56-57;
   God's forgiveness and, 64; God's
   presence and, 101; of Jesus for
   tormenters, 165; long-term view of
   formation and, 82; poem about, 182;
   unconditional love and, 97

Greer, Peter, 216
Grudem, Wayne, 151, 185-86n4, 205
Hagner, Donald, 36, 150
happiness, strategies for, 44-45, 57
hard-heartedness, 39-40, 39-40n5, 42
Harrison, Lawrence, 203
Hawthorne, Gerald, 120, 120n23, 124
Hays, Richard, 116n14
heart: inner life and, 25-26; Jesus'
    example and, 149; transformation of,
    68-69, 145, 148, 164
heart flow work: formation gaps and,
    56; righteousness and, 33-34;
    three-phase model of, 72; trinitarian
    prayer and, 131-32; truth encounters
    and, 154; willing-doing gap and, 31,
    33
Heatley, Bill, 58-59, 195-96
heaven, 32, 33n30, 63, 65-69, 68n18
Hellerman, Joseph, 163
Hewlett-Packard, 204
holiness, perseverance and, 64
Holy Spirit: abiding in, 155; as agent of
    sanctification, 33, 108, 129-30;
    awareness of gaps and, 75; believers'
    dependence on, 133; change in core
    beliefs and, 76; Christian living and,
    134; coming of, 107-8; conviction of
    sin and, 150-51; as copilot, 130-31;
    dependence on, 109n2; empowerment
    for ministry and, 129; formation
    change and, 55; as friend, 107;
    friendship and, 176; illness and, 59;
    indwelling of, 65; as Inner Tutor, 62;
    invitation to, 133; Jesus and, 113-15,
    118-20, 123, 130; kingdom of God
    and, 129n37; lifestyle changes and,
    220-222; as mentor and partner,
    129-32, 133; Scripture and, 139,
    140-41; willing-doing gap and, 17;
    wisdom and, 123-24; work and, 188.
    See also God the Father; Jesus; Trinity
HOPE International, 216, 219
hospitality, 23
Howard, Cheri, 209
Howard, Evan, 209
Hoyt, Dick, 108-9, 109n2

Hoyt, Rick, 108-9, 109n2
Hughes, James E., 211
Human Condition, The (Arendt), 164
humanity of Jesus. See dual natures of
    Jesus
humility, 147
illness, forgiveness and, 59
individualism, 89, 179
Inmac Corp, 153
inner life, 24-26, 24n11, 26n19, 82
Inside Out (Crabb), 24n10
intentionality, lifestyle patterns and,
    78-79
Isaiah (prophet), 39-40n5
Issler, Klaus, 9-10
Iverson, Daniel, 133
James (apostle), 178, 190n12
Jeremias, Joachim, 97-98
Jesus: abiding in, 155; Aramaic
    language and, 97; baptism of, 124;
    blessing of children by, 136-38; as
    builder, 189-92, 196-97, 204n36, 220;
    centrality of, 21; as champion, 15,
    15n1; character formation of, 60-63,
    83, 125; childhood of, 60-63, 123-24;
    disciples of, 176, 178, 207-8;
    emulation of, 127-28, 144-45;
    exorcisms by, 119, 119n20; faith of,
    116-18; forgiveness and, 164-65;
    friendship and, 178; at Gethsemane,
    50-51, 54, 57, 74, 119, 121, 178; God
    the Father and, 97-98, 110, 113-18,
    127; as great moral teacher, 18;
    healings by, 117, 141; as hero, 15-16,
    109-11; as high priest, 112-15; Holy
    Spirit and, 110, 113-15, 118-20,
    123-27, 125n31, 126n33, 130; as
    human example, 144-45, 144n8,
    146-49, 154; humility of, 147; at Last
    Supper, 54; at Lazarus's house, 47;
    leadership of, 147; as Lord of peace,
    183; money and, 210-11; Peter and,
    42, 171-72; on private property,
    208n44; prophetic commission of,
    178n38; resurrection of, 40-41, 70;
    rule breaking by, 25; scriptural
    knowledge of, 143, 143n7; as sinless

sacrifice, 115; sinlessness of, 121-22, 121n25, 128-29; skepticism about ministry of, 41; as source of rest, 35-36; on spiritual practices, 71n19; spiritual practices of, 76-77; suffering of, 63-64; temptation of, 120-22, 120n23, 128-29; as twelve-year-old at temple, 61-62, 123, 124; on unity, 180. *See also* dual natures of Jesus; God the Father; Holy Spirit; Jesus' teachings; Trinity
Jesus Film, 212
Jesus' teachings: abiding in, 48-49; as absolute, 21-23; as burdensome, 19-21; business setting in, 190-91; on divine and human spheres, 119; on forgiveness, 165-166; on heaven, 67; on Holy Spirit, 107; hyperbole in, 22-23, 64-65, 206-7; on inner life, 24-27; interpretation of, 21-23; kingdom of God in, 34-35, 149; on money, 184, 185, 210-11, 218; Paul's writings and, 51n18; prophecy and, 118-19; purpose of parables and, 141; rules and, 19-21, 26-27; on self-denial, 45; on selling all possessions, 205-6; on servanthood and humility, 171; on usury, 205. *See also* Jesus; *specific teachings*
John (apostle), 33, 178, 190n12
John the Baptist, 123
journaling, listening to emotions and, 46
justification, Christ's virtuous life and, 113
Kinnaman, David, 160, 161
Karen, Robert, 90-91
Keating, Thomas, 44-45, 57
Kettering, Keith, 32n27
kingdom of God: already and not yet of, 129n37; character formation for, 63-64; discernment of, 145-46, 148; as grand project, 149; Holy Spirit and, 129n37; in Jesus' teaching, 34-35; meaning of, 35; moral effort and, 64-65; prevalence of in Scripture, 149; righteousness and, 34, 34n32; wealth and poverty and, 211-14

koinonia, 177
Ladd, George, 34
Lambert, Elizabeth, 37-38
lamentation, 169n22
Lane, William, 112, 117, 119-20, 140
Larsen, David, 196
Last Supper, 54
Latimer, Walter, 196-97
Lazarus (biblical figure), 47, 178
leadership, 69, 147
Lewis, C. S., 42-43
Lewis, Scott, 212
lifestyle: character formation through, 77-79; meditative approach and, 136-42; money and, 208-10; routines and, 79-80, 79n33; Sabbath and, 80-82
Living Stones Foundation, 152
Lord's Supper, 175
love: attachment and, 90-91; barriers to, 89-91; deprivation from, 90; expectations about, 105; God as Abba and, 97-98; God's initiatives and, 101-3; Holy Spirit as agent of, 104; image of God and, 94-97, 100; languages of, 89, 105-6; moving toward source of, 91-94, 104-5; parental, 88, 90-91, 92-93, 108-9; receiving from God, 98-100; unconditional, 97, 98-100, 105
Lyons, Gabe, 160, 161
Maier, Gerhard, 140
Manning, Brennan, 99, 161-62
Marshall, I. Howard, 64
Martha (biblical sister of Mary), 47, 178
Mary (biblical sister of Martha), 47, 178
Mary Magdalene (biblical figure), 97
Matrix movies, 217-18
Matthew (apostle), 192
May, Gerald, 82
McKinley, John, 128
McKnight, Scot, 98
mediation, 170-74, 174-75n33, 176, 183
meditation, 136-42
Meilander, Gilbert, 179
microfinance, 216
Microwarehouse, 153

Miller, Calvin, 131
Miller, David, 192-93
miracles, 125-26, 126n33
mission: business as, 216, 217;
  forgiveness and, 164-70; friendships
  and community and, 176-81; Jesus'
  for us, 163-64; peacemaking and,
  170-75; in Sermon on the Mount,
  145, 148
money: business as mission and, 216,
  217; Christian perspectives on,
  185-86n4; common property and,
  208n44; dangers of, 185; debt and,
  202; discipleship and, 199-210;
  financial lifestyle options and,
  208-10; global income levels and,
  198n28; God's provision and, 197,
  199-200, 219-20; inequality and, 205;
  in Luke-Acts, 197-98; management
  of, 199-200; prayer and, 210; profits
  and, 204-5; prosperity gospel and,
  204n36; responsibility and, 185; root
  of evil and, 200-201; Sermon on the
  Mount and, 197-99; usury and,
  205-6; wealth and poverty and,
  202-4, 208-9; work and, 186-97;
  worship and, 184; Year of Jubilee and,
  205. See also generosity
Moo, Douglas, 64
Moreland, J. P., 180
Morris, Leon, 60-61
Moss, Carrie-Anne, 217
Mouw, Richard, 169
Muelhoff, Noreen, 168
Muelhoff, Tim, 168-69
Murray, Andrew, 136, 138
Nash, Laura, 193
nature, as source of wisdom, 143
Naugle, David, 29
New Year's Resolutions, 16
Nolland, John, 41-42, 208
Nouwen, Henri, 96
Novak, Michael, 185-86n4
O'Collins, Gerald, 117
Oden, Thomas, 112-13, 122
Oklahoma City bombing, 168
Oswalt, John, 39-40n5

Owen, John, 126n33
Packard, Dave, 204
Packer, J. I., 32
Palmer, Parker, 101, 180n41
parable of the four soils, 38-39n4,
  39-48, 57
parable of the good Samaritan, 26,
  214-15
parable of the king and two servants,
  165-66, 183
parable of the ninety-nine sheep, 94
parable of the prodigal son, 87, 92-93,
  96-97, 101-2
parable of the rich fool, 208
parable of the talents, 69, 197, 203-4
parable of the two builders, 149-50
parable of the vineyard, 97
Paul (apostle): on Adam and Christ,
  111; on anxiety, 51; on body with
  many members, 188; conversion of,
  70; on Damascus road, 97; on faith of
  Christ, 116, 116n14; on friendship,
  177; on generosity, 210; on God as
  Abba, 98; on Holy Spirit, 130, 149;
  on humility of Christ, 147; on inner
  freedom, 162; Jesus' teachings and,
  51n18; on kingdom of God, 34, 149;
  miracles and, 126; on mourning,
  169n22; on Spirit-filling, 125; as
  tentmaker, 192; trinitarian prayer of,
  131-32, 132n40; on truth seeking,
  144; on wealth, 200-201, 208-9; on
  worry, 199, 200
pause button, 49-51, 104, 133, 154-55,
  222
peace. See shalom
Peace and Safety in the Christian
  Home, 174-75n33
Peacemaker, The (Sande), 173n28
Peacemaker Ministries, 172, 174
peacemaking, 170-75, 174n31
Peel, William, 196-97
Perimeter Church (Atlanta), 202
Perkins, John, 215
Perriman, Andrew, 185
perseverance, 64, 70-71
Peter (apostle): change in life of, 33;

denial of Christ by, 42; as friend of Christ, 178; Gentile believers and, 70; on heaven, 65; Jesus' reconciliation with, 171-72; on leadership, 147; on private property, 208n44

Pharisees, 20, 24-25, 161-63

Pilgrim, Walter, 198, 204, 207

poetry, 104-5, 136-38, 156, 182

Pope, Randy, 202

poverty, 185-86n4, 202-4, 208-9, 211-17, 217n65

prayer: abiding in Christ and, 48; distressed gap and, 51, 54; forgiveness and, 170; friendship and, 180-81; giving and, 219; growing in, 151-53; illness and, 59; Jesus Prayer and, 154-55; journaling and, 46; money and, 209-10; pause button and, 49-50, 51; peacemaking and, 175; of recollection, 223; routines of, 79n33; scripture and, 136; trinitarian, 131-32; unconditional love and, 99; work and, 196-97

Presence and the Power, The (Hawthorne), 120n23

Prochaska, James, 71n20

prosperity gospel, 204n36

R. W. Beckett (business), 194

race relations, 175n34

Rae, Scott, 185-86n4, 193

Ramm, Bernard, 111-12, 112n7

Ramsey, Dave, 202

reconciliation, 22-23, 170-74, 175

rededication, 18

regeneration, 17

Renovation of the Heart (Willard), 74-75n23

reputation of Christians, 159-61, 182

retreats, 47, 102-3, 150-51

Richards, Jay, 205

righteousness, 33-34, 34n32, 135

road rage, 18, 74-75

Romania, 90

Roth, Bill, 45

rule following: versus character formation, 12, 27, 221; Jesus' teachings and, 19-21, 23-26; versus

righteousness, 135

Rule of St. Benedict, 79n33

Rutter, Michael, 90

Sabbath, 19-20, 20n5, 80-82, 83

salvation, Jesus' centrality to, 21

Samuel (biblical judge), 124, 139

sanctification: divine-human cooperation in, 32-33; Holy Spirit as agent of, 33, 108, 129-30; Jesus' centrality to, 21; in various Christian traditions, 32n27; work and, 187

Sande, Ken, 172-174

Satan, dismissive gap and, 41-42

savings and credit associations, 216

Schneider, John: on global poverty, 217n65; on moral proximity, 214-215; on prosperity, 204, 204n36; on rich of Amos's day, 209; on wealth creation, 185-86n4

Schreiner, Thomas, 64

Scripture. *See* Bible study

self-denial, 45

self-righteousness, 150, 160-63

Sermon on the Mount: anger and, 18, 74-75; exemplary practices and character and, 146-49; Jesus' metaphors in, 24n11; money and, 197-99; righteousness in, 33-34; themes in, 145-46, 148, 199-200

service, as love language, 89

shalom, 36, 36n37

Shumway, Cassidy, 37-38

Sider, Ron, 185-86n4

social justice, 187

Spence, Alan, 110

Spirit of the Disciplines, The (Willard), 211

spiritual disciplines. *See* spiritual practices

spiritual practices: character formation and, 75-77; identification with poor and needy as, 219; secrecy and, 71n19. *See also specific practices*

spiritual problems, misdiagnosis of, 11

spiritual warfare, 174-75n33

Spohn, William, 175

Stephen (early church leader), 108

Strobel, Lee, 18-19
Strobel, Leslie, 18
suffering, character formation and,
    63-64
Swinburne, Richard, 28n23
Swindoll, Chuck, 143n7
taxes, 191-92
temptation: character change and, 72,
    73, 74; of Jesus, 52, 109, 111, 113,
    118, 120-22, 148; resisting, 20, 128,
    146, 148; wealth and, 198; willpower
    and, 28
thanksgiving, 46, 199
Thomas (apostle), 40-41, 70
time, as love language, 89
Tom's of Maine, 213
touch, as love language, 89
Townsend, John, 76
Tozer, A. W., 152, 193-94
transparency, formation gaps and, 56
Transtheoretical Model of Change,
    71n20
Trinity, 131-132, 155n20
truth: deeds versus claims and, 150-51;
    encounters with, 150-51, 153-54, 155;
    sources of, 143-44; truth telling and,
    57, 58-59, 180, 181
Twain, Mark, 66
values, giving and, 211
virtue: ethics and, 26n19; Jesus'
    example and, 149
Volf, Miroslav, 174, 174n31, 188
Wallace, Daniel, 116n14
Wallis, Ian, 117-18
Waltke, Bruce, 25-26
Ware, Bruce, 62, 120-21
wealth. See money
Wesley, John, 218
What Would Jesus Do? 110
What's So Amazing About Grace?
    (Yancey), 159-60
Wheelan, Charles, 203
Wilhoit, Jim, 71n20
Wilkins, Michael, 24-25, 166-67
willpower: versus core beliefs, 28-32,

76; versus weak flesh, 119-20;
    willing-doing gap and, 18
Willard, Dallas, 31; on contempt, 74;
    on formation into Christlikeness,
    74-75n23; on grace, 32; on keeping
    the law, 33; on Scripture, 142-43,
    156; on self-righteousness, 162; on
    spiritual disciplines, 76-77; on wealth,
    211-12, 218-19; on work, 186
willing-doing gap: core beliefs and, 28;
    heart flow work and, 31, 33;
    possibility of change and, 16-18;
    questions about, 36; weak flesh and,
    119-20; willpower and, 18, 27-28
Wilson, Gerald, 56
Winter, Ralph, 80
wisdom: Holy Spirit and, 123-124;
    money and, 199-200; sources of,
    143-44
Witherington, Ben, 122-23
Wolterstorff, Nicholas, 164, 164n11
Wong, Kenman, 185-86n4, 193
words, as love language, 89
work: business awards and, 194n18;
    character formation and, 195-96;
    community and, 187-88; dimensions
    of, 187; evangelism and, 196-97; Jesus
    and business and, 189-92; job sectors
    and, 189, 191-92, 194-95; ministry
    focus in, 195; pastoral equipping and,
    196; prayer and, 196-97; spheres of,
    186-87; Sunday-Monday gap and,
    192-93; U.S. workforce and, 189;
    value of, 187-89; valued and
    undervalued roles in, 194
World Cup Soccer, 37-38
worldview, definition of, 29
worldview beliefs. See core beliefs
worry, 47, 199, 200, 202
worship, of God versus money, 184
Wright, N. T., 26
Yancey, Philip, 159-60
Year of Jubilee, 205
Zacchaeus (biblical figure), 207

Scripture Index

Genesis
1:28, *186*
2:2, *187*
2:2-3, *81*
2:15, *186*
3:1-5, *96*

Exodus
16:29, *20*
20:8-11, *19*
20:11-12, *81*
22:5, *205*
36:2, *26*

Leviticus
4:22-23, *72*
4:27-28, *72*
25, *205*
25:35-37, *205*

Numbers
28:26, *81*
29:1, *81*
29:7, *81*
29:12, *81*
29:35, *81*

Deuteronomy
23:19-20, *205*

Joshua
3:4, *20*
22:5, *26*

1 Samuel
2:26, *124*
2:35, *26*
3:2-19, *124*
3:10, *139*
16:7, *24*
18:1-4, *177*

1 Kings
3:12, *26*

2 Kings
4:8-37, *126*
4:42-44, *126*
5:1-15, *126*
6:4-7, *126*

2 Chronicles
18:2, *23*

Job
1:21, *68*
16:10, *23*

Psalms
1:1-6, *76*
1:3, *24*
22:26, *26*
31:23, *100*
51:11-12, *119*
61:3-4, *100*
62:2, *100*
62:6-7, *100*
63:7, *100*
91:1, *100*
91:4, *100*
94:22, *100*
139:7-12, *101*
139:23-24, *139*

Proverbs
4:23, *25*
14:23, *204*
17:17, *177*
27:6, *180*
27:10, *177*
31:18, *204*

Ecclesiastes
5:15, *68*

Isaiah
6:9-10, *39*
11:2, *123*
31:1-3, *119*

40:31, *130*
53:3, *165*
61:1-2, *118*

Jeremiah
17:7-8, *24*
17:9, *56*
31:31-34, *107*
31:33, *24*

Ezekiel
36:25-27, *107*
36:26, *24*
36:26-27, *188*

Joel
2:28-29, *107*

Amos
6:1, *209*
6:6, *209*

Matthew
1, *150*
1–13, *21, 36*
1:18, *123*
1:20, *123*
3:16, *118, 123, 124*
4:1, *118*
4:1-11, *111, 120*
4:2, *77, 111, 122*
4:3-4, *197*
4:4, *77*
4:4-10, *146*
4:7, *77*
4:10, *77*
4:11, *197*
4:17, *15*
4:18, *176*
4:21, *176*
5–7, *24, 145, 197*
5:5, *33*
5:11-12, *67*
5:11-16, *145*

5:13-16, *67*
5:14-16, *217*
5:16, *34*
5:17-20, *135, 145*
5:19, *53*
5:20, *20*
5:20-48, *52*
5:21-26, *74*
5:21-48, *145*
5:22, *18, 163*
5:23-24, *22, 171,*
  175
5:24, *172*
5:27-28, *24*
5:28, *24*
5:29, *20, 64*
5:30, *33, 64*
5:39, *20, 23*
5:43-48, *163*
5:46, *178*
5:48, *19, 33*
6:1, *69*
6:1-34, *146*
6:2-4, *77, 200, 210*
6:4, *71, 210*
6:5-6, *77*
6:6, *71*
6:9, *98*
6:10, *35*
6:12, *164*
6:16-18, *71, 77*
6:18, *71*
6:19-20, *22*
6:19-34, *197, 199,*
  210
6:20, *68, 199*
6:21, *24, 184*
6:22-23, *184*
6:24, *184*
6:24-25, *199*
6:25-34, *199*
6:26, *100, 199*
6:30, *116, 117, 199*
6:32, *199*

6:33, *34, 199*
7:1-2, *159*
7:1-12, *146*
7:3, *129*
7:3-5, *37, 38, 180*
7:5, *172*
7:7-8, *151*
7:12, *159*
7:13-27, *146*
7:15, *24*
7:17-20, *24*
7:21-23, *150*
7:24, *12*
7:24-27, *58, 69, 150*
7:25, *21*
8:20, *77*
9:9, *192*
10:3, *192*
10:10, *192*
10:19-20, *118*
10:42, *67*
11:3-5, *126*
11:15, *52, 102*
11:19, *204*
11:25-26, *146*
11:25-27, *48*
11:28, *87, 146*
11:28-30, *21*
11:29, *12, 33, 36, 81, 111, 147*
12:14, *165*
12:24, *165*
12:27-28, *24*
12:28, *114, 118, 119, 126*
12:31-32, *118*
12:33, *24, 77*
12:34, *31*
12:34-35, *24*
12:36-37, *199*
12:50, *163*
13, *34*
13:3-23, *38*
13:9, *102*
13:13-15, *39*
13:15, *52*

13:19, *52*
13:20-21, *52*
13:22, *52*
13:37-38, *217*
13:43, *217*
13:55, *189*
13:55-56, *190*
14:19, *116*
14:28-30, *126*
15:8, *24*
16:23, *120*
16:24-28, *45*
17:2, *115*
17:5, *142*
17:17, *111*
17:20, *117*
17:24-27, *191*
18:9, *64*
18:12-14, *94*
18:15, *163*
18:15-20, *183*
18:15-35, *174*
18:21-35, *170, 183*
18:23-35, *165*
18:32-33, *166*
18:35, *25, 166*
19:1, *207*
19:16-22, *219*
19:16-29, *34*
19:21, *206*
19:24, *34*
19:25, *34*
19:26, *171*
19:29, *34*
20:25, *147*
20:25-28, *171*
20:26-28, *144*
20:28, *147*
20:30, *155*
21:1-4, *215*
21:23-46, *165*
21:45, *141*
22:15-40, *165*
22:42-45, *126*
22:43-45, *147*
22:45-46, *143*
23:1-39, *178*

23:9, *98*
23:17, *75*
23:23, *210*
23:25-26, *24*
23:26, *220*
24:35, *143*
25:14-20, *203*
25:14-30, *197, 199*
25:21, *204, 218*
25:23, *69, 204, 218*
25:26, *204*
25:27, *205*
25:34, *67, 200*
25:34-40, *69*
25:35, *111*
26:4, *165*
26:37, *50, 111*
26:37-39, *52*
26:38, *50*
26:38-46, *120*
26:39-42, *116*
26:40-41, *54*
26:41, *74, 118, 119*
26:52-54, *77, 116*
26:65-66, *165*
26:67, *165*
27:6, *165*
27:20-23, *165*
28:9, *126*
28:16, *126*
28:19, *118*

Mark
1:10, *118, 123, 124*
1:12, *118*
1:15, *34*
1:20, *190*
1:29, *208*
1:35, *77, 141*
2:1-5, *141*
3:5, *39, 40, 111*
3:14, *77, 178*
3:28-30, *118*
4:3-20, *38*
4:11, *40*
4:11-12, *39, 52*

4:15, *52*
4:16-17, *52*
4:17, *42*
4:18-19, *52*
4:19, *47*
5:30, *118*
5:41, *97*
6:3, *41, 111, 189*
6:5-52, *39*
6:6, *41*
6:31, *77*
6:34, *111*
6:41, *116*
7:15, *24*
7:18-20, *24*
7:21-22, *189*
7:21-23, *24*
7:34, *97, 116*
8:16-21, *40*
8:17, *39*
8:17-18, *39, 165*
9, *127*
9:3, *115*
9:7, *142*
9:19-19, *165*
9:23, *116, 117*
9:24, *127, 132*
9:32, *42*
9:33, *208*
9:34, *171*
9:43-47, *64*
10:1, *77*
10:13-16, *136*
10:28, *208*
10:30, *204*
10:42-45, *144*
10:45, *77, 147*
10:46-52, *156*
10:47, *155*
11:12, *117*
11:22-25, *117, 127, 132*
11:25, *165*
12:6-7, *97*
12:10, *141*
12:33, *143*
13:11, *118*

13:31, *143*
14:1, *165*
14:33, *50, 178*
14:33-34, *147*
14:33-36, *52*
14:34, *50, 54*
14:36, *97, 116*
14:38, *118, 119*
14:65, *165*
15:34, *97*
15:41, *192*
15:43, *98*

Luke
1:1, *119*
1:14, *118*
1:15, *118, 123*
1:17, *123*
1:35, *118, 123*
1:80, *118*
2:5, *61*
2:11, *126*
2:40, *60, 61, 70,*
118, 122, 123,
124
2:41, *76*
2:41-51, *61*
2:46-47, *62*
2:47, *61*
2:49, *97, 123, 124*
2:52, *60, 70, 123,*
124
3:22, *97, 118, 123,*
124
4:1, *114, 118*
4:2, *77*
4:14, *114*
4:16, *77, 146*
4:16-21, *118*
4:17, *118*
4:18, *126*
4:21, *141*
4:36, *118*
5:10, *176*
5:16, *77*
5:17, *118*
6:12, *77*

6:19, *118*
6:23, *69*
6:29, *23*
6:35, *67, 210*
6:36, *33, 163*
6:38, *210*
6:40, *51, 144*
6:43-44, *24*
6:45, *24, 31*
6:46, *51*
6:46-49, *69*
6:47-49, *150*
6:49, *47*
7:34, *204*
7:36-50, *156, 170*
8:3, *192*
8:5-18, *38*
8:10, *39*
8:12, *52*
8:13, *52*
8:14, *52*
8:18, *52*
8:39, *116*
8:46, *118*
9:16, *116*
9:21, *41, 208*
9:23, *198*
9:23-24, *45*
9:29, *115*
9:35, *97, 142*
9:45, *41*
9:51, *208*
10:7, *51, 192*
10:21, *118*
10:21-22, *48*
10:29, *26*
10:29-37, *214*
10:36, *27*
10:40, *47, 178*
10:41, *47*
11:1, *77*
11:3, *98*
11:4, *15*
11:20, *118*
11:34, *184*
11:39-40, *24*
11:39-41, *210*

11:42, *210*
11:52, *53*
12:10, *118*
12:11-12, *118*
12:20, *75*
12:21, *208*
12:22-34, *197,*
199, 210
12:26, *199*
12:28, *116, 117,*
199
12:30, *199*
12:31, *199*
12:32, *69, 200*
12:33, *68, 184,*
199, 200
12:34, *24*
12:42, *199*
13:8, *77*
13:24, *64*
14:10, *20, 23*
14:12, *20, 23*
14:13-14, *210*
14:25-35, *198*
14:26, *22*
14:28, *190*
15:1-2, *178*
15:2, *92*
15:17, *87*
15:20, *87*
16:10-12, *199*
16:11-12, *208, 218*
16:14-15, *210*
16:15, *24*
17:4, *15*
17:6, *116*
18:11-12, *161*
18:17, *124*
18:22, *206*
18:34, *41*
19:1, *207*
19:1-10, *156, 219*
19:2-10, *191*
19:8-10, *207*
19:11-27, *199, 203*
19:13, *204*
19:15, *204*

19:17, *218*
19:19, *218*
19:23, *205*
19:38, *165*
19:41, *111*
19:41-42, *165*
20:13-14, *97*
21:33, *143*
21:34, *26, 47*
21:34-36, *52*
22:20, *107*
22:20-34, *175*
22:24-27, *144*
22:25-27, *171*
22:31, *42*
22:31-34, *172*
22:32, *42, 146*
22:33, *42*
22:35-36, *208*
22:39, *50, 77*
22:42, *116*
22:42-44, *52*
22:43, *54*
22:44, *50, 121, 171*
22:61, *172*
23:33-34, *165*
23:34, *15, 116*
23:46, *116, 118*
24:9, *40*
24:11, *40*
24:34, *172*
24:37-38, *70*
24:49, *118*

John
1:1, *126*
1:18, *126*
1:32-33, *123, 124*
1:42, *97*
2:1-2, *76*
3:6, *119*
3:16, *210*
3:34, *118, 126*
4:4-43, *77*
4:6, *111, 122*
5:1, *76*
5:19, *62*

5:19-20, *48, 114,
   115*
5:30, *48, 115*
6:15, *77*
6:27, *22*
6:63, *119*
7:3-5, *165*
7:19, *165*
7:20, *165*
7:25, *165*
7:28-29, *116*
7:37-38, *118*
8:28-29, *115*
8:32, *69*
8:37, *165*
8:40, *165*
8:42, *115*
8:43-47, *42*
8:58-59, *126*
9:34, *39*
10:10, *67, 69, 87*
11:5, *178*
11:35, *146*
11:41-42, *115*
11:53, *165*
12:1-6, *215*
12:6, *192*
12:16, *42*
12:27, *51, 54*
12:27-28, *115*
12:49-50, *60, 115*
13:1, *147, 163*
13:12-17, *127, 132*
13:13-15, *144*
13:15, *144*
13:23, *178*
13:29, *77, 210*
13:34, *163*
13:34-35, *144*
13:35, *163*
14:1-3, *66*
14:6, *142*
14:9, *126*
14:9-10, *147*
14:10, *114, 115,
   116*
14:12, *151*

14:12-14, *127, 132*
14:16, *17, 130, 133*
14:16-17, *107, 155*
14:23, *155*
14:24, *115*
14:26, *107*
14:27, *52, 172*
14:31, *115*
15, *38, 50*
15:4, *155*
15:4-5, *52*
15:5, *48*
15:7-8, *154*
15:9, *163*
15:9-10, *115*
15:12, *163*
15:12-13, *144*
15:15, *60, 61, 62*
16:14, *65*
16:32, *115*
17:1, *116*
17:4, *192*
17:5, *122*
17:7, *116*
17:7-8, *115*
17:18, *116*
17:21-23, *147, 176,
   180*
18:11, *115*
18:19-23, *23*
18:36, *77*
19:1, *165*
19:26, *178*
19:28, *141*
19:30-34, *111*
20:2, *178*
20:16, *97*
20:25, *41*
20:26-28, *70*
20:28, *126*
21, *68*
21:7, *178*
21:15-22, *172*
21:20, *178*

Acts
1:2, *118*

1:3, *34*
1:3-8, *129*
1:8, *107, 118, 129*
1:12, *19*
2:17-18, *107*
2:42, *177*
2:44-45, *208*
3:1-10, *126*
4:13, *33*
4:31, *129*
4:32, *208*
5:1-11, *210*
5:4, *208*
6:1-6, *208*
6:5, *108*
9, *70*
9:5, *51*
9:36-42, *126*
10, *70*
10:38, *118*
11:19-26, *70*
11:24, *108*
11:27-30, *208*
12:11-16, *154*
14:17, *26*
16:37-38, *192*
18:3, *192*
18:9, *51*
19:11-12, *126*
20:33-35, *192*
20:35, *51, 210*
22:25-27, *192*
23:11, *51*
25:10-12, *192*
26:14, *97*
27:1-2, *192*

Romans
1, *150*
1:21, *42*
1:30-31, *151*
3:22, *116*
3:26, *116*
5:1-5, *70*
5:5, *104*
5:12-21, *111*
5:18-19, *112*

6:11, *32, 144*
6:14-18, *32*
8:1, *103*
8:1-17, *107, 201*
8:3, *112*
8:5-11, *17*
8:13, *108*
8:15, *98*
8:17, *63, 64*
8:29-30, *129*
9, *149*
12:8, *169, 211*
12:10, *178*
12:18, *175*
14:10, *163*
14:17, *34, 149*
14:19, *65*
15:3, *144*
15:7, *144*
16:6, *103*

1 Corinthians
3:14, *69*
6:1-8, *173*
6:6, *163*
7:25, *51*
9:14, *51*
10:31, *172*
10:31–11:1, *173*
11:17-34, *175*
11:23, *51*
11:25, *107*
12:1, *129*
12:22, *188*
13:2, *117*
15:5, *172*
15:20-22, *111*
15:45-49, *111*

2 Corinthians
1:5, *63, 144*
3:6, *107, 188*
3:14-15, *26*
4:6, *144*
4:13, *117*
5:10, *69*
5:12, *26*

5:17, *174*
5:21, *112*
8:9, *147*
8:13-14, *205*
11:1, *144*
11:7-9, *192*
12:1, *51*
13:14, *129*

Galatians
1:11-12, *51*
2:16, *116*
4:6, *98*
5:16, *130*
5:22, *129*
5:22-23, *63, 149*
6:1, *172*
6:10, *214*

Ephesians
2:7, *68*
2:14-17, *172*
2:18-22, *172*
3:12, *116*
3:14-21, *131, 132*
4:3, *129*
4:4, *17*
4:12, *196*
4:15-16, *17*
4:16, *188*
4:18, *42*
4:25-32, *178*
4:28, *188*
5:2, *144*
5:18, *125*
5:21, *179*
5:25, *144*
5:25-26, *210*
5:29, *144*

Philippians
1:7, *147*
1:29, *63*

2:1, *129*
2:2, *177*
2:4-11, *144*
2:5-11, *122*
2:7, *122, 147*
2:9-11, *192*
2:18, *62*
3:9, *116*
3:10, *63*
3:17, *144*
4:6-7, *51, 52, 75, 199, 210*
4:8, *52, 144*
4:15-16, *192*

Colossians
1:17, *125*
3:2, *201*
3:12-13, *179*
3:15, *172*
4:1, *205*

1 Thessalonians
1:6, *144*
4:15, *51*

2 Thessalonians
2:13, *108*
3:6-13, *188*
3:7-9, *144*
3:16, *172*

1 Timothy
1:16, *144*
2:5, *172*
3:3, *204*
4:7-8, *52, 68*
5, *214*
6:7, *68*
6:10, *200*
6:17-18, *208*
6:17-19, *200, 210*
6:20, *201*

2 Timothy
2:12, *69*
3:16-17, *17, 144*
4:17, *51*

Titus
1:7, *204*
1:11, *204*
3:5, *108*

Hebrews
1, *112, 117, 140*
1–8, *15*
1:3, *125*
2:10, *15, 112*
2:10-17, *112*
2:17-18, *123*
2:18, *120*
4:9-11, *81, 187*
4:12, *140*
4:15, *111, 120, 144*
4:15-16, *112*
5:8-9, *60, 61, 62, 63*
5:8-10, *112*
8:10-11, *107*
9:14, *118*
9:15, *107*
10:16, *107*
10:24-25, *81*
12:1-4, *154*
12:1-6, *116*
12:2, *116*
12:2-3, *144*
12:3-4, *122*
12:10, *64*
12:14, *65*
12:24, *107*
13:3, *219*

James
1:2-4, *70*
1:3-4, *64*

1:13, *111, 120*
3:14-15, *171*
3:18, *174*
4:8, *52*
4:13, *204*
5:12-18, *154*
5:16, *180*

1 Peter
1:2, *108*
2:21-23, *63, 144*
2:22-24, *112*
4:1, *144*
4:1-2, *64*
4:13, *63*
5:2, *171, 204*
5:2-3, *147*
5:3, *144*
5:5, *181*
2 Peter
1:3-4, *131*
1:5-11, *70*
3:13, *63*
3:14, *65*
1 John
1:3, *177*
2:6, *144*
3:3, *144*
3:16, *144*
4:8, *99*
4:15, *155*

Revelation
2:1-7, *52*
2:26, *69*
3:17, *209*
3:20, *52*
5:10, *69*
20:6, *69*
21–22, *201*
22:3, *186*
22:5, *69, 186*
22:12, *69*

Other InterVarsity Press books by Klaus Issler

Wasting Time with God: A Christian Spirituality of Friendship with God

In Search of a Confident Faith: Overcoming Barriers to Trusting in God, with J. P. Moreland

For further information, visit
www.klausissler.com

Macgregor and Luedeke Literary
Represented by Chip MacGregor
macgregorandluedeke.com